TALKING ABOUT RACE

TALKING ABOUT RACE

Alleviating the Fear

EDITED BY

Steven Grineski, Julie Landsman,
and Robert Simmons III

Foreword by William Ayers

STERLING, VIRGINIA

Published by Stylus Publishing, LLC
22883 Quicksilver Drive
Sterling, Virginia 20166-2102

Library of Congress Cataloging-in-Publication Data
Talking about race : alleviating the fear / edited by Steven
Grineski, Julie Landsman, and Robert Simmons ; foreword
by Bill Ayers.—First edition.
      pages   cm
      Includes bibliographical references and index.
ISBN 978-1-57922-559-9 (cloth : alk. paper)
ISBN 978-1-57922-560-5 (pbk. : alk. paper)
ISBN 978-1-57922-561-2 (library networkable e-edition)
ISBN 978-1-57922-562-9 (consumer e-edition)
  1. Race—Study and teaching—United States.   2. Race
discrimination—Study and teaching—United States.
3. Blacks—Race identity—Study and teaching—United
States.   4. Whites—Race identity—Study and teaching—
United States.   I. Grineski, Steve, 1952–
HT1506.T35   2013
305.80071—dc23   2012048946

13-digit ISBN: 978-1-57922-559-9 (cloth)
13-digit ISBN: 978-1-57922-560-5 (paper)
13-digit ISBN: 978-1-57922-561-2 (library networkable
e-edition)
13-digit ISBN: 978-1-57922-562-9 (consumer e-edition)

Printed in the United States of America

All first editions printed on acid-free paper
that meets the American National Standards Institute
Z39-48 Standard.

Bulk Purchases
Quantity discounts are available for use in workshops
and for staff development.
Call 1-800-232-0223

First Edition, 2013

10   9   8   7   6   5   4   3   2   1

*To our students, colleagues, teachers, and neighbors
who have been fearless in their exploration of race and racism
and persistent in their work toward social justice.*

CONTENTS

PART FOUR: CLASSROOM DIALOGUES: MIDDLE AND HIGH SCHOOL

PART FIVE: CONNECTING TO THE COMMUNITY

ACKNOWLEDGMENTS

I want to thank those brave students who not only dared but wanted to talk about race and racism in the classroom, and those who followed Cindy Gomez-Schempp's advice and suspended their own reality so they could better consider the reality of others.

I want to recognize the work of writers, teachers, and activists like Mara Sapon-Shevin, Julie Landsman, James Banks, Bill Ayers, Jonathan Kozol, Richard Rothstein, Lisa Delpit, Greg Michie, Gloria Ladson-Billings, and Carl Grant, and their profound effect on my work.

And as always a special thanks to my wife, Lee, for her support and love; my wonderful daughters, Sara and Abby, who I am so proud of for being such good people; and my grandchildren, Noah, Libby, and Caleb, who remind me daily of the importance of love, kindness, and laughter.

—Steve Grineski

I want to thank all those on whose shoulders I stand to do this work: W. E. B. Du Bois, James Baldwin, Richard Wright, Ralph Ellison, Toni Morrison, Zora Neale Hurston, Lucille Clifton, Nikki Finney. They are wordsmiths and storytellers.

I also want to acknowledge pioneers in this work who continue to enlarge my perspective and trouble my mind in a good way: Noel Ignatiev, Michelle Alexander, Joe Feagin, Ta-Nehisi Coates, Michael Eric Dyson, Beverly Tatum, Asa Hilliard, Camika Royal.

I want to acknowledge the persistent love of my husband, Maury, and my son, Aaron, and my daughter, Johanna, and my grandson, Harry. To have them in my life is what steadies my world.

Thank you to my coeditors who make this book possible and their students brave.

Finally, thank you to activists every day who give their time and energy and heart to this work. We will change the world together, you just wait!

—Julie Landsman

I write for John. My hope and dream is that you will grow up in a world that allows you to understand the nuances of race and racism but not be limited by the obstacles it creates.

I write for my father—absent and incarcerated for the majority of my life. Your story motivates me and helps me to ask more questions.

I write for my mother. You are my rock and have always been there to deal with my reactions to racism but also ensuring that I understood its complexities.

I write for Detroit. You have taught me so much about resilience.

—Robert Simmons III

Unless
By Rose McGee © 2011

There is no tasteful decor or place-
setting where genuine beauty
and grace can shine peacefully
amidst the arrogance
of racism—none.

There is no space on earth where
round-the-clock guards or hidden
turfs shield pure hearts against multi-
onion layered peels
of racism—none.

There is no rushing call to action
or compassion as justice chokes
like withering rose blossoms
strangling from broken trust
of racism—none.

Unless . . .

. . . Digging deeper causes "closed eyes"
in denial to wake up and courageously
rise in unity with the "silenced voices"
who no longer fear making choices
that rid bullying acts
of racism—now.

Digging Deeper

William Ayers

Life is to be lived, not controlled; and humanity
is won by continuing to play in the face of certain
defeat. Our fate is to become one, and yet
many—this is not prophecy, but description.
—Ralph Ellison

Prophecy, indeed. The visionary poet Audre Lourde wrote, "When we speak we are afraid our words will not be heard nor welcomed. But when we are silent we are still afraid." It is better, then, she argues, to speak out (and to act up), to engage and to enter the fray. Why not? Since all life is risk, stepping forward affords at least the hope of something better, and stepping up is in fact the signature of every activist and agitator, every organizer or agent of change: to be able to see before us not just the world *as such*—the given world—but a world that *could* be or *should* be—a possible world. The activist lives to resist the deathless phrase of Margaret Thatcher: "There is no alternative." There are always alternatives, and the vocation of teaching (and of organizing) is a natural space for finding or imagining or teasing out or mapping or inventing a world that could be, but is not yet.

"All's well," calls the town crier as he makes his way through the sleepy streets, putting the people to bed for the night, but the activist replies: "Don't be so sure! Pay attention! Another world is both possible and necessary." The activist is on a steady mission of wide-awakeness, a project to invite us, and possibly to shock us into new awarenesses. It's in this spirit of resistance and hope that these authors and this book go in search of pedagogy of possibility seeking deeper and more hopeful, if more difficult, conversations about race.

Every age and each generation must somehow face the racial reality it's dealt. Once the urgency to end the North Atlantic slave trade defined the struggle, and everyone of good will fought that fight; the battle to abolish slavery altogether drew the next generation of freedom fighters. We're all abolitionists now, of course, but we are living here and now, not there and

xvii

then. The long and noble struggle against American apartheid achieved its greatest victories decades ago, and again, it's easy enough to celebrate the Civil Rights Movement and to declare proudly which side we're on in that great upheaval. But that settles nothing for today.

On November 4, 2008, after years of barriers breached and break-throughs won, this country—with its terrible traditions of racial oppression and white supremacy—elected an African American to the highest office in the land; ironically that astonishing achievement also marked the abrupt end of the multicultural movement. We won, and it's over—multiculturalism everywhere, access to everything. And still racism is entirely intact, white supremacy flourishing. What we see is a Noah's Ark kind of multicultural accomplishment—two of each, and the rest can drown.

So what is the freedom fight today? It is a fight for simple justice, for equity, for full recognition. Today prisons have sprung up like weeds in every corner of the American landscape. Aggressive, hearty, resilient, and resistant, a carceral system powered by its own self-justifying internal logic and mechanisms, mass incarceration and a vast prison-industrial complex with a distinct racial caste has become the fundamental feature of contemporary US society. There are more African-American men in prison, on probation, or on parole than were enslaved in 1850; there are more women, men, and children—over 6 million—under correctional supervision than were in Stalin's gulag; more than 50,000 men are held in isolation every day. And now, suffer the children: The United States sentences 2,500 children to life without possibility of parole—or to die in prison with no opportunity for review—and is the only country in the world to use that sentence for youth, a stark violation of international human rights law.

This is our predicament: prisons are an engulfing and transforming unnatural disaster, choking us to death, destroying our collective futures, limiting our sense of hope and possibility. And it starts with the young, and our fear of our own children.

The taken-for-granted in most teaching, the everyday-ness of too many public schools, and the common sense of so much of the educational project, relies on monologue, not dialogue, and answers rather than questions the comfort of pat conclusions and easy belief above exploration and curiosity. This is where we engage—right here, right now, just this. The most powerful and hopeful pedagogical gestures involve common exploration, deep questioning, and a commitment to dialogue. Dialogue above all asks us to speak with the hope of being heard and to listen with the possibility of being changed—it is by its nature, then, decentering, disruptive, uncertain, tentative, indeterminate, and risky. And yet it's the cognitive dissonance of dialogue that lights the fuse of possibility.

Our schools too often banish the unpopular, squirm in the presence of the unorthodox, hide the unpleasant. Much of what we call *schooling* forecloses or shuts down or walls off meaningful conversation, dialogue, and choice-making. There's little space for skepticism, irreverence, or doubt. While many of us long for teaching as something transcendent and powerful, we find ourselves too often locked in situations that reduce teaching to a kind of glorified clerking, passing along a curriculum of received wisdom and predigested and generally false bits of information. This collection offers a means to disrupt and reconnect, and a way forward.

Schools tend to teach political indifference, emotional and intellectual dependency, provisional self-esteem, one's proper place in the hierarchy of winners and losers, and the need to submit to certified authority. What, after all, are the lessons of report cards, grades, and the endless batteries of tests that play the part of autopsies rather than diagnostics? Don't trust yourself; seek approval from your betters. And what is the point of the established schedule and the set 50-minute periods, the uniform desks all in a row, the exhaustive use of time with no room to breathe and certainly no space to dream or wonder or wander or drift or reflect or imagine or pursue things to their deepest places or just be bored? You are not important and unique; be malleable and productive only in terms established by a higher authority.

The schoolhouse is a mini-society, both an open window and an evident mirror into any given social order. If, for example, you wanted insight into the workings of apartheid in the old South Africa, you could simply have peeked into the schools. There you would have noticed white kids attending small classes with up-to-date equipment, and well-trained teachers dispensing a curriculum complicit with white supremacist assumptions; you'd have also seen Black kids in overcrowded, collapsing buildings being force-fed a steady diet of obedience and passivity. Clearly the vast majority of youngsters were destined for the mines and the mills, the fields and the prisons, while the others were being tutored to administer and profit from the intricate webs of injustice.

On and on, across time and place, the principle holds: every school attends closely to its particular society. In any totalitarian society schools are quite naturally built for obedience and conformity, and whatever else is taught, obedience is front and center, the hidden or open curriculum on

every agenda; in a kingdom, schools teach fealty; in a theocracy, credulous-
ness and fidelity; and in a racialized society, educational privileges and
oppressions are distributed along the color line, and all lessons necessarily
bend toward xenophobia, illuminating everyone's place in the racial hierarchy. Education cannot be otherwise: schooling is never neutral.

Opening our eyes and beginning the conversation is the starting point.
We pay attention. We are astonished by everything before us: the beauty
and the ecstasy, as well as the unnecessary suffering and the undeserved
pain. And then we must act. Pay attention, be astonished, act, rethink,
and act again—repeat for a lifetime. And the starting point is these difficult
conversations.

Our schools, here and now, show us exactly who we are beneath whatever fear or anxiety, rhetoric or self-congratulatory platitudes we might
embrace. Look closely: One of the first things we notice is a strict social
hierarchy with youngsters attending separate and unequal schools based on
income, race, and class background. Some US schools are funded to the tune
of $30,000 or more per student per year, while other schools scrape by on a
tiny fraction of that. Not surprisingly, given our peculiar history, schools are
also segregated by ethnicity and race, which overlaps and interacts in powerful ways with class: Schools for poor immigrant kids or the descendants of
formerly enslaved people are walled off from schools available to the children
of white people. Savage inequality, that quite visible reality across the land,
is a defining characteristic of American schools.

All of these characteristics tell us more than we might want to know
about the state of the United States at the dawn of the new millennium.
If some of what we see is not as we would like it—aggressiveness, racial
and class segregation, war-likeness, conformity, chauvinism—we can always
search for justifications; we can retreat into mystification and our always
available, always precious, and highly mannered good intentions. Or we
might choose a more hopeful and honorable option: we might conclude that
some things *need* to be changed—we might even move toward joining hands
with others, naming the world before us as in need of repair, and mobilizing
ourselves as subjects in a living history and potential agents of transformation. We would be moving then, entering the deeply contested space of
school and social change, without guarantees, but with an expanded sense of
hope, confidence, and possibility.

In a school focused on the needs and dreams of the broad community,
we would be inspired by fundamental principles of democracy, including a
common faith in the incalculable value of every human being. We would

recognize that the full development of each individual is the condition for the fullest development of all, and conversely that the fullest development of all is the condition for the full development of each.

Faith in the value of each human being, a deep embrace of our common humanity, has huge implications for educational policy: racial privilege is wrong, class separation unjust, disparate funding immoral. There is simply no justification in a democracy for the existence of one school for wealthy white kids funded generously, and another school for the children of formerly enslaved people funded meagerly. That reality offends the very idea that each person is equal in value and regard, and reflects instead the reactionary idea that some of us are more deserving and more valuable than others.

The democratic injunction has big implications for curriculum and teaching as well, for what is taught and how. People in a democracy must be able to think for themselves, to make judgments based on evidence and argument, to develop minds of their own, and to ask fundamental questions—Who in the world am I? How did I get here and where am I going? What in the world are my choices? How in the world shall I proceed?—and to pursue the answers wherever they might take them. In a democracy we must all learn to refuse passive acceptance and easy obedience in favor of initiative, courage, imagination, creativity, serious conversation, and more. These qualities cannot be delivered in top-down ways, but must be modeled and nourished, encouraged and defended. Dialogue, conversation, going deep—these practices and dispositions are the hallmarks of education in and for democracy.

The best teaching encourages students to develop the capacity to name the world for themselves, to identify the obstacles to their full humanity, and the courage to act upon whatever the known demands. In an educational project that values democracy, teachers devote attention to the creation of community, to posing questions and exploring options, to wondering and wandering. This suggests a pedagogy of equity and engagement, one that is driven by and serves the needs of the rising majority, the currently marginalized communities, and the victims of empire. It insists that we reject and resist the top-down, irrelevant, straitjacket schools we have, and that we notice, construct, or revive models of liberatory education: participatory democracy, problem-posing and question-asking curriculum, dialogue, and going deeper.

With our eyes open, we cannot sensibly accede to a regime of test and punish, certainly not the widely discredited "No Child Left Behind" initiative, nor the rebranded but essentially identical "Race to the Top" program. The underpinnings of each of these campaigns is the explicit charge to American kids to "be competitive" in the narrowest field, to outperform and hence to enlist in the effort to dominate others. These programs teach nothing about the full development of human potential, nor about justice, joy, or peace—it's all business, and the business is not good.

The "achievement gap," the shameful distance between students that fractures along lines of race and class, is a big stick in this campaign, but it is nothing more than a carefully constructed mechanism of power that simply cannot be abolished in its own terms. Standardized testing is calibrated precisely to reflect students' class experience and social capital: the best predictor of how a student will do on any high school standardized test is how she did in her first test in third grade, and the best predictor of how she will do on that first test is her parents' income. This is not some unfathomable mystery that simply can't be cracked, even as it has become the focus of anxiety and remediation and, of course, more research and more intervention. Politicians are *shocked, shocked* that the gap can't be overcome, while many thousands of academics and researchers enlist in a kind of jobs program, continually circling around it, probing and scratching their heads. Testing in American schools is not only culturally biased in obvious ways, but it's a self-perpetuating and fraudulent validation machine designed so that those with more social capital and privilege will land on the top of the pile.

As education is increasingly framed as a commodity purchased in the marketplace rather than a public good and a human right, it is reduced to a social Darwinist model of competition, sorting, and external criteria for success, and it's desperately enacted in classrooms across the country. We are told repeatedly that we benefit from the greatest democracy and the greatest amount of freedom, which makes us the envy of the world, while in our schools we see the iron hand of authoritarianism—more intrusive, more demanding, more concerned with the tiniest details of education. Teachers, families, children cannot accept this forever. We can and must build, from the bottom, a new twenty-first-century education that is vital and engaged, responsive to the needs of humanity, and geared to the challenges of now.

Nothing is settled, surely, once and for all, but a different order of question presents itself: Who should be included? What do we owe one another? What is fair and unfair? And always, the enduring questions in education remain: Education for what? Education for whom? Education toward what kind of social order? This is where we begin—and the models and examples developed here can become powerful aids and tools in that effort.

INTRODUCTION
Our Separate Voices, Our Combined Vision

Julie Landsman

One fall evening I was giving a talk to about 300 people gathered in a library center in an inner-ring suburb of Minneapolis. About 85% of the crowd was made up of primarily white teachers as my talk was in conjunction with my book *A White Teacher Talks About Race*. A young black man was recording this for a cable TV station. As the question and answer portion of the evening went on, I kept suggesting that it would be a good thing for teachers to initiate some discussions around race and racism in their classrooms. One after another, teachers protested that such conversations might "get everyone angry" or "get students too riled up" or "make everyone too uncomfortable." After 10 minutes of this, the young man put down his video camera and asked if he might take the microphone.

"What are you all afraid of?" he asked. "What is it that scares you about having a discussion that many of us who are not white have all the time in our lives?" The audience went silent for a moment. I asked this young man's question again, "What is it that keeps us from having these discussions? What do we think will happen? Students want to have this dialogue, yet we are hesitant to the point of simply avoiding it. Why is that?" Gradually the teachers began to talk, about their fears of saying the wrong thing, about their concern that students might fight with each other or disrespect each other. I knew that there were white as well as black and brown teachers who encouraged such discussions in their classrooms all the time. These discussions happened with every age group.

My belief, after holding a number of similar gatherings and after years of consulting with schools around the country, is that *not* providing a frank, open, and honest space to explore issues of race comes from an advantage that we white people have, yet are rarely conscious of having. We do not have to explore the effects of racism in order to live lives of relative welcome in this country. We do not have to warn our children about how people might react to them or might discredit them ("You only got into this school because you are black, brown, etc."). We do not have to learn what to say when a store staff member follows us or a police officer stops us for no reason as we drive in a white area of the city or suburb. We have people who look like us represented in the curriculum in the schools where our kids go, and people who look like them teaching them. We swim in this invisible privilege and so become uncomfortable when anyone points it out to us. Yet it seems deeper than simply being ill at ease around race. We have a visceral fear of such discussions: We feel it in our stomach tightening, our palms sweating. Yet this fear is preventing white kids, as much as or more than students of color, from getting a real, critical, and deep education that will serve them well in their global futures. For all our students, then, it is essential that we deal with whatever it is that scares us about the topic of race and racism. Then we can become fearless in the classroom. It is essential for the well-being of all students, that they learn the truth of history, the variety of literature, the contributions of scientists, the artistic brilliance of all cultures.

I can't help but wonder if deep down we know the debt we owe students of color along with their parents. Perhaps this is the reason we do not want to trouble the murky waters. Is it a fear of having to confront the reality of race and racism and genocide that were part of this country's founding? Is it fear of unleashing the reactions of our students of color as we go through our education in race and racism? Or is it rather that we fear, in such discussions and in such cultural participation, that we may not have the edge, we may be inarticulate and will not have the upper hand? Perhaps we are ignorant of those whom we teach and do not want to reveal this. Whatever the reason, whatever the basis to the fear, it is up to all of us to set our fears aside and plunge in. It is up to us to look at our schools as places to bring a social activist and justice curriculum to our students. It is up to us become comfortable with being uncomfortable. We owe it to the future of our young people to explore what it is in us that resists the acknowledgment of racism today in the United States and in our schools. Until we explore this, until we tell the stories of those who live it and have lived it, nothing will change.

The teachers and professors, community activists and social workers in this book have been exploring the topic of race and racial justice for years. They do this with preschool students and college students, as professors and as first grade teachers. They are unflinching in their desire to grapple with race in their theater classes, their middle school social studies blocs, their ninth grade suburban classrooms. They use hip-hop and photography, film, challenging texts, activist service learning, tutoring experiences, and constant family involvement to keep the discussions alive and to encourage contemplation as a precursor to progress. They create safe spaces in their rooms, their community centers, and their homes for this to happen. And no matter how tough the talk, no matter how confusing the responses may seem to these educators, they are unflinching in their insistence that we dig deeper to arrive at a solution, a truth, a resolution to a problem.

In this book we hope to alleviate the fear that the young man who listened to the members of the audience that night asked about. In the words of high school students in their letters to us, in poems, in descriptions of things that went right and things that went wrong from teachers and professors, in the unique way each author here approaches the topic of race, we hope you find an impetus to create an ongoing space in your classroom, in your American Legion hall, in your library, for words from the heart that contain honesty and truth.

I know that in so many schools this is not being done. I know from reading articles and talking to teachers and principals that there is often little acknowledgment of the place racism holds in the lives of students. I know that unless we change this, unless we join those creative thinkers in this selection and others all over the country who are trying to bring the topic out into the open, racism and the color line will continue to be the most significant issue prohibiting our country from advancement and prosperity.

When I think of my grandson, Harry, now three years old, I want a different world for him as he begins school. I want him to be able to attend his neighborhood school in Flatbush, Brooklyn, with the Haitian, Jamaican, and African-American kids he grew up with, and that it be filled with the best equipment, the most extensive technology system, the finest teachers and the firm yet warm principal he needs to flourish. I want him to talk about skin color from kindergarten on, and even before that, in his pre-school. I want his teachers to be fearless and rebellious if need be in bringing to him an abiding love of the truth that will last his lifetime. I want school to be fun, and not rote and full of "rigor" because he is in an inner-city school and it is assumed that kids in such a school need a military-type education. I want him to be critical and original and open and curious because his teachers are all these things. I want the subject of race to be natural to him, without defensiveness or denial or fear or silence. I want him to have friends who are white as well as of color, so that he is not the one white kid in a school that is primarily kids of color, just as I would want a black kid to have black peers wherever he goes to school. So, while I believe community schools are important, and this is Harry's community after all, I also believe that true integration of neighborhoods brings with it a richness of integration that benefits Harry and everyone else.

As I write these things down, I feel a dangerous drop in mood. I feel anxiety that this will not at all be the case. I worry that race will continue to be a taboo topic, that there will be assumptions made and actions taken based on the color of a student's skin. Suspensions for black kids will be up, graduation rates will be down. And all this time, the important conversations that could change this, that could reverse trends and redo entire curriculum content, that could restore art and culture in schools, will not happen. It takes some painful, persistent work to make the changes. It takes political and social will to get at the racist practices that govern the lives of so many of our students.

I was invited recently to give a talk about the "achievement gap" by a group who had been meeting monthly for four years and had never talked about race in all that time. How do we manage to do this? How stubborn is our resistance to having these conversations, and to keep going back to the table for our lifetime to work things out? For Harry's sake and even more for the sake of the children in our communities who feel alienated from school way too early in their young lives, the discussions have to happen, and soon. We have to ask for those around us to feel the urgency that many of my friends, both white and black, are feeling. For generation after generation we have avoided this talk. In Harry's generation, perhaps, we will deal with it head on—for him and for all of us.

Steve Grineski

"How can we ever teach in open, inviting, and multicultural ways if we cannot even talk about race and racism?" This was a question asked by one of my students during class discussion in a Social Foundations of Education class at Minnesota State University Moorhead (MSUM), a small, regional university in northwestern Minnesota. This question would come to frame much of my teaching for years to come.

MSUM is located in Moorhead, Minnesota, a small town of about 38,000 largely white and middle class residents. Of the 6,000 K–12 students who attend the local school district, 18% are students of color and about 32% of students qualify for free or reduced lunch. These figures more than double for students enrolled at the alternative school.

My Social Foundation of Education students are almost exclusively white, working- and middle-class, and grew up in small, outstate communities with curbed opportunities to experience racial, ethnic, and economic diversity. This social construction has limited their ability to think critically about schooling, race and racism, and privilege. To begin to "re-see" schooling as a panorama of stories made up of varied student perspectives, my students are asked to engage in a process of unlearning, learning, and relearning. This process could not be more important when it comes to talking about race in this context.

Being a white teacher and teacher educator for over 38 years who teaches predominantly white students situated in mostly white communities, I am presented with a unique, difficult, and challenging invitation when asking students to reconsider how they have been socialized to think about racism's place and space in schools. I want students to become bold and fearless teachers who not only honor the lived experiences of their students, but also work for transformative and meaningful social justice change.

A first step in working toward this end is having my students engage in race and racism conversations around what "creates discomfort." Like so many students, they worry about saying the wrong thing or being careful not to insult someone. Readings like Julie Landsman's "Bearers of Hope"; our work with students from the local alternative high school; and the all too many local, regional, and national news events provide the needed relevant and meaningful curricula to move past these initial and cautious feelings. Students complete individual writings, then share these writings with partners and small groups before we talk in large groups. I ask students to think about their own stories as they wonder about the "why" of their discomfort and what the intended and unintended consequences of this thinking will be for their future students—the stories of others. We also have conference calls with progressive educators such as Julie Landsman, Robert Simmons, Bill Ayers, and Mike Klonsky, who provide additional insights for my students. Regularly I bring the conversation back to the question posed by the insightful student who asked, "How can we ever teach in open, inviting, and multicultural ways if we cannot even talk about race and racism?"

Sadly, in October 2011, an opportunity occurred in our community that provided my students with much to consider in talking about race, racism, and schooling. While disciplining an African-American student, a local white school administrator used the racial slur "Buckwheat" to name this young man. This assistant principal apologized to the student and his family and received a reprimand from the school district. He was required to create a corrective action plan, including sensitivity training. When I asked about 100 Social Foundations of Education students for their responses, many thought it was not that big a deal and that the punishment was appropriate.

Comments were made about political correctness, but also feelings of visceral anger and outright empathy for the student surfaced. I asked the students if they knew the historical significance of the term *Buckwheat* and, although some were familiar with the *Our Gang* television show, they still did not see the significance of the remark. I asked if they were familiar with the dominant, negative, and hugely oppressive racial caricature used to portray black children—"Picaninny"—and most did not. Ironically, a student did comment on this obvious lack of knowledge. At this point we went to the computer lab to research these terms. I asked the students to do some writing about what they learned and then to consider "re-seeing" the original story. I began the next class period by having students write responses to some challenging ideas written by Cindy Gomez-Schempp in the October 27, 2011, issue of the *High Plains Reader* titled "Those Little Rascals":

> And it is our educational system which fails to teach us enough about racism, its function, and its effects on every aspect of American life, that leads to unjust outcomes like the one in this case. A community of people who have been shielded from the ugly history of genocide and racism that helped found this nation is much more likely to feel a kinship to the guy being crucified for calling a black kid "Buckwheat" than outraged persons calling for his dismissal.

Many students began to do some unlearning and relearning, although for some it was a struggle. Through this community event, students in my classroom moved further in talking about race and racism and its schooling effects, as issues of privilege, power, oppression, luxury of ignorance, and assumption of rightness not only surfaced but framed our learning. I believe they got closer to understanding racism's place and space in our schooling and how and why it can and should be eliminated.

And yet more recently the continued lived-experience curriculum was undesirably offered to my students in the form of a *Forum* story dated May

30, 2012, "Burning Cross in Yard Sends Racist Message." In a small Minnesota town about three hours north of campus, where 92% of the residents are white, and 1.5% are biracial, an eight-foot burning cross with racist writings was placed in the front yard of a biracial family. Although the Greater Minnesota Racial Project has been working in this area for over eight years to educate residents about respecting differences, their work is obviously still needed. The director was quoted as saying, "We have to talk about these things . . . it's about being sensitive and respectful for every human life." Interestingly, she began her remarks with a call for conversation.

Many times events like the cross burning provide a springboard for critically examining social history, although this study can be met with student responses that America is *doing better* than in the past, and that these kinds of events are just the way things are and most likely will always be. I challenge students to reexamine these privileged responses and to actively imagine landscapes filled with stories of people searching for alternative and additional solutions to what some think is "just the way it has to be."

The national stage provides another lens to examine talking about race, racism, and schooling. The elimination of Mexican-American Studies at Arizona's Tucson High School caused the loss of an innovative social justice curriculum that forever altered the lives of many students: 93% of enrolled students graduated from high school, with 85% attending college. This action literally ended important conversations about words, ideas, events, and important contributors. While most of my students sadly did not engage in this kind of valuable learning, they viewed its inclusion in the curriculum as important and agreed with progressive educators that the program should be reinstated.

This study led us to talk about the censorship of ideas within classrooms, included and excluded voices, and how teachers can act in socially responsive and just ways. It also renewed my commitment, for educational, moral, and global reasons, to engage my students in authentic learning about as many cultural groups as possible. While we were studying the Tucson story, a student commented on the lack of library materials at the alternative high school in which we work—another kind of silencing. This led us to develop a book drive, access Parent-Teacher Association funding to purchase books, work with the local public library to secure donated books, and use the university as a resource for book shelves. As a result of this action, the school now has a much improved library for its students. This project demonstrated that collective action can work toward solving social inequalities, an important kind of learning that is all too often not included in teacher education curricula.

I am privileged to be the grandfather of two children. Noah (5) and Libby (2.5) live with their mom (our daughter Abby) and dad (Jeremy) five blocks from my wife and me in south Moorhead. Most likely Noah and Libby will attend school in the Moorhead District, along with mostly white and middle-class students who will be taught by mainly white teachers. Although Moorhead is benefiting from an ever increasingly diverse population and widening socioeconomic status (SES) groupings, given our location, climate, and dominant culture, broader diversity change will come slowly.

A vision comes to mind when I think about the schooling I want for Noah and Libby and their schoolmates.

> Teachers in this kind of schooling will treat children not simply equally, but fairly by providing each student with the curriculum, instruction, and materials they need to successfully learn, and experience well-being and positive life chances.
>
> Teachers in this kind of schooling will honor the contexts (e.g., SES) that shape and surround the lives of each student and use these contexts to better understand families and act supportively in their communities.
>
> Teachers in this kind of schooling will engage and empower all students through relational and critical teaching that takes full advantage of their gifts, talents, and interests.
>
> Teachers in this kind of schooling will have well-deserved reputations as social activists who work tirelessly for social justice within and outside the school walls.
>
> Teachers in this kind of schooling will fearlessly and boldly promote racial integration and harmony through honest dialogue among all students, teachers, administrators, and community members.

My dream is that this book will cause concerned adults and students of all kinds to "re-see" the places and spaces where racism occurs in our schools and communities, and then collectively vision a new racial landscape where dropout rates for students of color flatten, all students experience a "windows and mirrors" curriculum, and all kinds of arts are used to celebrate the many gifts and talents our students possess. This vision can lead to social, economic, and educational policy making whereby all students are valued and encouraged, celebrated and challenged, and unconditionally accepted. And maybe a good place to start is by asking, "How can we ever teach in open, inviting, and multicultural ways if we cannot even talk about race and racism?"

Will Noah and Libby and their classmates have this kind of schooling and these kinds of teachers?

Will you join us in this conversation?

Robert Simmons III

The tragic murder of Trayvon Martin took me back to my childhood growing up in Detroit at a time when Malice Green was brutally murdered at the hands of several Detroit police officers. There was outrage from large segments of the African-American community about his death, as this death took place mere months after the beating of Rodney King and the social uprising in Los Angeles. Yet there seemed to be a dangerous silence, not around the function of race in the case of Malice Green, but about our general feelings about race and racism in Detroit. As such, I would argue that this same style of discourse has framed the awkward silence about race and racism within the Trayvon Martin death. The cynic in me wants to harken back to a question I asked shortly after the murder of Malice Green—are African-American men still worth three-fifths of a person? However, this question would cover a small slice of the issue. Perhaps the most appropriate question we should be asking ourselves is, why are we so scared to have a conversation about race outside the context of some tragedy?

In the same way that my heart went out to the family members of Malice Green, I had the same feelings for the parents of Trayvon Martin. As the national media covered this story, and the groundswell of support was expressed through public demonstrations, I was determined to remind myself, and others, that the fate of Malice Green and Trayvon Martin could easily be that of my 18-month-old son, or myself. As a sign of solidarity with the public demonstrations, in addition to my participation in several of these events, I placed several items on my office door at the university that focused attention not only on the murder of Trayvon Martin, but on the larger issues related to racial profiling. The implications of these items on my door could have led to a larger discussion in our department about the connection between racial profiling and education, or a much deeper dialogue exploring our role as faculty at a university in Baltimore where the school-to-prison pipeline is alive and well. Instead of a productive dialogue about the issues at hand, someone in my department had determined that the postings on my door were somehow offensive. Because I found out about these concerns after the complaint was initially raised with my department chair, and the complainant went so far as to contact several other administrators in the School of Education and the university, I was bombarded with a complex set of emotions—anger, frustration, sadness, and confusion.

While the "offensive nature" of the postings on my office door was determined to be unfounded by numerous university administrators, and I was not forced to remove anything, I have continued to reflect on the meaning of this incident as well as its connection to the focus of this book.

My previous experience speaks directly to the issues of race in various educational contexts, as well as effective ways to think about and consider these issues, as discussed in this book. While my worldview doesn't quite allow me to understand or comprehend what was so offensive about the contents of what was on my office door, I would have been more than willing to engage in a dialogue about it. However, I was not given this opportunity and can only assume that the person who was offended wasn't all that interested in my thoughts. With his or her silence toward me in

mind, and the deliberate attempt to mute my views on this particular subject, I am reminded of Eric Holder's assertion that discussions about race in
the United States continue to be uncomfortable for some and painful for
others. I am not sure that the person who registered an objection to the
postings on my door is uncomfortable with race or experiencing any pain.
What I am sure about is this: That person's unwillingness to communicate
with me regarding the "offensive nature" of the postings on my office door
are aligned with Holder's assertion that "we are a nation of cowards" when
it comes to talking about race. Am I implying that this person is a coward?
I am not sure. Am I implying that this person's actions were cowardly? Yes.

Although some time has elapsed between when this incident took place
and the writing of this introduction, I continue to question the motives of
the person who raised these claims. But more importantly, I look deep into
the eyes of my 18-month-old son and wonder what would happen if this
person were to encounter my own son wearing a hoodie. Would he be pro-
filed as an intellectual or identified as a thug? Would he be challenged to
think critically in a classroom or would he be shuffled off to special education? Would he be allowed to maintain the innocence of childhood or be
forced to declare his guilt or innocence as a member of the school-to-prison
pipeline? Regardless of how these questions will be answered during his lifetime, the focus of this book encourages us all to engage in a dialogue about
race that might make us less cowardly when faced with something we don't
understand or someone who is different than ourselves.

A Drive-by in Frogtown
Paul C. Gorski

> *for Gwendolyn Brooks—a reflection on being*
> *one of the Lovers of the Poor*

I barge into Frogtown with a busload
of proud progressives. Our tie-dyed, peace sign
rugbies are tucked into pressed khakis,
pleated and resistant
to the messiness of difference.

> —I've been to Frogtown—
> or through it, at least.
> Once read about it in the *Pioneer Press*.
> Consumed cautionary tales from friends concerned
> for my well-being, my watch, my car
> windows, my whiteness:

> *Another shooting at University and Victoria.*
> *Gang life rampant among Hmong youth.*
> *They don't like white folks in Frogtown.*
> *They don't even speak American!*

> But I subscribe to *Mother Jones.*
> I'm in Code Pink.
> I own *Bowling for Columbine*—
> special edition DVD.
> I dabble in Mandarin;
> I've considered adoption.

A guide, tall, pale, grinning, greets us:
Welcome to Frogtown!
I half expect her to say
Don't feed the natives!

Aside from our gawking
Frogtown is quiet. A crisp fall
Sunday.

I can't help feeling as I zip
myself into my parka and bury
my hands in its pockets,
that I'm lost here,
the way a socialite is lost at a hoe-down,
never knowing what he's missing.

But now I understand:
I am the person I criticize.
A pet paying entrance
to the petting zoo.
A liberal elitist in the least
elite sense of the word.

A tourist
in my own hometown.

PART ONE

GETTING GROUNDED

BLACK SILENCE, WHITE NOISE

Race and Labels

Johnnetta S. C. Ricks and Imandeep Kaur Grewal

We are friends and intellectual colleagues in the Educational Studies PhD program at Eastern Michigan University (EMU). We are teachers but of students at different levels. Imandeep teaches educational psychology at the university level for EMU and Johnnetta is a former high school mathematics teacher for Detroit Public Schools (DPS). Over the course of our relationship we have spent time critically reflecting on our teaching and learning experiences. As such, the common theme that consistently surfaces for both educational settings is the effect that race and labels have on learning communities. Johnnetta is concerned with how to effectively use her educational experience as an African-American woman educated by an urban public school system to inform her work as an educator, scholar, and activist. Imandeep, an East Indian woman, is concerned with how labels impact perceptions that affect classroom culture in conversations about racial and ethnic diversity at the university level.

Black Silence, White Noise

Johnnetta S. C. Ricks

Black silence is the product of the American Civil Rights Movement. As an African-American woman, I represent *Black silence:* the use of tact and restraint when faced with injustice associated with race. *White noise* represents the assimilated rage displayed by those who have benefited from the laws, policies, and cultural shift caused by the Civil Rights Movement. As a beneficiary of the Civil Rights Movement, I was educated in an integrated public school system and attended predominantly White universities for my bachelor's and graduate degrees. This essay focuses on the *Black silence* and *White noise* related to my educational experience in the United States.

The Origin of My Black Silence and White Noise

My parents were both participants in and beneficiaries of the Civil Rights Movement. As part of the great migration of African Americans from the southern United States, my parents were educated in the segregated public school system in Chattanooga, Tennessee. With outdated textbooks formerly used by White students contributing to their educational experiences as high school students, their participation in protest marches and in sit-ins at hostile, racially segregated lunch counters in downtown Chattanooga provided a foundation for their lifelong activism.

In spite of the challenges of attending segregated schools, with state-mandated segregation laws guiding student enrollment, separate but unequal facilities and inferior resources as the norm in their schools, they have always contended that they received a top-notch education facilitated by top-notch educators—always African-American from the teaching staff to the administrators. My father graduated from Tennessee State University (TSU). As for my mother, before earning a bachelor's degree from the University of Michigan, she worked as a waitress at a segregated lunch counter in Chattanooga and as a domestic in the homes of White families in Nashville. The money she earned was used to pay for business school in Nashville, which during that time consisted of learning to type, write in shorthand, and take dictation.

My parents married two months before my father graduated, and, with his degree from TSU in hand, they migrated north from Chattanooga, Tennessee, to Kankakee, Illinois, and then to Flint, Michigan. Moving north with the hope of a future not tainted with the blatant racism of their past, their embracing of a *Black silence, White noise* framework is my foundation for my own positionality. As such, I have come to understand their *Black silence* through nonviolent methods of protest to facilitate social change but also the embracing of *White noise*—their adoption of America's dominant culture of individualism.

My Racially Privileged Reality

During the late 1960s and early 1970s, General Motors (GM) in Flint, Michigan, was recruiting people to work in one of its many auto plants. The opportunity for employment in one of the factories or associated supplier companies drew people of all races and ethnicities to Flint. As a result, I spent the first five years of my childhood living in a racially diverse housing development. My best friend, Julia, was Mexican American. She taught me Spanish, and together we terrorized our community on our tricycles and Big Wheels. My circle of friends included a White hearing-impaired girl who taught me sign language and an African-American boy who convinced me that if we dug a hole in the ground deep enough, we could get to Hell and ask the Devil why he was so mean. This racially diverse representation of friends has been an ongoing theme in my life that was supported by attending racially integrated K–12 schools. I believe that my openness and ability to relate to others of different races and ethnicities was heavily influenced by my early childhood and the education my parents received. In addition to the exposure to people of other races, I had educated parents who were fully engaged in my cultural, social, and intellectual development.

My parents provided their three daughters, Donna, me (Johnnetta), and Loudean, with a safe and happy childhood enriched with traditional mainstream American books and stories such as Cinderella and Snow White. But those stories of White princesses and princes were balanced with the reality of the real world that included injustice, violence, hatred, and its aftermath. After reading an American classic novel such as *The Grapes of Wrath* by John Steinbeck, I was expected to balance my perspective of my country and the world by reading *Nigger: An Autobiography* by Dick Gregory. My perspective on race and racism in the United States was heavily influenced by the juxtaposition of the fairy tales read to us at night balanced by the ugly stories of both my parents' past and of America's past, which include the Ku Klux Klan burning a cross in my father's backyard, a warning for the family to end their civil rights activities.

As I witnessed my father's progression up the public education ladder as Mr. Ricks, I was reminded by my parents' stories of the many fellow African Americans who were not addressed as *Mr.* or *Mrs.* but as *boy* or *gal,* and who were subjected to humiliation and violence on the job. Mom often told stories of her former job as a waitress at a segregated luncheonette in Chattanooga that included her coworker, Billy, an African-American busboy, being kicked down a flight of stairs by the luncheonette's owner simply because he could. Billy, of course, would return to work after such abusive encounters due to the limited choices of employment for African Americans in Chattanooga as well as the South.

Upon entering school as a kindergartner, I found myself in classes that were roughly 60% Black and 40% White. I learned to read with the Direct Instructional System for Teaching and Remediation (DISTAR) reading program. According to the creators of DISTAR, Bereiter and Engelmann (1966), DISTAR was created specifically for underprivileged students in order to close the literacy and achievement gap between underprivileged and middle-class White students. I was not underprivileged in terms of income, but I did fit the predominant assumption that I was underprivileged in terms of being a member of a socially oppressed racial minority group. I also attended a school that served a significant population of both financially underprivileged and racial minority children. My parents had evaluated the DISTAR program in graduate school and fully supported my participation. According to Mom, I was reading before Christmas, less than four months after entering kindergarten. My parents made it very clear to me that the context by which DISTAR was created and implemented was racist and classist because at the time it was not being evaluated by testing the program on all children. Primarily inner-city minority children were used to evaluate the program, with White middle-class children being excluded from the program evaluation process. Thus, the creation of DISTAR was grounded in an assumption of inferiority. My parents also made it clear that, despite the context of the program, if I was reading by Christmas, the benefit of learning to read so soon after enrolling for school outweighed the original context of the program. My parents' decision not to voice their concerns regarding the context of DISTAR is a perfect representation of Black silence.

My Black Silence and White Noise

The racial diversity of my schooling continued through high school. I attended Flint Central High School (FCHS) in the late 1980s. FCHS was approximately 60% to 70% Black and 30% to 40% White, Latino, and Asian. My first experience with Black silence was with my tenth grade physics teacher, Mr. X. Mr. X was a White male in his mid 60s. My physics class was predominantly African-American and kind of rowdy. Contrary to my textbook, my physics teacher, Mr. X was teaching the class how to find the lengths of vectors by measuring them using rulers. The physics textbook used the Pythagorean theorem to find the lengths of vectors. When I realized the method that Mr. X used was different than the textbook's, I waited until after class and asked him why he was not teaching the class to use the method used in the textbook. Mr. X stated, "Because you are too stupid." I promptly informed Mr. X that I was not stupid and that he was going to teach me how to use the mathematics-based method for finding vector length as shown in the physics textbook. We agreed that we would meet after school every day for my individualized instruction. I remember distinctly being both hurt and offended by Mr. X's assessment of my intellect as well as the intellect of my peers and felt that his negative assessment was based on race. But I remained silent and did not report him to his supervisor, nor did I inform my parents of his foul disposition toward me and the other students. My plan was to learn the material, earn the grade, and move on. Black silence helped me to learn and pass physics, but it did not help my classmates.

White Noise

After my negative experience with Mr. X, I decided to participate in the magnet program offered by Flint Community Schools. Every student in the district had the option to participate in the magnet program, including my classmates in Mr. X's physics class. Each school had a specialty. Flint North-ern High School (FNHS) specialized in mathematics and science. I decided to complete my remaining two years of mathematics and science at FNHS. My experience in Mr. X's class was not the only factor that influenced my decision. One of the factors was that there were no African-American teach-ers teaching any of the higher-level mathematics classes at FCHS. At that time, the majority of my teachers were White with the racial demographics of the teaching staff at FCHS approximately 60% to 70% White and 30% to 40% African-American, Latino, and Asian. All of my college preparatory classes were taught by White teachers. When I stayed after school to receive additional help, I heard the African-American teachers talking to each other and complaining about how they were never given the chance to teach the college preparatory courses. I used my post–civil rights privilege of White noise and exercised a choice that my parents never had. I went to another school across town from my districted school, FNHS, without giving my race a single thought. FNHS did have a few African-American teachers teaching college preparatory classes, in particular the trigonometry teacher who became my favorite, Mr. McClean.

As a beneficiary of the opportunities created by the Civil Rights Move-ment, I now feel obligated to authentically and critically reflect on my roles as an educator, scholar, and activist. How may I use my roles as an educator, scholar, and activist to create access for those coming after me? Is there a place for Black silence and White noise in the future of the United States?

I will use the opportunities created by those who came before me by acknowledging my truth as I navigate the roles of educator, scholar, and activist as well as helping others to discover and acknowledge their truth as it pertains to their life's role. When one discovers and acknowledges the truth that is that person's purpose on Earth, he or she can then begin to negotiate the use of Black silence and White noise within their own racial and social construct.

How Do We Teach Future Teachers About Diversity?

Imandeep Kaur Grewal

The silence is deafening and predictable. So is the palatable rise in tension and the roll of some eyes to indicate impatience with yet another attempt at conversation about race. This is the reaction I have witnessed with little variation over the last thirteen years of teaching cultural diversity in the classroom as part of an educational psychology course for pre-service teachers. Passion and engagement in this topic is limited to a small number of students, most of whom are minorities. Some statistics—like the fact that 92% of teachers are White, or by the year 2020 there will be no majority group left in America (mostly as a result of immigration and also because of increased number of interracial marriages)—grab student attention. Discussions on the intersection of race, income, and language with educational achievement, however, seem to be less interesting or critical for a majority of them. I have often found myself blaming the students for their lack of critical consciousness surrounding race issues in education and felt frustrated in teaching the chapter to the extent that I have wondered about the usefulness of introducing the topic of race. Is it better to introduce the topic of race, even if I only have a lecture or two to really dig into the expansive issues surrounding it? Is this minimal and often superficial level of discussion useful or does it simply reinforce stereotypes?

While it is easy to blame the majority of the students for their apparent lack of interest (and sometimes open hostility) in the topic, it serves little purpose. The more relevant question, I have come to only recently realize, is to ask why so many of the students are uninterested. Is it because their experience of growing up as part of the majority culture gave them little to no experience of being denied rights and services and so they are unable to understand (or empathize with) the rampant discrimination and dehumanization experienced by many of the minority students? Then what about those students who have been raised in very homogeneous societies and have had little to no experience with discrimination, but have a deep understanding and empathy for issues of discrimination? Are they born with this ability to understand the experience of the "others"? Is it the influence of their families? (Class discussion makes clear that this is rarely true.) Was it a critical experience in their lives that opened the doors to this understanding? Can that experience be given in class?

Soon after 9/11, I had a Muslim student in my class who chose to wear the burqa (full body covering). In an informal discussion with her after class, she shared with me that she felt that whenever she entered a class, the students assumed she was a terrorist or was associated with one. Seeing this as an opportunity to provide the class with a critical experience, I asked my student if she would be willing to share her feelings with the class and answer any questions they might have for her. She was both excited and fearful of the experience. She was excited to share her feelings and fearful of the students' reaction. I assured her that we would set clear ground rules (any question was okay to ask as long it was motivated by the purpose of expanding understanding rather than by value judgment). The student went all out and bought food (haleem) and drinks for the class. The discussion began tentatively and as all the students began to trust the process, the discussion grew deeper and "riskier." The class wanted to know whether she was being forced to wear the burqa by her husband. No, she said. It was her choice. In fact, her husband was not very happy that she chose to wear the burqa. It was one of the most successful and satisfying classes I have taught (although technically I didn't teach it!).

Trust is an essential ingredient for successful race dialogue, as is comfort (or confidence) about voicing one's ideas and feelings. Both trust and comfort need time to develop within a group. Comfort (or confidence) is influenced by experience. For the vast majority of teacher education professors who are White and have no experience teaching in urban schools and the vast majority of teacher education students who are White and have little to no urban experience, except as "tourists," this ingredient is missing. More importantly, the majority of teachers are graduating with little to no knowledge or skill on how to effectively teach students who do not look or behave like them, which reinforces the role of schools as perpetuators of inequality. A possible solution that I propose is to locate teacher education programs in urban schools and capitalize on the urban teachers who are outstanding as long-term mentors. Through collaborative urban teacher mentorship programs, future teachers will gain exposure to students and teachers of different races and ethnicities. Working with racially and ethnically diverse students and teachers will help mentees to navigate a critical reflection that challenges previous perceptions related to race and culture.

Conclusion

Imandeep and Johnnetta have shared their experiences teaching in both the university and K–12 school settings. They agree that labeling regarding race and ethnicity is the primary influencing factor affecting conversations about race and ethnicity. Their experiences as teachers support their theory that labels with regard to race and ethnicity drive policy decisions and contribute to the cultivation of learning environments built on trust and collaboration versus learning environments grounded in instability and fear.

Reference

Bereiter, C., & Engelmann, S. (1966). *Teaching disadvantaged children in the pre-school.* Englewood Cliffs, NJ: Prentice Hall.

WORKING WHILE WHITE

Observations, Missteps, and Suggestions

Amy Phillips and Anita Bender

As a preface to the following material, we would like the reader to know who we, the authors, are, and why we chose a conversation format for this chapter. Anita Bender is an adjunct instructor in the Women's and Gender Studies Program at Minnesota State University Moorhead in Minnesota. Amy Phillips is an assistant professor in the Social Work Department at the University of North Dakota in Grand Forks, North Dakota. We are longtime friends and we are both White.[1] Together we have over 30 years' experience working in community- and university-based antiracism initiatives and teaching courses and workshops containing content related to race, privilege, oppression, and antioppression. The universities at which we teach are predominantly White. We are both on individual, but mutually supportive, journeys to develop our capacities to act out of antiracist/antioppressive perspectives.

Although professional and personal responsibilities often get in the way, we believe that intentional conversations should routinely take place between instructors trying to create antioppressive classrooms. Because this effort takes place in the context of constantly changing campus and community environments and involves a dynamic, organic process, we must as instructors be willing to engage in authentic, intentional reflection to understand

The authors would like to thank the following colleagues for their feedback on this chapter: Susan Peterson, assistant professor of Social Work at Minot State University; Kandace Creel Falcón, assistant professor of American Multicultural Studies and of Women & Gender Studies at Minnesota State University Moorhead; and Michelle Stevier-Johanson, writing center, tutoring, and supplemental instruction coordinator at Dickinson State University.

how to change and develop our practice. Being "reflective practitioners" (Schön, 1983) is key to improving our work and developing antioppressive classrooms. The following conversation is a small portion of a larger conversation we had—and continue to have.

Conversation

Amy: When talking about being a White instructor teaching about race, oppression, and other related topics, there are many places we could start! How about curriculum?

Anita: Okay. I think it's is easy for us, in Women's Studies, to focus on issues around gender and to not pay attention to intersections of race and class and other forms of oppression. I am very conscious about choosing books, videos, and other materials that offer a number of different perspectives. What happens, though, is that this decentralizes the White perspective, which I think throws students off—and sometimes throws me off too! If you are White, the different perspectives help you realize how accustomed you are to viewing and experiencing your White perspective as the norm. I feel like one of the things that happens is that a White, middle-class, heterosexual, Christian perspective is seen as the norm and we forget we are racialized as White folks, we forget that we are gendered if we are not female, or we don't see class issues if we are middle class. Class is seen as about being poor. Not only is it important to decentralize the White perspective but also to acknowledge that we have racialized, classed, and gendered identities. It is not a neutral experience. So the key is to help students reflect on and own their identities.

Amy: And whenever we are called on to reflect about who we are, we also need to realize that those identities shape how we see the world.

Anita: Yes. And it is interesting because I chose a book for class, *Women's Lives: Multicultural Perspectives,* which offers multiple perspectives, and the White students' first reaction was to be very frustrated. We would read some of the essays by women of color and the White students would say that the authors were bringing in a lot of "their own issues" and not discussing what is central to being a woman. But what they meant was the authors weren't talking about being a *White* woman, right? So when authors, or anyone, are talking about how race informs their perspectives on gender and sexism, this can be seen by students as the authors trying to impose their own issues, as getting in the way of us talking about the "real issue" of gender. We have to turn this around and get students to think about what they are saying, but they can't do that unless they have reflected on their own identities and how their own social locations really inform their perspectives on gender, race, and so on.

Amy: Right.

Anita: What can happen is that White students can distance themselves from the readings in several ways. One is that they say, "Well, I can't relate to this because it doesn't have anything to do with me, my experiences are totally different, I can't relate to it," and so they end up stepping back and disconnecting. Or they appropriate what they're reading and they begin to own that experience as their own experience, which then doesn't acknowledge that there is something going on that is not theirs to own. Or they begin to feel sorry for people: "I am glad that I am in a family that is so much more open about women" or "My parents never ever squashed my voice as a woman and so I am really glad that I was brought up in a family that treated everybody equally." There are these ways in which students become very paternalistic about it. I've had to have conversations about how we are reading and talking about the materials and the ways in which we can distance ourselves from them. Hopefully these discussions help students understand the stories without distancing themselves or appropriating the message.

Amy: So are you saying that we have to figure out how to help students identify the lens through which they are reading the stories and we, as instructors, have to do some modeling of that self-examination and self-reflection?

Anita: All the time.

Amy: That seems key to creating an environment in the classroom for students to feel safe talking about race—hearing us talking about our journeys and the lenses we've seen through. I want to model that reflective journey and that openness in discussing race, racism, and other topics, but I know I have struggled with figuring out how to best present my journey in a way that is going to create a safe space for everybody. I still struggle with how to say certain things or what to say or what not to say. I also think it's important to not present myself as the expert who has arrived at a place where I can easily talk about our race, class, or sexual orientation—that I am perfectly comfortable, that I know exactly the right thing to say and how to create safe space—because I don't feel that way! Do you?

Anita: No.

Amy: There is an interesting balance between personal sharing and modeling self-reflection as the instructor, but still making the statement, if not overtly, that I haven't yet figured this all out yet and that it can still be uncomfortable for me or I don't always have the know-how to say the things the right way. But at the same time, they are looking to us as the experts!

Anita: Yes, and I don't want to undermine my authority, which is a weird thing to say (laughs), because I do talk a lot about the way in which we are constructing knowledge together in the class. So it is a careful balance of personal sharing and modeling self-reflection, while at the same time maintaining the authority I need to facilitate the class.

Amy: There's also an interesting connection between identities that give us power and our ability to be vulnerable in the classroom. Because I'm White, heterosexual, educated, and middle class—even though students may not know all that about me—these identities already privilege me and give me power generally, but specifically in the classroom and with undergraduate students. So I feel I can, for good or for ill, fall back on that privilege and power, which gives me a little bit more leeway to be vulnerable and to make mistakes. And there are also the powers I have by virtue of being the instructor of the class—legitimate power because I was hired by the university, reward power because I give grades. There are so many bases of power I have that I am conscious of those giving me a certain comfort level when it comes to talking about race in the classroom. So if I make a mistake, such as a White student saying something in the classroom that may be offensive to a student of color, but I don't address it immediately, or don't address it at all, I still feel like students perceive me as being the expert. And they will consciously or unconsciously let me off the hook for that . . . you know what I'm saying?

Anita: Yeah, I think you're right.

Amy: They may be thinking, "Oooh, I didn't like what that student said but maybe there is a reason for Amy not addressing it." Then I struggle with viewing my privilege and power as a way of not being accountable to myself and to the class, because I could use my position to avoid addressing classroom dynamics that need to be addressed. This also gets me thinking about another aspect related to "use of self" in the classroom. In an undergraduate group work class I teach, the students have to go through a very serious growth group process where each group member identifies a personal prejudice they have and then talks about it with her or his group. These are groups that have been set up very intentionally, and confidentiality is very important. I am purposefully not there most of the time during their group sessions so they have the freedom to talk openly. They have to identify a personal prejudice against groups who have been affected by systemic oppression and then explore where the prejudice came from—its influence on their relationships with other people, its relation to their potential work, and come up with some beginning strategies for addressing that personal prejudice. I know that part of my job is to talk about my own personal prejudices and to model that for them. So I will have a conversation with the class before we get into the group process about having struggled with prejudices and where I think some of those prejudices came from and how they have affected me and how I still work on dismantling those prejudices. I know this is an important part of the teaching process, to model that and to talk openly about it, but I also get concerned that it's normalizing prejudices: "Well, our teacher has these prejudices, so it's really okay for me to have them." I also talk about how my prejudices have gotten in the way for me, what they prevent me from being able to do, my own journey of trying to develop strategies to deal with them, minimize their effect, but I also worry that because of those bases of power that I mentioned earlier, they are translating *my* having prejudices as a validation of their own prejudices. And some students believe or want to believe that because they are becoming social workers, they are not prejudiced.

Anita: This is where I think some of the danger lies when we are working through our own personal prejudices. What we have to do is put the conversation within the context of the system, because if we don't, then it makes the whole topic personal rather than systemic.

Amy: Talk some more about that.

Anita: I feel my own struggle with personal prejudices is because we live in this landscape that is incredibly racist and so we can't get away from it. All of us have to battle with systemic oppression and so it's not a matter of whether I'm racist or classist, it's a matter of how I walk in the landscape, how I choose to deal with the landscape of racism, sexism, and other forms of oppression. I don't want my struggle reduced to merely a personal prejudice because that prejudice can only be fully understood within the context of systemic racism.

Amy: Yes!

Anita: For me the importance is to always connect my own personal battle with the larger piece of the system. They can't be separate. It's not about being in RA, "Racists Anonymous," because it's not just a personal battle. It's also about changing the system.

Amy: Yes, we are members of various institutions and systems, and they contain embedded forms of oppression that reinforce those prejudices.

Anita: Yes. So for example, as a teacher I can strive to create a bias-free classroom. I can work to make sure that everyone is welcome and that everyone has the ability to thrive in the classroom. But the reality is I don't get rid of racism by being a good teacher. I have to understand about how racism operates systemically. In Women's Studies and Social Work we think about it in terms of activism and systems change.

Amy: Absolutely. That's right. But I also want students to do that self-reflection and self-examination. I don't want students thinking, "Oh, it's a larger problem than me and I personally don't have to worry about it because I'm not prejudiced." It's an interesting paradox in that it's both us as individuals and "the system" that is larger than us. It is outside of us but we are also part of it. Right?

Anita: Yes, yes. Do you ever worry about the safety of students when you are talking about your own prejudices or asking students to talk about their personal prejudices? For example, is there ever a time when you feel that acknowledging prejudices around race is something that students of color shouldn't have to hear? I know that these kinds of conversations won't be a surprise to students of color—I'm sure they negotiate them all the time. But is there a way of creating space in the classroom that is different than everyday conversation, because the reality is we're trying to create a space where people can be more vulnerable and talk honestly.

Amy: Yeah, I worry about that. I will talk about the fact that I plan to discuss my personal journey around dealing with my prejudices and I apologize for them having to hear something that may be difficult, particularly coming from me the instructor, the authority figure. But I don't want them to see me as being "off the hook," or as someone who hasn't struggled with prejudice. So to work toward a safe space, I will talk with the whole class about personal safety and respect, and that they can come to talk to me individually if they are feeling uncomfortable or unsafe. For any student who wants, I will have individual conversations with them before the growth group starts and talk with them about the purpose of the group, and say that if there is anything at any point along the way that is beginning to feel uncomfortable or disrespectful, I want to know. I feel more purposeful about doing this with students of color because of the homogeneity of the classroom, the university, the community, the region of the country that we are in. I set up parameters that are meant to ensure safety and respectful environments, but ultimately I have to rely on their willingness to be respectful and to create a safe environment amongst themselves.

Anita: The issue of safety is such an interesting one. Frankly, the more you begin to talk about race, the more potholes there are for White students to step into. There is more opportunity for people to really say some things that are incredibly offensive. Then I am always left with these moments of

"Do I say something or don't I say something, do I address this or don't I address this?" I have made some missteps. In one class, there was a student who was talking at length about her involvement with an organization in a Native American community and in the middle of her description, she referenced how there were a few of the residents of the reservation who weren't drinking and who were really working. I still to this day wish I had gone back and said "You know, I just need to check in with you about this. I think we need to unpack what was just said." It was irresponsible for me not to address it.

Another example of a misstep was my use of a video about a young African-American woman who did a study where she had young kids of color choosing between a White doll and a Black doll and asking them which was the "good doll" and which the "bad doll." The purpose of the video is to look at the ways in which racism socializes all of us into these racial rules and to look at internalized oppression. But in a classroom of mostly White students, with only a couple of students of color, it made those students of color much more vulnerable. The White students did not have the ability to identify systemic racism and instead they became paternalistic and made statements like "Oh, my God, look at how awful they feel about themselves, isn't that awful?" as if there is no internalized racial superiority, right? The only way you can safely talk about any kind of internalized racial oppression is if you look at internalized racial superiority at the same time. Any video about racialization needs to include discussion of internalized racial superiority as well as internalized racial oppression. That's why Jane Elliot's "Blue Eyes/Brown Eyes" is such a powerful video.

Amy: So it's not just about talking about racism in the abstract, but acknowledging its presence in the classroom. This is part of creating safe space. What are other ways for White instructors teaching undergraduate classes to create safe space for everyone in the class? For example, in the class that I teach, there is a lot of discussion about ground rules, and those are actually written out and students sign them. And of course those ground rules connect to the values and ethical standards of social work and group work practice, which have to do with social justice, mutual respect, and confidentiality.

Anita: I also use journaling as a way of talking about race and racism in the classroom. It helps me identify issues that I need to talk about in class.

Amy: Yes, you can have some personal conversations with students via journals and draw out larger issues that need to be addressed.

Anita: Exactly. So this is how I know what students are thinking about the readings, because they may not be saying it out loud, but they are saying it in their journals.

Amy: That's good. So it may be necessary to have some personal dialogue between the instructor and the student via journals or essays or minute reflection papers so the instructor can understand how the students are reacting to the reading and how they are interpreting the texts. And I think there is a pacing of the class that we have to be aware of, so that you're not launching right into "You are White and you have power and privilege" in the first week of class! There's a scaffolding process that goes on to prepare students for some of the more difficult material or self-reflection that you are going to ask them to do, right?

Anita: And trust within the group has to be built. I mean, you can't create a safe environment by just saying, "Okay, it's safe now." Even the ground rules don't make it safe—it's how the classroom dynamic plays out, and it's students acknowledging that not only the instructor, but they too are held accountable for that dynamic.

Amy: Yes, everyone is responsible for a safe environment. And what would you say about the assertion that we both have a point of view that we don't hide? I don't think students would say that they don't know where we stand on issues of racism or other forms of oppression. I think they know that we believe social justice is important and that pursuing it means believing that institutional racism exists. That we believe that there is such a thing as White power and privilege that is embedded in institutions and systems. These are basic assumptions that our classes are based on, would you agree with that?

Anita: Yes, I would. Acknowledging our points of view and assumptions are important to creating classroom safety and openness. But, you know, it's not as easy for a faculty of color. One of our colleagues of color was talking to me about how it's not unusual for some students to accuse her of being biased in terms of her course content. They say they want more perspectives than hers and she finally said, "Well, the perspectives you are talking about you hear every day. I am giving you one that is not heard very much." She was getting push-back from White students and her voice was being delegitimized because she is a woman of color. We need to help students uncover the dominant discourse about race in our society and ask them questions that help them reflect on their own perspectives.

Amy: So using questions may be a way of helping students unpack the dominant perspectives they are voicing that they may not even be aware of.

Anita: Yes, but that's not always easy to remember to do! Sometimes I move too quickly to tell students what perspectives their statements may be reflecting rather than asking questions to help them get to it themselves. The skill of being able to ask good questions is an important one to develop. Many times it comes to trusting the process. I think sometimes the reason we *tell* students things as opposed to asking questions is that we don't trust that they are going to be able to fully unpack all the layers.

Amy: Right! And so part of it is trusting this process of inquiry and good questioning, helping them uncover what they already know and exploring that a little bit more.

Anita: Exactly.

Amy: So we've discussed self-awareness, self-reflection, vulnerability, honesty about our own journeys, the questioning process, creating a safe space—all of this is interconnected. And along with that, I think it's good to have our own peers available to help us process what we're doing as instructors.

Anita: Yes!

Amy: I can't think of how many times I have had to talk with other instructors who also teach this course about situations in the classroom and how to handle them.

Anita: I think that when you are doing this work, a lot of times you feel you are very much alone and that's why it's important to have others to talk to.

Amy: Are there additional things we want to talk about in terms of being a White instructor?

Anita: I remember one time when I was at the beginning of my journey. I was in a workshop talking about race, and I said that, as a White teacher, I don't think I can do it, I don't think I can lead these kinds of conversations because I don't have the expertise to know about it—as if I couldn't talk about racism because I was White! And so I think that it's even more important for us to model our willingness to struggle with it because otherwise what happens is we leave it up to the people of color to teach us about racism.

Amy: And it's up to us to acknowledge the privilege and power that accrues to us as being White even in the context of the classroom. Otherwise, the conversation becomes how people of color are disadvantaged and we miss the flip side of White power and privilege. So we have to be able to talk about that and acknowledge it as White instructors. Anything else?

Anita: I think we've covered a lot—having these kind of conversations is important for instructors who talk about race in the classroom. It reinforces the importance of the work.

Amy: I agree!

Note

1. We agree with Sandra Lawrence and Beverly Daniel Tatum that "White" is a racial identity and that the identity development process "involves becoming aware of one's 'Whiteness,' accepting this aspect of one's identity as socially meaningful and personally salient, and ultimately internalizing a realistically positive view of whiteness which is not based on assumed superiority" (from Lawrence & Tatum, "White Racial Identity and Anti-Racist Education: A Catalyst for Change," pp. 1–2. This piece can be found online at http://wiki.uiowa.edu/download/attachments/31756797/White + Racial + ID.pdf.)

In our chapter, we have deliberately decided to capitalize the word *White* when referencing White people in order to reinforce the fact that "White" is a racial identity, although not seen that way by most White individuals. However, as Anita's colleague, Dr. Kandace Creel Falcón, has pointed out, many people prefer to capitalize Black but not white as an effort to reinforce Black as a political identity and in an effort to move it from margin to center. We also respect that convention.

Reference

Schön, D. (1983). *The reflective practitioner. How professionals think in action.* London: Temple Smith.

COMPLICATING WHITE PRIVILEGE

Poverty, Class, and Knapsack

Paul C. Gorski

I n my favorite photograph of my Grandma Wilma, taken during her early teens, she stands outside her Kitzmiller, Maryland, house. The house's exterior, cracking and worn, hints at the working-poor life she and her family are living in Appalachia. Evidence, too, is her attire: full-length overalls, dusty and stained, hang over a plain white T-shirt. The tips of dirty shoes peek out from the bottoms of the legs, which appear too long for her short frame. The casual do-gooder might look at the photo and think, *I don't know how people lived like that, in those dirty clothes and broken-down houses,* not realizing that poverty continues to wreak havoc in Appalachia and throughout the United States today.

I study Grandma: the way she stands, shoulders back, perfectly postured; the way she rests her hands on her hips, elbows winged out, claiming her space; the way she teases the camera, chin flirtingly downturned, eyebrows arched over smiling eyes; the way she manipulates the photographer, as if to say what she never, never, *never* would actually say: *I'm bigger than this— bigger than these overalls, bigger than this house, bigger than this town, bigger than you. I know it and I know that you know it. And that's why I'm smiling so big you barely can capture me in a single frame.*

She was right, you know. Like many of her peers in that coal-mining town, Grandma *was* bigger than all of that—than what many people assume women like her, from towns like Kitzmiller, are capable of being. She was valedictorian of her high school class and favorite confidant to a network of

friends spanning two towns. Like many of her neighbors, Grandma was bigger in spirit, bigger in talent, bigger in smarts than what that little coal town should have been able to contain. But she also was poor. She was terribly poor despite the 14-hour shifts her father, my Great-Grandfather Henry, worked in the coal mines, chipping and digging and coughing up dust.

I have spent considerable time over the years on the front lines of the "white privilege" brigade, committed to challenging myself and other white people to think critically about the upper end of the racial hierarchy in the United States and its schools. During that time I have attended and conducted numerous workshops about white privilege and its effect on education; participated in and facilitated a variety of dialogues on racism and whiteness; and acted against white privilege in myriad, although not always effective, ways.

It has been a relatively short time—just more than twenty years—since that term, *white privilege,* was popularized by the feverish circulation of a now-famous essay written by my now equally famous friend and colleague, Peggy McIntosh. She titled her essay, "White Privilege: Unpacking the Invisible Knapsack." The white privilege *concept* wasn't new, of course, nor was it uniquely Peggy's, a fact she has explained with great humility through the years. Scores of People of Color throughout the brutal history of European colonization had spoken and written about the *concept* of white privilege for generations before Peggy wrote about the power whiteness afforded her. W. E. B. Du Bois, Gloria Anzaldúa (whose book, *Borderlands: The New Mestiza,* knocked me on my proverbial ass and changed everything I thought I knew about social justice), James Baldwin, Harold Cruse, Rayna Green, Hinmatóowyalahtq'it (also known as Chief Joseph): Each, despite never using the term, wrote or spoke about white privilege before doing so was hip; when nobody grew wealthy writing and lecturing about white privilege; and, in some cases, when speaking truth to white power put People of Color at *grave* risk. Rayna Green continues to do so today. Still—and this, in and of itself, is a marker of privilege—it took Peggy's essay to plant the concept firmly into the mainstream diversity education lexicon, which is another way of saying *White people seemed intrigued enough by the knapsack not to dismiss it.* And so the notion of *white privilege* stuck; it appears as though it's here to stay.

I dove into the white privilege discourse as part of my training as an antiracism educator in the mid-1990s, just a few years after my white educator peers had started shuffling through their knapsacks. The shuffling often occurred back then, as it does today, in white caucus groups, organized dialogues among white educators. During these dialogues we more or less took turns pouring the contents of our knapsacks onto the floor before encouraging each other to "own" whatever came out and insisting that we take responsibility for racism. Rarely did we get around to talking about what it meant to be an antiracist. Rarely did we use those dialogues to grow ourselves into more powerful educational change agents. This, I think, persists as a problem in white caucusing and other forms of race dialogues today: too much conversation about how hard it is to be a white person taking responsibility for white privilege; way too much thinking that the dialogue, itself, *is* the antiracism rather than what *prepares* us for the antiracism.

However, looking back now, having observed how conversations about social justice education have evolved in the past twenty years, what stands out to me most about those early conversations about "white privilege" is this: Even then, in those few years after *white privilege* had entered white educators' "diversity" lexicons, the rules of the conversation already had been firmly established. Many were the standard "be respectful" rules, some of which—"speak from personal experience," for instance, which could limit participants' opportunities to speak to *systemic* racism—actually *privileged* white people in conversations about white privilege. The most heavy-handedly enforced rule, and the one we, in the white privilege brigade, still seem determined to protect with the greatest earnestness, dictates that *Nobody shall, during a conversation about white privilege, mention any identity that is not a racial identity or any oppression that is not racism.* To my knowledge there is no official rulebook governing dialogues about white privilege. If such a rulebook did exist, though, I am sure that *this* rule would be printed in bold italics.

᠊ᢌ᠊

Not more than a year ago I visited fellow teacher educators Althea Webb and Bobby Starnes at Berea College, a work college nestled into the hills of Appalachian Kentucky. During the trip I accompanied Althea and Bobby on a drive into the mountains, where coal companies continue to desecrate a once-pristine landscape by tearing off mountaintops, removing the coal, and in the process spoiling what, by some measures, is the most diverse ecosystem on Earth. I only recently had begun to explore my own Appalachian heritage, something rarely acknowledged on my mom's side of the family despite the generations of young men our lineage lost to whooping cough, black lung, and other ailments associated with coal mining. It was during that trip that Bobby, herself a product of Appalachian eastern Kentucky, pointed out, after the umpteenth-or-so time I mentioned how *my mom's peoples are Appalachian,* that Mom's peoples being Appalachian meant, in point of fact, that *you, Paul, are Appalachian, too.* And I thought I wasn't a blusher.

Why, I wondered, had it never occurred to me to identify with Grandma, the person I admired more than anybody else I knew, as Appalachian? I pondered and journaled. I commiserated with my mom and with Grandma. I literally lost sleep. And then it hit me and it came down to this: white privilege.

ॐ

Kitzmiller remains, as it was when Grandma lived there, a virtually all-white town. Grandma remembers one African-American man who lived there for a short while when she was a kid. She learned later, she once confided in me, that the Ku Klux Klan was active in the town. She assured me, though, that none of our relatives were Klanspeople and that it seemed more like *a club for men to ride around in sheets* than anything else.

A few years ago, while helping Grandma prepare to relocate to Georgia, I sat sorting through personal effects left behind by her mother, my late Great-Grandma Grace. Hidden in an old toolbox beneath a dozen years' worth of labor union dues stubs I found a contract between an American Indian tribe and the town of Kitzmiller, apparently brokered by my Great-Grandfather Henry. The agreement granted the tribe access to a hill on the outskirts of town for a few months each year, probably on land that once constituted its ancestral territory.

A few more years ago, my Uncle Ross, along with my cousins, Ryan and Rebecca, moved to Kitzmiller, a familiar and, more importantly, *affordable* place from which to launch a business from home. The homecoming lasted mere months before Ross invited an African-American business partner to his home for a meeting. Neighbors complained with subtle threats. Ross and Ryan and Rebecca moved to Florida.

ॐ

Some people, including those who are hostile to antiracism efforts or who, perhaps, are open to antiracism efforts but new to conversations about white privilege, might argue that my Grandma and, for that matter, any white person mired in dire poverty, cannot also be considered "privileged." It is not uncommon for white people to dismiss the problem of racism by pointing, instead, to class. *I'm not white, I'm poor,* or *the* real *issue is poverty.*

I disagree. And because I disagree, I often begin the workshops I facilitate on poverty and education with two clarifications. First, the fact that we are discussing class does not mean that class is the *real issue* or that we can excuse ourselves from understanding race and racism, too. Secondly, racism and economic injustice are linked inextricably in US history. Slavery, colonization, Manifest Destiny, Jim Crow, "separate but equal": Each is an example of racial injustice driven largely by economic interests. We simply cannot understand class in the United States without also understanding racism. Class or, more precisely, *economic injustice* is the real issue, but so are racism and sexism and heterosexism and ableism, and the many intersections of these and other oppressions.

So do Grandma and other poor white people have white privilege? Yes, absolutely. Next to Ross's African-American colleague, Grandma is privileged. Next to the American Indian tribe that had to negotiate with white people for access to their ancestral land, Grandma is privileged. Next to the many poor and working-class People of Color in Appalachia who are not welcome or *safe* in towns like Kitzmiller, Grandma and every other poor white person enjoys some level of white privilege.

‍‍‍‍‍‍‍‍‍‍‍‍‍‍‍‍‍‍‍‍‍‍‍‍‍‍‍‍‍‍‍‍‍‍ح

I am tempted, here, to silence myself. I am tempted to revert to the absoluteness with which I was trained to enforce the white privilege rulebook.

Ah, ah, ah, I hear myself thinking. *We're talking about whiteness. We're talking about racism. Don't you see how your privilege allows you to avoid talking about race by hijacking the conversation and steering it toward class?*

Here, then, is the rub: We, in the white privilege brigade, often, and somewhat generically, in my opinion, like to say that racism is about power. That word, *power,* might be the most often spoken word in conversations about white privilege and schools. Rarely, though, do we speak to the *nature* of power beyond the types of privilege so eloquently expounded upon by Peggy. This is where critical race theory, with its frameworks for deconstructing racism, has flown past the white privilege discourse. Critical race theorists centralize the fundamental questions too often left unasked in conversations about white privilege: What, exactly, does *power* mean in a capitalistic society? Why, in a capitalistic society, do people and institutions exert power and privilege? What are they after?

So yes, yes, undoubtedly *yes.* Grandma has white privilege. But it's a *relative* white privilege. It's not the same white privilege that I have or that Peggy or Tim Wise has or, for that matter, that any white person has who manages to build a financially solvent career out of writing or talking about whiteness. I feel the tug—believe me, I do—of that race-only white privilege rule. Still, no matter how I slice it, I come back to this: Class matters, even when it comes to white privilege. This is why I have come to believe that the white privilege brigade has been wrong to police the complexities of class (and, for that matter, other forms of oppression) *out of* conversations about white privilege and schooling.

Worse, by doing so, we also have failed to interrogate the hierarchy of privilege among white people, including white antiracists. And there is much to interrogate. For example, Grandma doesn't stand to benefit economically from the "white privilege" industry; from the books and speaking engagements and T-shirts and bumper stickers that have generated considerable wealth primarily for white people who never have experienced the kind of sustained poverty Grandma has experienced.

Neither is Grandma in line for accolades or kudos honoring her "bravery" for being a white person willing to talk or write about "white privilege," a concept that, again, white people co-opted from the literatures and narratives of activists, scholars, and educators of Color. I often share with Grandma my admiration for who she is. However, she cannot afford to attend the White Privilege Conference, one of my favorite gatherings of social justice educators and activists, in order to participate in a white caucus group. She does not have books to sign or lectures to deliver at pricey events. I, on the other hand, might, upon finishing this essay, be celebrated for writing yet another piece about white privilege. It could help me get tenure.

No, Grandma's white privilege is nothing at all like my white privilege. It certainly doesn't resemble the white privilege enjoyed by Bill Gates, or even that enjoyed by Martha Stewart. *Pretending* that she shares that level of white privilege, or that a working-class white third grade teacher experiences the same white privilege as a property-class white lawyer or professional keynoter is, well, nonsensical. And it certainly isn't conducive to an authentic movement for racial justice because it limits the extent to which we allow ourselves to understand the messy complexity of racism. It limits, as well, the extent to which we succeed at fostering a movement to which working-class and poor white people feel connected.

I couldn't afford to feed my kids last night. You attended a lecture about racism on the university campus—last time I was in that vicinity I was accosted by campus police—then, after asking the lecturer to sign your copy of her book, you met friends at a bar to continue the conversation over drinks. Now you want me to tell *you* about *my* privilege? Um, you first.

As I mentioned earlier, I do understand the drive to minimize the ways conversations about white privilege are hijacked, reframed, or devolved into a *woe-is-me-as-an-antiracist-white-person-with-racist-parents* affirmation for "good" white people. I recognize that the learning curve can be steep; it certainly has been for me. This is why the race-only rule persists and why it is enforced so vehemently.

Ah, ah, ah. . . . We're talking about white privilege now.

At some point, though, we do ourselves and our movements a disservice when we refuse to consider class privilege within white privilege or, if you like, white privilege *privilege*. This is a matter of consciousness, of depth in understanding. It also is a matter of strategy, of effectively growing movements for educational justice by acknowledging the varied ways in which people experience oppression. More than anything, though, it's a matter of honesty and ownership on the parts of white educators who, like me, find themselves in a position to bolster their economic privilege through white privilege work. We must ask ourselves whether these conditions—struggling against white privilege and profiting from that struggle, something Grandma cannot do—are compatible.

∽

As I continue to study my favorite photo of Grandma, I ask myself this: Who, exactly, do I see? What of whiteness, of poverty, of Appalachia, of me do I see in Grandma? Is she white in the same way that I am white? Risking censure from the white privilege brigade, I offer the only honest answer I can muster: *No.*

Perhaps with that answer I am breaking with white privilege convention or providing white privilege deniers the ammunition they need to point, again, to class as *the real issue.* Still, the acknowledgment feels like a triumph, like a step toward a more honest conversation. And that, after all, is the only real way to racial justice.

4

BREAKING THE CYCLE
OF COLOR BLINDNESS
IN HIGHER EDUCATION

Caprice D. Hollins

Like life, racial understanding is not something
we find, it is something we create.

—Dr. Martin Luther King, Jr.

In our society it's usually socially acceptable to talk about our attitudes, values, and beliefs associated with class, gender, religion, age, ability, and, in some settings, even sexual orientation as long as we don't stereotype and spew epithets in the process. For the most part, we are able to enter into discourse around common adverse experiences that accompany being a member of one or more of these groups without having others deny that those experiences occur. However, when it comes to race, we have adopted a color-blind approach that essentially proposes we are somehow immune from noticing skin color and in the process negate the fact that it, too, matters. It's not the simple fact that our skin color varies that causes people to cling so tightly to color-blind ideology but more so the inequalities that go along with those variations that keep them unwilling to enter into discourse. The discomfort often linked to the shame and guilt white people sometimes feel, paired with the tension that comes about in cross-cultural interactions, has made talking about race almost taboo in our culture.

Research as early as the 1940s has shown that children at a very young age begin to notice racial differences. As they become aware of the world around them they develop a natural curiosity about why things are the way they are. Although there is evidence that parents of color talk with their

43

children about race to prepare them for experiences of racism, many parents of white children don't see the need. They are unprepared and often get caught off guard when the most innocent of questions are asked, like, "Mommy, how come that man is so chocolate?" usually said loud enough for the "chocolate man" to hear. Children are frequently met with an immediate "shhhh" and clear embarrassment from their parents. It is in these early childhood moments that they are socialized through verbal and nonverbal messaging and are taught that exploring racial diversity is off limits. As they grow older they learn to keep their curiosities about racial differences to themselves for fear of disappointing their parents or being met with a disapproving eye. Over time, with the help of socialization through media, they are left to make sense of racial differences on their own.

Early experiences like this one often foster anxiety in adults, causing them to avoid having conversations about race altogether. What was once a fear of disapproval from parents grows into a fear of disapproval from friends and colleagues. They fear that someone will get hurt, or that they might say something that will offend. They worry that they will be seen as incompetent or that conversations will create a division. Even worse is the looming fear that they will be seen as a racist. When you consider that people spend a lifetime developing their identities and that those identities are often tied into being a good, kind, loving, moral person who treats everyone the same, it becomes easier to understand why people resist seeing themselves as color conscious. In an effort to prove that they don't judge people based on skin color, statements like "We are all human," "I treat everyone the same," "I don't notice skin color," and "My best friend is black" become the mantra that replaces the much-needed race conversations and our cross-cultural relationships become proof of our truth that we don't notice racial differences. Although color-blind ideology keeps fears hidden, it is the most harmful in that it inhibits us from exploring unconscious stereotypes, bias, behaviors, and beliefs that often lead well-meaning white people to perpetuate racism and widen the racial divide.

College professors are not exempt from these fears, nor are they immune to the process of socialization that leads to color-blind thinking. Many don't grow up having conversations about race and are not taught ways in which race matters in their own educational experiences. Having little experience, education, or training in race relations, combined with their fears, leaves many ill prepared to infuse race content into their curriculum. More often than not, they end up teaching what they have knowledge and experience in, what feels safe, and what they will be seen as competent in. As a result, many higher educational institutions end up perpetuating a cycle of producing "color-blind" graduate students who are unprepared to live, work, and serve in an ever more diverse society.

If we are ever going to break the cycle of color-blind thinking, it's important that our higher education institutions take part in the process not just at an institutional level but also in the classroom. When I first started to teach, I tried to teach the way I had been taught. I had an image in my head of what being a college professor entailed. For me that meant being an expert of my subject matter. I believed that I had to have thorough knowledge of my content area and feared that if students asked a question that I was unable to answer I would be discovered as a fraud or imposter. Over time and of course with experience, I have learned that the best way to teach my students is to be willing to learn with and from them. Even today, after almost twenty years of studying and teaching specifically in the area race relations, I am making mistakes and learning from my students every day.

A couple of days ago I was facilitating dialogue with a group of seventy-five participants. I attempted to make a point about the tensions that often exist between whites and people of color and offended a person of color in the process. Because of his light complexion, I referred to him as white. I quickly felt my anxiety and discomfort rise when he informed me of his multiracial heritage. I didn't know what else to do in that moment except (a) apologize for my assumption; (b) validate his common experiences of not being seen; (c) stay focused on the effect it had on him rather than my intentions at the time; (d) use myself to model the challenges that having this conversation brings by naming out loud my anxiety and discomfort in the moment and sharing how I, too, am on this journey toward cultural competence; and (e) thank him for the graceful way in which he entered into dialogue with me. Because there is no formula or cookbook approach, this may not work in every situation. However, what does work more often than not is to stay in the here and now, be authentic in the conversation, keep feelings of defensiveness to a minimum, and remain open to learning.

When it comes to infusing race and other diversity conversations into the curriculum, professors who have little if any experience engaging in these types of discussions are bound to feel terrified of what might go wrong if they do. These fears become barriers to their own growth as well as the personal and professional growth of their students. The other day my very shy ten-year-old daughter told me she had tried out for a part in the school play. She said, "Mom, I wanted to go last because we had to dance in front of everyone but I ended up having to go first. I was so scared but I did it anyway because I wanted to get the part in the play." I said to her, "Honey, that's what courage is—when you do something anyway even though you feel afraid." There are ways in which college professors can infuse diversity into the course content and create meaningful dialogue that is rewarding for both the student and teacher if they are willing to take risks and make mistakes. Although the risks are higher than facing your fears of dancing in front of your ten-year-old peers, the rewards of overcoming our fears are similar in that we grow in our competence and develop confidence in the process.

There is a multitude of culturally relevant resources to support teaching and learning that were not available even twenty years ago, making it easier to engage students in conversations about race. Simple things like finding books by authors of color, showing videos that address diversity, looking at history and the role that people of color played in the subject they are learning, using vignettes, discussing current events, bringing in outside speakers, and discussing our history of racism can all lead to rich and meaningful dialogue. What is not so easy is navigating the treacherous waters that come with race conversations, particularly when emotions are high and the tension is thick in the room after someone has offended or been offended. When I'm facilitating well in these moments, I approach the conversation with the following principles in mind:

1. I'm not an expert. I don't know that anyone is. It's impossible to know all things about all cultures because issues related to race are just too multifaceted. Approach the conversation with the idea in mind that although you may have some expertise, you are not an expert. Seeing yourself as having to be an expert in race relations before you are willing to engage others in conversation will likely leave you feeling forever content inadequate and therefore never prepared enough to lead your students in dialogue.

2. Take risks. No matter how much practice you have had in engaging others in conversations about race or how much research and reading you've done, you are bound to come face-to-face with a challenging situation you have never faced before. It simply comes with the territory, so be prepared to be unprepared to face it, be comfortable with the discomfort that these conversations bring about, and be open to learning from whatever happens.

3. Be open to learning. No matter how much you try to distance yourself from the experience, you will be emotionally affected by what

occurs between your students. Be willing to be a part of the process that unfolds in the classroom. When you share your experiences, what you are feeling, or what is going on with you in a given moment, it gives your students permission to do the same. At the same time, keep in mind the power you hold as the professor and the unconscious needs your students have to be able to trust you to manage the process. Share enough to model the vulnerability that this work requires, but not so much that they no longer trust you with their fears and anxiety.

4. Engage in the here and now. When tension exists, take risks and address what is going on in the moment. Don't ignore the nonverbal or verbal cues that you pick up on that occur between your students. Students are aware of the dynamics playing out in the room regardless of whether you are willing to engage in it. When you don't talk about it you risk students leaving the classroom and talking about one another rather than providing them the opportunity to learn and process together what is occurring in the room.

5. Focus on impact versus intent. It is not uncommon for someone who has offended to put the responsibility to "listen for understanding" on the person who has been offended. Statements like "It was just a joke," "That's not what I meant," and "You're twisting my words" change the focus to the intention of the individual who offended rather than the effect the words had on another person. This becomes a missed opportunity to deepen awareness of self. It's helpful to talk to students early on about intent versus impact before the need arises.

6. Consult with colleagues. Whenever I plan to engage students in a way that I have never engaged them before, I always talk with at least one or two colleagues who can help me think through my ideas.

Following are some examples of questions that you might ask students to assist you in facilitating conversations about race. It's important to note that when someone's words or actions become the focus of conversation, it's essential that you circle back around to that person to find out what he or she is hearing and how it is that person is affected.

1. I noticed that people reacted when Lisa made the comment that she doesn't think racism exists any more. Let's take a moment to talk about what her comment elicited in you.

2. What's the laughter about that followed Michael's statement that he doesn't notice race?

3. Patricia, I noticed your facial expression change when Danita said she is treated differently because of the color of her skin. What was going on for you in that moment?

4. I notice that I'm having an internal reaction to this conversation. I find myself feeling uncomfortable with where this is going. Is anyone else experiencing the same thing? Let's slow things down and talk about it.

There is no substitute for practice and at the same time no matter how much experience you gain, no strategy will ever be full proof. However, taking an emotional temperature in the room allows students to talk about what is going on for them and why. It allows them to bring in personal experiences as to why they feel or think the way they do and will help bring context to the conversation. Students' resistance or openness to race conversations often stems from their individual experiences. Once you know what is going on with students, you can then bring in content that helps deepen their understanding about a common collective experience related to power, privilege, and oppression that occurs for people of color because of their race.

As college professors, it's important that we don't let our fears overshadow the mission of our institutions to prepare students to become professionals in their fields of study. We must move beyond delegating diversity conversations to the instructor who teaches "the multicultural class" and begin to see infusing race content into the curriculum as the responsibility of every faculty member. It is in this way that we can break the cycle of color-blind thinking and do our part to eradicate racism.

PART TWO

WHEN IT GOES WRONG, WHEN IT GOES RIGHT

5

A SMALL REQUEST WITH A BIG ANSWER

Can I Borrow Your Copy Code? And Other Pitfalls of Teaching in a Large Public School District

Laura Zelle

Expectations for a student are expressed in both nonverbal and verbal ways throughout the day in any school environment. Most teachers communicate loud and clear that they expect every student to reach their full potential. But what happens when teachers are told by the school leaders not to do this? What happens when teachers are told not to expect each student to live up to high expectations? It is a serious issue when we start writing some children out of our psyche of high expectations, especially when they are only in first grade.

My experience within one of the largest public school districts in Minnesota was disheartening at best. There were many positive lessons I learned every day. However, most of these were from the students in my class, rather than the adults in leadership positions. I met students who brought their whole enthusiastic self to my classroom, ready to be loved, taught, socialized, ready to explore, misbehave, struggle, and reflect. I also learned about institutional racism, low teacher expectations, and perpetual stereotyping. These were combined with significant budget cuts decade after decade, eventually leading to my exit from public education.

I was hired to teach remedial reading. I worked with students from all different backgrounds, some from immigrant families who were absorbing English quite well and moving through our reading curriculum at a steady pace with success. I remember a few young girls in particular who loved to read the popular chapter books like *The Baby-sitters Club* series and *Amelia Bedelia.* They couldn't get enough. Once they acquired the basic reading skills, they were off and running. There were never enough copies in the library, and the books quickly lost covers and corners were bent due to high usage. One girl from Laos would always come and ask me what certain words meant as her eyes rapidly read every line on the pages. She would get annoyed with me if I couldn't give her the definition right away because it slowed her reading pace. She was an eager learner, making progress every day.

Another factor about my school was that we were working under a complex integration initiative that had been around since the 1970s. This initiative bussed students from low-income neighborhoods to our schools throughout the district to equalize the needs of students and desegregate the district overall. We had whole pockets of neighborhoods bussed to our school. Some families had five or six students at our school and I was well acquainted with them. I wanted to ensure that these families received my information. They lived farthest away, they weren't the families who could afford to send their children to summer camp, and they were eager for new ideas to educate their children. I knew my students were good readers. I saw how they learned to love books. They always asked me for the next recommendation because I was their teacher. After all, we had a relationship in the classroom. That was my role.

Spring conferences were approaching and teachers were getting ready to share information with parents. As part of my preparation, I was planning to hand out a summer reading list to my families, a common way to encourage these parents to provide plenty of reading opportunities while students, their sons and daughters, were not in school. Because of a tight budget, our administration looked for ways to save money. One of the ways was to reduce the number of photocopies teachers could make. Our staff was allocated a limited number of copies for the whole year. The rule was also meant to identify those teachers who relied heavily on worksheets instead of other pedagogical methods. Perhaps a mentor program would have worked better to inspire new teaching methods for teachers. The practice of allocating copies to each teacher quickly became part of a bartering system between us. Swapping allocated numbers was a hot commodity and a necessary act for those of us communicating constantly with newsletters, handouts, or the required individual student reporting paperwork.

As most teachers did by the spring, I looked to bargain with a colleague so I could make more copies than I was allotted and pass out my summer reading list to *all* families to encourage them to visit the library over the summer. I searched and asked around and was unsuccessful. After these other avenues failed, I decided to approach my principal and see if there was some way I could override my allotment and make the copies.

I sat down with my principal and made my simple request for additional copies. Her response threw me off guard. It clearly showed her thoughts and her expectations about the students in my class. I was told to "just make enough copies for the neighborhood families," which in this case were mostly the white families that lived in the middle-class neighborhood surrounding our school. My principal went on to say, "The other copies will just be wasted on those other kids, and we don't have money to waste."

Really? That's what it came down to? The choice of who should receive the information and who shouldn't was based on a stereotype? I realized that the reading list was not going to make or break a kid's summer or catapult me into the teacher of the year award, but the flippant attitude of a leader guiding me toward deciding who should or should not have more attention and more information bothered me. I began to wonder what other decisions were being made with this kind of thought, this kind of institutionalized racism? Who was recommended for special education classes? Who was recommended for an accelerated track? Which families were contacted to volunteer?

I walked out of her office and immediately went to discuss what I thought I heard with a colleague of mine who happened to sit on the Diversity Committee with me. I asked her if this seemed racist to her. I wanted to know if she picked up on the same nonverbal racist attitudes that our principal and others in leadership positions held. She was not surprised in the least. She had encountered that same type of low expectations. We discussed what we should do. Can we approach this subject, peel back the layers of racism in decision making, and suffer the consequences of confronting a person in power? I almost wish I had asked my principal for something bigger for these families, so that her response couldn't be dismissed because of the ordinary content of the request. Her response signified the lens that she walked the halls with every day. Which students get disciplined more? Which students are scrutinized more and which students are given the benefit of the doubt? All these quick interactions or quick responses performed multiple times every day create expectations or lack of expectations for every student.

Eventually, I left the district, but not education. In the end, I didn't confront anyone, but built my network of like-minded colleagues that honored students because of who they were, not because of where they lived. In the end, I wish I could have tackled some of the bigger racist issues playing out in my school. In the end, I never made the copies. I moved on to the next task for conferences. I would encourage any new teacher to take a vigilant stand endorsing high expectations for all students. Let your expectations be known by both your words and your actions. Let this simple sentence be your mantra: Build your network of colleagues that can support one another and give each other your copy code number.

—

6

VIGNETTES ON EDUCATION AND RACISM IN MY LIFE AND THE LIVES OF MY CHILDREN

Ruth Newton

I have written these true stories from my life and the lives of my children to encourage readers to carefully consider the words that proceed from their mouths. As well as words having great influence, one's attitudes are also very influential when interacting with others. I hope that the reader will more carefully ponder his or her words and attitudes after reading these brief vignettes.

I begin with a short description of myself and my family. I am a married Native American Ojibwa mother of three adult children. My husband is non-Native and the father of my children. My children have grown up primarily in the White world—they have been educated in the public school system and presently work in that world. My oldest daughter works in secretarial positions. My middle child, a daughter, is a registered nurse and my son works in manual labor positions. They are all enrolled members of the Minnesota Chippewa Tribe.

Although my children have been acculturated within the White community, they have also been immersed in Native culture as their mother (me), maternal grandparents, three uncles and aunt, and extended family are Native Americans and reside on the reservation.

Vignettes From the Lives of my Children

David Ray

I begin with a story concerning my youngest child, David. He entered kindergarten at five years old. He turned five on May 11, 1989. Thus he was a young five-year-old when school began that September. When my husband and I came to the first parent–teacher conference, I was upset that David's desk was positioned such that he had an empty desk on both sides of his desk. Apparently, he was considered by his teacher to be a disruptive child and needed to be seated in an isolated position.

Although I was upset, I did not express any of my feelings to the teacher, who was White. I felt intimidated because I was in a White public school setting. I have to wonder how this relates to my public schooling experience where all of the teachers were White and held all of the power. (I will say more about my public schooling later.) I simply accepted her discipline of my child, even though I did not agree with it. Later during that year, my son told me that he did not like school and did not want to go. I wonder today about the effect that kindergarten teacher had on my son. Did she consider his racial identity when disciplining him? Or was she subconsciously taking into account his identity and treating him unkindly in regard to the discipline strategies she used?

David's teacher knew that I was Native and my husband was White. How much did his parentage come into play? I wondered about that; when I was a teenager, I had myself been called "a f---ing half-breed" by my White boyfriend's father. As one may postulate, that relationship was doomed from the start. My boyfriend's father constantly reminded his son that I was a half-breed. The relationship ended despite our feelings for each other. The cause of it was the father's hatred of Native Americans.

There is one more story from my son's life that I wish to share with readers. David was employed by a roofing company. He worked very diligently, was punctual, and earned favor with the supervisor, who was White. David continued to get up and go to work every day. Replacing roofing on houses is very difficult work. Employees work very long hours in extreme heat and other grueling conditions. Despite the hard physical labor required for the job, David remained a trusted employee who worked hard and accurately.

After many months of employment, he finally confided in me. He related how one of the White employees, along with a number of other White employees, were harassing him throughout his employment there. Some comments that were made a number of times centered around rain. In the roofing occupation work is cancelled when it rains. On many days when David arrived at the workplace, the leader of the employees who were continually stressing my son with remarks about Native Americans said, "Hey, David. You must have done a rain dance because it's raining." Then they all laughed as he walked by them. It was not much later that he stopped going to work. I tried to encourage him to keep working but he would not change his mind. I did not realize at the time that this kind of racist harassment was happening every day. I thought it was a rare occurrence. In the end, he quit a job that he was skilled at and at which he was earning well above minimum wage with the prospect of advancement. The supervisor apparently was aware of what was happening to David as he said, "Hang in there, David. Don't let me down." He knew David was a dependable, hard worker and wanted him to continue working there.

David quit the job because of the daily racist harassment. Sadly, this situation is not unique to David. This kind of racist harassment has occurred over and over throughout history and still continues. One would think, and many do, that racist comments and behaviors were "taken care of" with the Civil Rights Movement. I have heard that. However, I know that that is not the case. The battle against racism is still being fought. I feel that this is my way of fighting racism—by telling my stories.

One significant factor I need to mention is that my children are very different in terms of physical appearance. My oldest child, Sarah, looks White. She has light brown hair, like my husband, and hazel eyes and has a very light-toned skin complexion. My middle child, Sally, has medium brown hair and brown eyes and her skin has a light-brown tone about it. With Sally she can pass for White or Native. My son, David, is a very different story. He has black hair and dark brown eyes and is very dark skinned. He definitely appears Native. There is no question in one's mind about his nationality.

Sally Mae

Their varying skin tones and other physical characteristics affect how people react to them. For example, when Sally was in her senior year of high school she attended a primarily White school. There were a few minority children in the school however; only a very, very few were Native children. At this time Sally was taking a history class. One day she came home from school in tears. She began to tell my husband about her history teacher's habit of telling degrading jokes about Native Americans. She said that almost every day he began the class with a degrading joke about Native people. He apparently did not know that Sally was Native American because if he did he surely would not be telling such jokes, would he? One joke he told was that Native American people were the result of mating between Black people and sheep. My husband went to the school the next day and spoke with the high school principal. The teacher apologized to Sally as well as to the entire class. Hopefully, this teacher and Sally's peers have learned how damaging thoughtless, cruel jokes can be.

Sarah Jean

A further story about how my children's physical looks can and do affect their lives involves my oldest daughter, Sarah. Sarah is the child who does not look Native. She favors my husband's side of the family. Sarah was employed in the same small town where my daughter, Sally, was attending her senior year of high school. One day as Sarah and her coworkers were on a break outside the building, there was a large semi-truck with a car that had been crashed on the truck bed, in the parking lot. Someone loudly said, "Hey, look there's a car that must be on its way to an Indian car lot." Everyone, except Sarah, began to laugh hysterically. One consistency about Sarah is that she will never allow dehumanizing jokes about Native Americans to pass easily without her commenting about the inappropriateness of them—which she did in this case. She let her coworkers know that she is Native and did not appreciate the degrading nature of the joke.

She has encountered these kinds of jokes many times in her life. I have often thought that perhaps her physical characteristics put White people at ease because they think she is one of them. Therefore, they feel comfortable enough to make terrible jokes about Native Americans. However, Sarah will not tolerate such jokes as family on her maternal side is Native American. I am very pleased that my daughter defends her Native heritage and always endeavors to educate others on how devastating such jokes are.

Sarah has also suffered many, many humiliating comments from her former in-laws. Her ex–mother-in-law and father-in-law stated a number of times directly to her, "White and you're right." When she would thank them for something, they never failed to respond with, "I'd do it for a White girl." I'm not quite sure of the meaning of this remark; however, I know it was racist. Her former in-laws were definitely racist. Her husband was as well. When he first met Sarah, he did not know she was Native American because she does not look Native at all. Because Sarah did not realize it was an issue, she did not mention her heritage. Her husband fell in love with her despite the way he was raised (to be a racist). He treated her quite well in the beginning of their marriage but at the midpoint he began to mistreat her. Then toward the end of the marriage he was treating her absolutely horribly. For example, he required that she give him her entire paycheck and he decided how much he would give her to buy cigarettes. But he would purposely never give her enough to buy cigarettes for the two weeks until she would be paid again. She told him that the amount he gave her would not be enough until she was paid again. He said that he would buy her more when she was out of money. Then when she was out of money he would play mind games with her. One thing he really enjoyed was telling Sarah he would not buy her any cigarettes (after she was out of money—because he would not give her enough!), while all of the time he had already bought the cigarettes and had them. Finally, after about two hours of this he would give them to her. He was quite cruel, but only to Sarah.

Vignettes From my Life

First Story

When I entered first grade at seven years old, I lived on the White Earth Reservation with my Gramma and Grampa. There was no kindergarten so that is the reason I began in first grade. Entering school was a very traumatic event for me. I was a very, very timid and extremely shy little girl. My classmates were Native children and my teacher was White. Thinking back to those days, I suddenly realized that Mrs. Phyllsticker was not a teacher with whom one would ever feel close. She was quite reserved. Her demeanor was that of professional teacher, yet not observably caring. I believe she cared about us as her students but simply did not demonstrate that in the class-room. I was thinking that she may have been more suited to working with older children. Yet, as I pondered further, I don't think she was well matched with the teaching profession. Thus, the match between my teacher and me was not ideal.

At some point in the beginning of first grade I remember needing to use the bathroom urgently, yet being afraid to raise my hand to ask permission. The first time this happened, I did not ask permission and eventually uri-nated in my clothing. This set the pattern for the remainder of the year. I repeated this process many times throughout this first year until finally my teacher recommended that Mom take me to the doctor. The doctor could find nothing medically wrong with me. His diagnosis was that I must have "weak kidneys." Eventually, I stopped this behavior but I have no memory of when, why, or how.

I know that Mrs. Phyllsticker did not speak to me or my mother about this behavior. I wonder what might have happened if she had just spoken to me about this. What if she had assured me that when I needed to use the restroom I would be allowed to? I know that in many elementary classrooms today there is a disconnect between the White teacher and Native student. What if I had had a Native teacher? Would I have felt comfortable enough to ask her to use the bathroom? Would she have talked to me about what was going on with me? Would this problem have been resolved much sooner and saved me a lot of grief? Or what if I had had a very caring teacher, whether she was White or Native?

I am convinced that a genuinely caring teacher makes all the difference in the world to any child, but especially to Native children. I have witnessed firsthand the effects of caring and uncaring White teachers in the all–Native American school that I taught in for three years. The differences between classes with a deeply caring teacher were visible to all.

Additionally, in regard to my educational experience, I remember that when I arrived at school I felt like I was in a completely foreign world. Although my classmates were Native children, all of the teachers in the school were White. There was one Native teacher's aide. Yet, because White people held the power, they had control of every aspect of school. Thus, school was such a different world when compared to my home world. The language and culture of school was vastly dissimilar to my world at home. I felt very much "out of place" when at school. There was no sense of belonging or community. There was absolutely no feeling of classroom ownership by the students. This had to have contributed to my feelings of not being comfortable at school and, when combined with my timidity and shyness, both worked together to exacerbate the problem behavior I had.

One further aspect I would like to mention concerning a caring teacher is that there is a caring philosophy in the nursing profession that is now being applied to the teaching profession. It is postulated that teachers must embody a caring attitude toward those they teach. I do not mean to imply that all teachers are uncaring; however, a caring attitude is now being promoted as a necessary characteristic that teachers must develop. In regard to my issue I wonder how a caring teacher would have managed my problem behavior.

Second Story

The School of Teaching and Learning is my workplace. I have been employed there for almost eleven years. I have a colleague with whom I have taken master's level classes. Thus we've known each other for over ten years.

This colleague is White. She also teaches at the same university as I do. During my third or fourth year of teaching, my colleague gave birth to a beautiful baby girl. One day she brought her newborn baby to work. As I walked by her office, I saw that another colleague was sitting in her office holding her baby. They were both looking intently at the baby and talking about all of her sweet characteristics. I truly love babies and children, so I stopped by and when there was a pause in the conversation, I asked, "Can I hold the baby?" I was very excited and happy at the prospect of holding a baby again as I had not had any babies in my life for many years. My colleague who had been holding the baby began to hand her over to me when the baby's mother said, "Whoa, hold on here. Are your hands clean?" I was stunned. I immediately stopped reaching for the baby and slowly said, "Yes" as my colleague who was holding the baby looked at me with an expression of pity and surprise. Her expression communicated to me, "I can't believe she just said that." The baby's mother then stated, "Well okay, just checking. You can't be too careful." I immediately felt that she was insinuating that my hands might be unclean. The phrase "dirty Indian" promptly came to mind because I am Native American and she was fully aware that I am.

After that I really wanted to just run away. She had taken away all of the happiness and joy I had initially felt at the thought of holding a precious baby again. I could hardly hold back the tears as I held the baby. I held the baby for only a few moments before handing her back and quickly continuing on with my initial task before stopping at her office.

As far as I know, my colleague never learned how much she had hurt my feelings. I deliberately chose the phrase "hurt my feelings" when describing this kind of racism. Because I considered this person as more than just a colleague and more so a friend, I did not use "offend"—although that is what she did. I think that hurting someone's feelings is a more intimate description and presents a truer depiction of what took place. In my eyes, this type of racism is far more destructive than when a stranger offends another person.

I think what is completely amazing, and quite sad, is that this incident occurred in a university and that this university places emphasis on diversity—and specifically diversity in regard to people of color. Students of color are actively sought for attendance. Furthermore, the event took place in the education department! How contradictory! This racist incident transpired in the most relevant department for helping students to understand other cultures. The education department is the primary place for diversity enlightenment—diversity in regard to those who are mentally challenged, physically disabled, or of a different ethnicity. It seems quite inconsistent to say the least.

I will never discuss this directly with the colleague who hurt me deeply. Since this occurred, she has never said anything of this nature to me again. I do not believe she ever will, as our relationship has since grown in many positive ways. I forgave her almost immediately, as my faith promotes. I believe that unforgiveness hurts the person who will not forgive. I do not want to live my life with unforgiveness.

Conclusion

The primary reason for sharing these stories with the readers is that I wish to communicate how very important it is to be aware of what one says. Words can be uplifting, encouraging, positive, and helpful. Conversely, words can also be damaging, destructive, negative, and hurtful. Therefore, I caution the reader to always carefully consider his or her words as they promote life or death. Words are very powerful and must be used wisely.

THE COLOR OF OUR SKIN

Naomi Rae Taylor

Mercedes, my ten-year-old daughter, and I were at an outside swimming pool. Mercedes's beautiful red earth/brown skin glistened in the sun. Her long Pocahontas-like braided hair lay in the middle of her back. My skin was on a timetable of light golden brown that only occurs in the summer months. I am relaxing on a lawn chair while Mercedes comes running to me to say that a little girl said to her, "How can *she* be your mom? You are Brown and she is White?" I felt upset. It hurt me that at this time in our history in 1999, my daughter has to put up with being challenged because her skin tone is different from her mother's.

The whole scene sent me back to 1984, when I was at a pool with my mother and sister, Giselle. My mother's looks have always reminded me of Snow White, her pale smooth skin, long dark hair, and her bright red lipstick. Giselle's skin is a gorgeous rich brown color with a hint of golden caramel hues especially in the summer. Her hair would be stereotypically classified as *nappy*, but I prefer to call it *textured*. We were playing in and out of the water when Giselle yelled out in front of everyone, "Mom, look at me jump off the diving board!" As my mother relaxed deeper into her lawn chair, Giselle came running to her in tears. A little girl said, "That's not your mom! (*laughing*) You don't know your colors."

So again, a year before the twenty-first century, I had to face the same challenges my mother did of comforting my daughter because of a cruel comment about our skin color. I made a vow that day to have more intentional conversations about race with my children. I also made a concerted effort to provide Mercedes with Black dolls and Native American dolls, and multiethnic books and music to reflect her multiracial heritage: half African-American, one-fourth Cherokee, and one-fourth White. Mercedes, now at age 22, self-identifies as mixed. All the while as I sought to protect my children from the ignorance of the world, I struggled inside to help not only them, but myself, feel an identity, process the past, and talk about our multi-hued backgrounds. I have been more explicit about all of this with all of my children and interesting conversations have begun to happen on a regular basis.

My four-year-old, Julia, and I were on our way to meet a colleague of mine. Julia asked me, "Mom, is she Black or White?" I said, "Neither, she is Columbian, kind of like Tia Maria, who is Mexican." Later as I reflected on my response to Julia, I realized that I compared Columbians and Mexicans as if the two cultures are synonymous. I am thus often reminded that my journey is ongoing even in the year 2013 as I continue to learn about the similarities and differences between various cultures.

Julia further asked if she was Black *and* White "like we were." I found this conversation a little daunting. At such an early age my daughter was classifying people in the world as Black or White or a combination. When I began conversations about race with Julia at the age of 2, I showed her a variety of books of Black and multiracial children with different skin tones. A *Newsweek* (Bronson & Merryman, 2009) article titled "See Baby Discriminate: Kids as Young as 6 Months Old Judge Others Based on Skin Color. What's a Parent to Do?" echoed my experience with Julia. It described that babies as young as six months noticed differences in skin color. That article just made me more determined to find ways to have discussions and conversations about race.

When appropriate, I share the context of my own story with some of my students, friends, and family members. I teach at a college and find students hungry for these discussions. Yet most people do not know how to respond to this question: Should a person of biracial background have to self-identify as a minority? I have also asked some biracial, multiracial adults and children how they self-identify to explore this further. I learned that they are dealing with this in a number of ways: self-identify as "other," check multiple boxes, or select the minority category only. In my own case, when confronted with this situation, I am beginning to gain pride in my biracial heritage. It is not sufficient for me to only claim or check only the African-American box, and I cannot neglect and ignore my White side. Just as I have intentional conversations with my children, I continue these conversations in the classroom and in the community.

I volunteered at Wilder Foundation, in a youth program called Youth Leadership Initiative. I met with the mixed-heritage group to share my story and my continuing desire to learn the most effective ways to dialogue about race. I asked these 9th–12th graders to share about themselves, how they self-identify, and what it means to them to be of mixed heritage. The students openly shared their ambiguity, hurt, and pain. Some had pride in one culture but not the other. Some shared that at an early age they learned to "code switch." Code switching was explained as meaning that when they are with White family or friends they act White, and when with their Black family or friends they act Black. This whole notion of acting White or Black was another conversation starter for great dialogue. Yet given their struggle, it was clear to me and to them that this time together with other students in their situation was a time they felt supported and cared for. During our time together the students expressed these current concerns:

- How to address the situation when a parent or friend is different than me
- The need to understand racial development stages (see Ladson-Billings & Tate, 1995)
- How to deal with the intense peer pressure to identify as one race
- The need for learning about history of their culture and instilling in all people a pride and understanding of that history
- The importance of preparing children—all children—to understand their cultures and others without judgment
- How to be comfortable acknowledging what we don't know and being willing to learn
- How to answer and respond to the question "What are you?"

Just a few years ago while meeting a friend of my husband, he later told me that his friend said, "She seems nice, Willie, but what is she?" Here is my personal response:

I am Naomi Rae Taylor.
I am a child of God.
I am a woman.
I am a wife.
I am a mother.
I am a teacher.
I am biracial.
I am Naomi Rae Taylor.

My initial reaction to the "What is she?" question was defensive. I was reminded that I am not yet resolved to my situation and the pain it caused me: growing up biracial yet having only the White side of my background acknowledged by my family. My story is further complicated by the fact that my identity was mistaken. My mother of European ancestry assumed, due to the pale color of my skin at birth, that my father was Mexican. I learned at the age of 23 that my father was African-American. While explaining this story to my children, Christian, my five-year-old son, said to me, "Mom, you are beautiful inside and out, that is all that matters." Here was a five-year-old who struggled with identifying as Black due to being light-skinned like his mother telling me that I was beautiful!

As I teach graduate-level courses for adults who are working with P–12 diverse student populations, I begin with topics that enable them to tell their own cultural stories. Too often teachers want quick fixes and strategies to successfully work with children who are labeled as "culturally different" yet struggle with acknowledging their own culture. To avoid White guilt, blame, and shame from students who are White and lack defining their own culture, I often begin with my own story of who I am. How deep I share depends on the day, but often as trust is built or felt, I make myself more vulnerable and in turn have received the gift of others sharing their stories. Creating a safe place is vital for students to be willing to critically self-explore and to share with others.

I make the statement that "we all have culture" in my first class. My students, many of whom are White, often look around the room wondering what their culture might be. I share multiple definitions of culture in class that date back from E. B. Tylor in 1871 to Elise Trumball in 2008. My mentor, Dr. Rosilyn Carroll, once taught me about the Culture Wheel activity and I now use it with students to complete an exercise on how to identify and provide specific examples that make up who we are as individuals and as part of a group. The categories of the Culture Wheel are Race, Time, Customs, Traditions, Holidays, Languages, Gestures, and Values. I have used the Culture Wheel activity with students ranging from the high school to graduate level as a way to be able to clearly define with concrete examples various dimensions of their culture. The fun and learning that takes place always amazes me as individuals often have homework or follow-up work to do to complete the spokes. Also within the group the similarities and differences are highlighted in conversation across the room. As the teacher, I too participate in all of the activities that I expect my students to do.

Once they are grounded in the idea that we all have culture, I move on to the following list of questions. These have proven effective in small and large groups in getting conversations of race and culture started on a concrete, real-world level.

Possible Discussion Questions:

1. How do we as teachers unknowingly affirm particular students and not others? How can we become aware of this and change our responses?
2. What is an appropriate or sensitive way to ask someone about his or her race, ethnicity, or culture?
3. Do you consider some people to have a race and others to be individuals alone? How do you self-identify your own race or ethnicity and culture? Do you identify yourself as part of a race or culture, or not at all? How do you choose if you are more than one race?
4. How would you respond if someone asked you, "What are you?" Or questioned you about another person by asking, "What is she or he?"

Another activity that I have adopted after attending a session at the White Privilege Conference is called "Taking a Personal Inventory." This activity is set up with an inner and outer circle. For each question the inner and outer circle person has two minutes to respond. Here are the ground rules for "Taking a Personal Inventory:"

Some Simple Ground Rules

I will respect the views and experiences of others.
I will speak in the first person, about my thoughts, my feelings—about myself.
I will respect confidentiality if it is requested.
I will try to listen to and appreciate the experiences and feelings expressed by others.

Each person takes turns responding to seven questions:

1. What is your ethnic and cultural heritage? What are you most proud of from that heritage? When were you first aware you were a member of that group?

2. Growing up, what kind of contact did you have with people from different racial and ethnic backgrounds?

   When were you first aware that there was such a thing as racial and ethnic differences?

   What are your earliest memories of people of color being treated differently than Whites?

   Recall an incident if you can; how did you feel?

3. How did important adults in your life (parents, teachers, coaches, clergy, etc.) help you understand and interpret your experiences with racial groups different from your own?

   What did they tell you about specific groups (e.g., African Americans, Asian Americans, Arab Americans, Latino/a Americans, Native Americans, Jewish Americans, Multiracial Americans, European Americans, etc.)? What was their main advice about these groups?

4. What was the cruelest thing someone from a different race ever did to you?

   What is your greatest fear about what they might do? Where do you think this fear comes from?

5. How has racism kept you isolated and separate from others?

   If it were possible, how would you limit the effects of racism and prejudice in your life?

6. Name a time when you stood up for your rights or the rights of others. What did you do? What do you wish you had done? What can you tell me (us) about your family or your growing up that would help me (us) understand where you got the strength and courage to do what you did?

7. How would your life be different if it were not affected by prejudice and racism?

Debrief the experience with the whole group. On a blank card write a response to this question: What can I do in concrete steps, especially after question 7, to commit to doing to get closer to the vision of 7? Be sure to include your address and turn the card in to the facilitator.

Within six months of completing this activity I send the students their note cards as reminders to keep dialoguing about racism. My experience in debriefing this exercise with groups has been raw in the sense that some students become tearful as the questions evoke painful memories while some become angry that their K–12, undergraduate, and graduate courses have thus far excluded the topics of racism, white privilege, and culture from the curriculum.

One of the most important aspects to emphasize is that culturally relevant community building is vital in a classroom in order to foster the safety, trust, and risk-taking from students. Gloria Ladson-Billings (1994) coined the term *culturally relevant teaching* and defines it as "a pedagogy that empowers students intellectually, socially, emotionally, and politically by using cultural referents to impart knowledge, skills, and attitudes" (p. 18). Usually for the first two class sessions I model culturally relevant community-building activities. Then I ask students to get into triads or pairs and they must sign up to lead a culturally relevant community-building activity in a following class session. My favorite "first day of class" culturally relevant community-building activity I use in class is called "My Name." I read aloud the vignette "My Name" from the book *The House on Mango Street* by Sandra Cisneros (2009). I read the vignette aloud with expression. Then I share what I have come to know about my name: Naomi Rae Taylor—*Naomi* in Hebrew means "pleasant spirit." When I learned this and shared this with my mother, she said not during my teenage years! Originally my mother was going to name me Rachel, but did not think I looked like a Rachel so she used Rae to substitute. My birth name was Schumann. It is German and I had no pride in keeping Schumann since that was my mother's father's name and he was a racist and never had anything to do with his two biracial grandchildren. My current last name, Taylor, is from my husband.

If the group is small, everyone shares with each other what they know of their own name; if the group is large, they each turn to a partner. Another option is to have partners introduce each other and to share one interesting aspect of their partner's name to the group.

My story begins with how race was so ill defined for me growing up. Then it encompasses the experiences of my children. Now that I am the head of two generations in my family, I can help my children and mijo construct our culture together. My hope is that they may choose to proudly self-identify—whether it be as a member of their race or ethnicity, or their gender, religion, or sexual orientation. I hope that they find strength in the various dimensions of their diversity. This global world is no longer somewhere else. It is in our homes, schools, workplaces, and neighborhoods. How I have learned to embrace and love my particular global self is a footprint I proudly leave as my mark on this earth. I believe with making this an essential and central part of my classes I can pass on to my students the joy of exploring their own culture and race and the importance of having tough conversations among themselves and with their students.

References

Bronson, P., & Merryman, A. (2009). See baby discriminate: Kids as young as 6 months old judge others based on skin color. What's a parent to do? *Newsweek.* Retrieved from http://www.thedailybeast.com/newsweek/2009/09/04/see-baby-discriminate.html

Cisneros, S. (2009). *The house on Mango Street: 25th anniversary edition* (2nd ed.). New York: Random House.

Ladson-Billings, G. (1994). *The dreamkeepers: Successful teachers of African American children.* San Francisco: Jossey-Bass.

Ladson-Billings, G., & Tate, W. F. (1995). Toward a critical race theory of education. *Teachers College Record, 97*(1), 47–68.

White Privilege Conference. Retrieved from http://www.whiteprivilegeconference.com/

8

A DEVELOPMENTAL APPROACH TO CIVILITY AND BYSTANDER INTERVENTION

Jennifer McCary

Nikki tried to sit and breathe inconspicuously as she gathered her thoughts around what she was hearing. While she sat at the shuttle stop, she was outraged as she overheard several students talking about the university becoming more lenient in their admissions process and allowing anyone in now. Nikki tried not to tune into this conversation until she heard one young man say that he has noticed an increase in Latino and Black people on campus, and he was beginning to take extra precautions. Nikki was outraged; however, she remained silent as she was one of two students of color standing at the shuttle stop. The students were not being loud; in fact, it almost seemed that they were trying to be discreet because they were aware of their company. Nevertheless, Nikki could clearly hear their conversation and knew that other bystanders at the shuttle stop overheard this as well. As the shuttle approached, Nikki decided to walk back to her residence hall. One of the males from the group of students that she overheard noticed her change of heart and asked, "Are you boycotting?"

As Nikki walked, she began to reflect on her experiences on campus, wondering why she was becoming increasingly more aware of her race. Nikki decided that she was going to ask her friends if they felt race mattered on campus and what their experiences have been. As she sat around with her roommates, Lisa and Crystal, she casually mentioned what happened at the shuttle stop. Immediately, the room erupted.

"He said what?"

"Why didn't you call us?"

"What did you say?"

Nikki said, "I didn't say anything. What was I supposed to say? I was standing with a group of people who were expressing their clear frustration with me even being a student here. What would I look like saying something?"

"Well did anyone else standing around say something?"

Perplexed by this line of inquiry, Nikki responded to her friends— "There were a few people who looked uncomfortable with what they were hearing. Most of them were White too, but no one said anything. Although I was bothered, I can't say that I was surprised. I deal with comments like this all the time on campus, including in the classroom. Just last week, one of my faculty members called me in to meet with her about one of my grades. She sat me down and told me that I did poorly on my midterm and wondered what was going on with my family. I questioned what she meant, and she asked me if there was something going on at home, such as my grandmother becoming ill, that might have been distracting me. Thoroughly confused, I asked her what my grandmother would have to do with my midterm grade. She explained that she was just curious if something was going on with my guardian or a family member that would be keeping me from my studies. I convinced myself that I was reading too much into that statement and simply replied no. I told her that I did not fully understand the material and that I should have taken more time to prepare for the exam. She told me that if I needed more time then I should register with disability services. Exhausted with the conversation, I took my exam and left her office."

As Nikki and her friends sat in silence for a few seconds, she continued by saying—"These examples are the reason that I brought up the shuttle incident in the first place. I have never felt like a minority, but these constant comments are becoming too much, and I'm considering transferring to a place where I don't stand out as much. Are either of you experiencing this stuff, or am I being too sensitive?"

"No, I don't think that you are being overly sensitive. I have undeniably had some of the same experiences. But Nikki, transferring is not the answer. No matter where you go, you are going to have to face comments that don't sit well with you. We say things about other people sometimes in the privacy of our room that wouldn't be so favorable either. Nikki, if you want to transfer, do it. But don't leave without telling someone why. Last year, we had about four friends transfer after our first semester for the same reason.

How will this place change if we all keep leaving without challenging the culture?"

With a sense of outrage emerging in the room, Mary suggested, "We need to report what that boy said to you tonight. As a matter of fact, I think that we should go and talk to some of the people that we know in Multicultural Affairs, Residence Life, and Student Activities to see if we can do a program on how bystanders can report things on campus. People need to know that bystanders have the power to intervene and change things. Nikki, you shouldn't have to walk home because you felt intimidated by the crowd on the shuttle. We shouldn't have to watch the cleaning staff, which happens to all be Black, be treated like crap because they are seen as 'the help' by the students. We should not feel like we are battling stereotypes in the classroom or seen as the exception when we succeed in the classroom rather than it being the expectation of us."

Emerging Issues

The feelings that Nikki expressed are not all that atypical of a student of color at a predominantly White institution (PWI). Smedley, Myers, and Harrell (1993) found that students of color at PWIs, unlike their White peers, experience stress in five areas—social climate, within-group stresses, interracial stresses, racism and discrimination, and higher levels of achievement stresses for females. Furthermore, Swail (2007) suggested students of color face additional challenges at PWIs:

- Not having enough professors of their own race
- Noticing few students of their race on campus
- Racist institutional policies and practices
- Difficulty having friendships with nonminority students
- Rude and unfair treatment because of race
- Discrimination
- Being accused of "acting White"
- Doubts about their ability to succeed in college

Despite our "best" efforts, students of color still feel unwelcomed or like they never really have a place on PWI campuses. Could this be because our focus has been on diversity and not civility? Colleges and universities search for solutions to help students become more actively engaged in diversity, inclusion, and creating a positive campus environment. However, it seems that students need to be hearing more messages about civility, morality, and how their ability to intervene is actually the key to more inclusive and diverse communities.

The challenge of fostering an atmosphere of civility on college campuses has been largely framed by levels of incivility that has become more evident on college campuses, especially in residence halls (Tiberius & Flak, 1999). As such, Tiberius and Flak have suggested that college campuses have become places where speech or action is disrespectful or rude and ranges from insulting remarks and verbal abuse to explosive, violent behavior, as opposed to a level of civility framed by being polite, respectful, and decent (Clark & Springer, 2007). Nevertheless, if we redirect our efforts to remind students that they control more than just their own college experiences, we may be able to change some of the bias-related incidents that happen on our campuses.

Increasing Awareness

As we begin to discuss what civility and bystander intervention is all about, we first must recognize that everyone is a bystander, every day, in one way or another, to a wide range of events that contribute to the marginalization of certain groups on campus. All students have the right to feel safe and respected when they are on their college campuses. It is everyone's obligation to stop discrimination or harmful behaviors that hurt the community or its members. Taking basic steps on reminding students of the importance of being polite, respectful, and decent are the beginnings to facilitating conversations around race or intervening when uncomfortable situations occur.

Much like Nikki's roommates in the case study at the beginning of the chapter, people find themselves passionately engrossed in conversations around race. A part of this passion stems from the fact that race, whether we realize it or not, makes up a large part of our identity. Many students of color usually identify with race before identifying with gender or any other categorizing quality. Therefore, when something is said in a classroom setting or in passing that alludes to a problem with someone's racial identity, people can grow defensive. Both students of color and White students may find themselves equally motivated to speak up when it comes to conversations around race based on their identity development or lack thereof. Contrariwise, students can sometimes find themselves silenced during conversations about race for fear of feeling ignorant, isolated, or ignored.

Students must begin to understand reasons why they don't intervene. In Nikki's situation, there were several people standing at the shuttle stop who overheard this conversation. Undoubtedly, someone besides Nikki was uncomfortable. We must explore what disables our students from being the person to challenge such harmful behaviors on campus. In those few intense moments at the shuttle stop, bystanders overheard someone expressing his opinions about students of color on campus. Every bystander may have gone through a different series of emotions; however, each one in that short time processed at least two of the following thoughts:

- What is the risk of me speaking up?
- Could someone potentially be hurt in this situation?
- Am I in the mood to intervene?
- Will this bring up a past experience or bad memory for me?
- Am I able to defend myself?
- Will someone else say something? If so, it would save me the hassle.

We must teach our students how to move from a place where they are processing these thoughts to a place where they are deciding to act.

Confronting Uncomfortable Conversations

Moving from thoughts to action is hard whenever faced with a dilemma. Intervening on someone else's behalf means that you are assuming some responsibility for the situation. To do that, you have to exhibit respect for someone whom you may not know. In some cases, respect has nothing to do with it; instead, your personal morals are telling you that speaking up is the proper thing to do. In order to act responsibly, people have to reason with themselves to come up with at least one thought telling them that they have to intervene.

To consider

1. *How will I balance my concern for this individual with my own welfare?*

   A critical moment for people when trying to decide if they should intervene is if they are jeopardizing their own welfare in any way. Students will consider if their decision will affect them academically or physically, but most importantly, if their actions will be socially acceptable to their peers. If students fear rejection, retaliation, or any consequence for intervening, then they won't. Even if they are concerned about another person, they will always put themselves first.

2. *If I remain silent, will someone get hurt as a result of my unwillingness to help?*

For students to intervene despite any perceived risks for their own welfare, they must feel that someone can be physically, mentally, or emotionally harmed if they remain silent. Students will evaluate the situation and decide if this is a clear emergency. Any ambiguity could result in them deciding to steer clear. Latané and Darley (1970) suggest that if a group of bystanders are witnessing an emergency, it is less likely that any of them will help. Their theory, *the bystander effect*, assumes that the more people witness an emergency, the less likely it is that someone will intervene because people convince themselves that nothing is wrong because no one else is responding. However, if a person is alone and witnesses an emergency, he or she is more likely to intervene by at least calling authorities for help. In Nikki's case, there were several students at the shuttle stop. Therefore, others may have felt that nothing was wrong since no one else spoke up. They may have also assumed that someone else would help.

3. *Do I feel like being bothered with this?*

As strange as it may seem to include this question, people are more likely to help others when they are in a good mood. If you are already having a bad day, why would you willingly engage in a situation that can make your day worse? If someone is in a bad mood, this is not the person that we want intervening because his or her emotional state could potentially lead to a more harmful situation. If a person is in a bad mood, he or she should simply identify someone else who can assist.

4. *How do I even begin to confront racist behaviors on campus?*

This is the most difficult question. It is the moment that takes you from thoughts to action. When dealing with race, people should be careful that they are confronting the behavior and not the character of the person. As mentioned early, people get defensive about their identities. The reality is that in some cases when bystanders are intervening, they won't know the first thing about a person anyway. It is important to keep in mind that you can call people out for their actions without accusing them of being bad people. You want them to understand that what they did had an effect on others and that it will not be tolerated in the community. This goes along with any example of intervention in both on- and off-campus situations. In any conversation, you just want to address the behavior and allow that person to ponder his or her responsibility in the situation.

Follow Up

1. If you were a student at the shuttle stop and overheard this conversation, what would your response be?
2. Do you feel that Nikki (or any other student) should transfer because of an incident like this?
3. If you received a report from Nikki outlining the details of this event, how would you respond? Keep in mind that Nikki does not know the young man's name.
4. What are some things that you could do to educate students on the concept of civility?
5. How do you promote the concept of bystander intervention?

Commentary

In response to question three, you will want to be certain to consider who will be designated to respond to this incident. Does your institution already have a bias or harassment policy in place, and will it require some form of adjudication if the young man is later identified? Additionally, you want to keep Nikki's feelings in mind throughout this process.

Some institutions notify the entire campus community that an incident has occurred and is being investigated. This is a good way to send a message that bias behaviors will not be tolerated on campus. Nevertheless, if Nikki could potentially be singled out by this form of communication, you may want to consider alternative methods in getting this information out to the campus.

You want to take these types of incidents as an opportunity to educate the entire campus. This allows everyone to have a developmental moment around sensitive topics. It also helps in reaffirming the mission and values of an institution, while promoting larger lessons on civility.

References

Clark, C. M., & Springer, P. J. (2007). Thoughts on incivility: Students and faculty perceptions of uncivil behavior. *Nursing Education, 28*(2), 93–97.

Latané, B., & Darley, J. (1970). *The unresponsive bystander: Why doesn't he help?* New York: Appleton-Century-Crofts.

Smedley, B. D., Myers, H. F., & Harrell, S. P. (1993). Minority-status stresses and the college adjustment of ethnic minority freshman. *The Journal of Higher Education, 64*(4), 434–452.

Swail, W. S. (2007, February). Campus climate and students of color. *The Newsletter for Higher Education Professionals,* 4–6.

Tiberius, R. G., & Flak, E. (1999). Incivility in dyadic teaching and learning. *New Directions for Teaching and Learning, 77,* 3–12.

PART THREE

CLASSROOM DIALOGUES: PRESCHOOL, ELEMENTARY

9

WHITE SKIN AND PRINCESS HAIR

Exploring Race in a Preschool Classroom

Brigid Beaubien and Linda Williams

It was the kind of day, in a Midwest winter, that made both the teacher and children think that summer was but a distant, abstract memory. Dark clouds heavy with snow allowed not even the tiniest bit of sun to shine through. Ice built up on both sides of the windows and steam rose from manhole covers trying to escape the frigid temperatures. There, in an urban classroom, were twenty African-American preschoolers with their white teacher. The classroom was a bright spot in the otherwise gray day filled with light, color, and happy noises. It was free play time and each of the children was engrossed in different activities. The teacher and one of her four-year-old students sat close together at the child-size table, on child-size chairs, working intently on practicing how to make a capital Q for Quincy, the young man's name. Quincy's hand was gently enveloped by the teacher's as they repeatedly made circles—"with one important, fancy swish," she had said. There was obviously a great deal of warmth between the two—they sat close together and he would lean his elbow on her thigh as they were talking about the writing. He stared intently at his teacher, studying her face as she discussed the merits and importance of that "swish" making it more than just a circle but a letter. He giggled at the noise she made for the swish and again placed his hand under hers to begin another set of circles. Suddenly, he untangled his hand and moved his fingers across the top of her hand. Wondering what he could be doing she looked down to find him carefully studying her hand. After a few moments Quincy looked up at his teacher with amazement and loudly announced, *"You're white!"* Several children snickered while several others came over to see for themselves. The teacher's hand was pulled by several children at once as they explored her whiteness. Moira announced that she knew all along that teacher was white. Sheketa, Quincy's cousin, wondered how he could be so dumb and several others agreed. A few children were quietly observing, wondering where all this was going and what the teacher was going to say. Quincy looked up at the teacher with questioning eyes and again stated, "You're white." The only person more surprised than Quincy was the teacher. After years of teaching in an urban classroom as one of a very small number of white teachers at her school, she had been pretty sure her race was something that most children came into her classroom understanding. Children regularly arrived each September quickly telling her their Daddy, or Grandpa, or Mother, thought she wasn't a very good teacher because she was white or that she shouldn't be teaching them because she wasn't black. She was used to that—but here, Quincy just realized that she wasn't like him—that there was a difference. This felt profound to the teacher and she didn't want to make a mistake—but she also wasn't sure how to proceed.

During the 2008 election it was common to hear television pundits talk about a "postracial" country and refer to the need for a conversation around race, making it sound like we were all going to sit down one Tuesday at 3 o'clock and chat it out. Obviously, this is not going to happen. So how do these needed conversations about race take place? They can occur in a multitude of public and private spaces, but conversations taking place in early childhood classrooms, with the very youngest of children, could potentially have the most substantial long-term effect on these conversations. While much of children's racial socialization and attitudes are grounded in the beliefs that occur in the home as children enter preschool, the school community often presents the first opportunity to join this racial conversation in public space. Racial conversations occur every day in the preschool classroom. Often teachers either ignore the conversation or take a surface, almost passive way around the dialogue, losing the opportunity to open and create the discussion of race in a comfortable, safe, learning space. This is exactly where the teacher found herself with Quincy and his classmates. If she said too much it became a big deal; if she said too little she wasn't laying the foundation for positive conversations in the future.

Racial socialization, defined as the "subtle, overt, deliberate and unintended mechanisms by which parental attitudes and behaviors transmit world views about race and ethnicity" (Hughes, 2003, p. 15) takes place in different ways among different racial groups, depending on where the race and ethnicity is placed on the hierarchy of power. White, middle-class parents often give messages such as "everybody's the same" or "everybody's equal" and avoid direct conversation about race (Bronson & Merryman, 2009). White, middle-class teachers may follow this example in the classroom and gloss over opportunities to speak more directly about race with children, believing that this stance will help all children negate the negative messages of a racially and ethnically stratified culture. Another belief often held by white parents and teachers is that a racially diverse environment is enough to communicate a desire for integration and diversity. Often white parents feel that they do not need to talk directly about race because they may send their children to racially mixed schools. Overt talk about race is avoided because it is seen as rude or uncomfortable. The parents hope that their children will form unbiased opinions about their diverse classmates and that their children will become "color-blind" (Bronson & Merryman, 2009). Concurrently, a white teacher may think that her presence in a mostly or all-black school environment may be sufficient to communicate her own beliefs about integration, racial harmony, and racial equality. Her admonitions that "we are all the same" may unconsciously reinforce her own beliefs in color blindness. Research shows us racially diverse environments do not automatically educate students about other races or help students form friendships across racial lines. In fact, research shows that integrated environments often result in reinforcing negative stereotypes about the "Other" (Moody, 2001).

So what should the white teacher in the opening vignette do? Fortunately, this teacher was very experienced and also had participated in antiracism work. She knew the position from which she spoke and its inherent socially constructed and assumed power. She knew that Quincy's abrupt statement was a window into his developing maturity as he learned to classify attributes of people just as he was learning to categorize circles and lines into specific letters. It would have been pointless to tell Quincy "we're all alike" or that "it doesn't matter." Quincy's eyes told him there was a difference between himself and his teacher—and it was a difference he had heard about and around which he was constructing his own knowledge. It was also a difference that other children had spoken about and whose ears had now been alerted by Quincy's exclamation. So in response to Quincy's, "You're white," his teacher simply said, "I am." This plain statement invited more exploration by Quincy and he stared at her face examining it in a different way than he had just moments ago. "Does it change anything?" she asked.

He thought for a moment—no, he didn't think so. "If I'm white," the teacher said, "what are you?" "We're black" came a chorus of children. A discussion of who was what color began and the teacher took the opportunity, like many in quality preschool programs do, to explore what color each person really was. Scrapping her plans for the rest of the morning she brought out skin-colored paint and after tracing each child's hand, they mixed paints together to exactly replicate each person's skin tone. When it was all said and done, it was determined that the teacher was really peach with red flecks, white blotches, and brown freckles and not really white at all. Quincy was mocha mixed with just a touch of cinnamon, as was his cousin, Sheketa. Moira was a combination of ebony and olive. Discussion around the phenomenon of skin color helped the students where they were: struggling with the blanket categorizations of skin color that belied their knowledge about what they saw with their own eyes. It also gave them language around color and skin tone that allowed them to work with categorization more precisely, as their developing minds reached for increasingly more specific definitions. And while this portion of the conversation did not attend directly to all the political and social dimensions as to why some people were called "white," and others "black," it did confirm this: that it was all right to talk about race and skin color in this public space.

Throughout that frosty winter week, the classroom was abuzz as color and race continued to be discussed. The teacher had quickly written a letter to the parents to let them know about the classroom discussion and to invite any parent wanting to discover their color to come in and paint their hand. Several did this and lively conversations about skin color were heard among parents, students, and teacher. Questions arose such as whether a person's color changed as he or she grew up and why Sheketa, for example, wasn't the same color as her mother. The conversations ranged from serious to silly, but the teacher kept the dialogue organic and focused on the experience of the participants. She wanted each conversant to trust his or her own understanding and she consciously chose not to bring in books or outside resources that would have shifted the power to the authority of outside experts.

At the end of the week, five-year-old Moira tripped over a toy and hit her head on one of the tables. As she burst into tears, the teacher scooped her up and sat her sobbing charge in her lap, rocking and soothing her gently. As Moira began to calm down she rubbed the teacher's smooth brown ponytail between her thumb and first two fingers. Once Moira was fully recovered she said to her teacher, "You have princess hair."

What did Moira mean by this revelation? Was she comparing her teacher's hair to images she had absorbed from the media? Did her teacher's hair most resemble the hair of fairy tale princesses, fashion dolls, or beauty queens? Was it hair that Moira herself wanted? Did Moira on some level associate her white teacher's hair as a symbol of power and femininity? Again, the teacher thought quickly about how to respond. She knew she must somehow acknowledge Moira's experience, while gently engaging the boundaries of her schema. "And you," the teacher responded, "have the hair of an African queen." This response seemed to satisfy Moira as she leaned her carefully parted and braided hair against her teacher's shoulder.

Preschoolers are wonderful phenomenologists. As they explore the dimensions of human beings, they are learning to distinguish characteristics such as gender, color, race, ethnicity, wealth, age, and so on, and assign attributes to each category. In this identity-forming process, they are looking for what is "me/not me," sometimes looking for confirmation in common characteristics, or sometimes disconfirmation in difference. From a cognitive point of view, preschoolers are rapidly enriching their mental representations of their experiences, organizing their worlds into useful schemata that help increase their understanding. From a sociocultural point of view, they are apprentices to the task of learning how to interpret the data they are acquiring through observation and participation in the tasks of daily living. They look to significant others—family, peers, caregivers, and teachers—to know how to understand, respond to, incorporate, or disassociate the data from the interactions they observe and participate in. In their research on young children and intergroup bias, Patterson and Bigler (2006) make use of both the cognitive and sociocultural points of view. They suggest that preschoolers are highly influenced "to show preferences for groups that adults emphasize in their language and behavior, even in the complete absence of explicitly evaluative messages about groups" (p. 858). In other words, young children observe very closely the behaviors and the subtle use of language of the adults around them to both augment their schema and know how to respond. Thus, it was important for Moira's teacher to affirm Moira with both her deeds and her words. A safe place was created for Moira to recover from her accident and this place was the teacher's lap, where Moira perhaps absently began touching her teacher's hair. It was in this context that Moira brought words to the sensory phenomenon by describing her white teacher's hair as "princess" hair. By responding as she did, the teacher hoped to engage Moira's metaphor by utilizing the motif of royalty. More importantly, she hoped to find a place of similarity from which Moira could construct her own sense of belongingness.

It is perhaps redundant to ask for the hard conversation about race in this country. There is no one conversation to be had. Rather, what we learned from observations in a preschool classroom is that these conversations are happening in classrooms every day. The level of conversation increases, however, when teachers are thoughtful, reflective practitioners who are able to talk openly and honestly with students, according to the students' developmental needs. Effective educators are also able to hold honest conversations with parents, other teachers, and administrators regarding the importance of homegrown, student-prompted conversations about race and ethnicity. The more these conversations are encouraged throughout classrooms, the more our students will be served not only to talk about race and racial issues, but also to perhaps be in a position to do something about the persistent inequities in our schools and communities.

References

Bronson, P., & Merryman, A. (2009). *Nurtureshock: New thinking about children.* New York: Twelve, Hachette Book Group.

Hughes, D. (2003). Correlates of African American and Latino parents' messages to children about ethnicity and race: a comparative study of racial socialization. *American Journal of Community Psychology, 31*(1/2), 15–33.

Moody, J. (2001). Race, school integration, and friendship segregation in America. *American Journal of Sociology, 107*(3), 679–716.

Patterson, M. M., & Bigler. R. S. (2006). Preschool children's attention to environmental messages about groups: social categorization and the origins of intergroup bias. *Child Development, 77*(4), 847–860.

10

LESSONS LEARNED

Creating a Safe Space to Navigate a Challenging Topic

Pam Booker

"Pam, I'm calling to offer you the position." I was elated. The week before, I had interviewed for the Community Cultures position at a K–6 elementary school created for the main purpose of voluntary integration. The students came from one urban district and two suburban districts in Minnesota. Students were admitted by lottery, and enrollment each year was always close to 50% students of color and 50% white students. The two foci of the school were Environmental Science and Community Cultures. I had been a classroom teacher at the school for a number of years, but felt that this position was the ultimate next step in my career. I would have the opportunity to work with all of the students in the building, and the responsibility to teach kids to see differences without judgment. Another part of the position was to provide professional development in culturally relevant teaching for staff in the building. It felt as though my passion for teaching, learning, and equity were coming together in a job that was made for me.

The Physical Environment

The classroom I inherited was a dream space. It was located at the front of the building with picture windows facing the front doors. That room could set the tone for the entire building as visitors entered, and I wanted to make sure it lived up to that purpose. I also wanted to make sure the room represented an inviting space: a welcoming and inclusive place where students (and adults) could share their thoughts and experiences with each other with respect and compassion. There was a stove and refrigerator in the room, plenty of cabinet space, and natural lighting. Four bulletin boards and two long whiteboards lined the walls. There were tables and chairs to enhance collaborative and cooperative learning opportunities. Bookshelves held multiple supplemental materials for teachers. The room also housed other multicultural resources such as posters, artifacts, and trade books, many written in the students' home languages. I wanted to make sure that this was an environment where all of my students would see themselves reflected. I made sure to display materials that represented the cultural groups who were part of the school community. I made use of many of the cultural artifacts that were at my disposal to display in the room. Things like musical instruments, baskets, textiles, and dolls were accessible for students to touch and explore. I also made sure I had left enough wall space in the room and in the halls outside the room to display authentic student work. Our ways of being with each other (classroom norms) in the space would be designed and agreed upon by the students.

Instruction

Before each nine-week quarter began (this was a year-round school), I made it a point to meet with the classroom teachers whose students would have Community Cultures as their specialist time. I asked about what topics they would be covering, particularly in social studies, and how I could support the standards they needed to cover. The classrooms were multiage except kindergarten. The other grades were 1–2, 3–4, and 5–6. At times the topics would vary among each class and multiple grade level standards had to be taught. Many teachers would want me to teach specific topics, while others would let me choose what standards I wanted to focus on. I always made sure that what I was teaching would somehow be connected to what the students were learning in their classrooms.

As every new class entered my classroom, the very first thing we did was build community. I was used to working with a group of fifty students (two classrooms combined with two teachers team teaching) in my own multiage classroom. Now I would be seeing over 400 students in a year. I made it a point to learn their names and find out something about them: what they enjoyed about school, what hobbies they had. I realized early on in my teaching career the importance of building relationships with my students. I told them I had high expectations for them and wanted them to learn so that the possibilities for them would be endless. I greeted each one of them as they entered the classroom and said good-bye as they left, sometimes just asking how school was going for them or what plans they had for the weekend. These seem like little things, but I always believe that kids know if you really care about them or if you don't. They need to be affirmed and encouraged. I also communicated what was being taught and why. I expressed that we were there to help and support each other and that it was all right to be ourselves in the space. We were going to learn about different cultures, and that we would talk about things that were different. But different is just different, not less than.

It was okay to disagree. I also realized early on that I needed to model this behavior as well. Every Community Cultures class began with a read-aloud. This was standard for every grade level, and soon became the expectation of the students. They came in and immediately gathered at the section of the room called the "story rug." I always read sitting in a rocking chair as the students gathered around me. The stories were always connected to our topics and contained diverse characters. When choosing the books I read, I also was purposeful in choosing stories that would give students multiple perspectives. I was always conscious about whose story was being told and by whom. Often we had the most enlightening conversations by reading someone else's story. Connections were made with characters who culturally were the polar opposite of many of the kids in the room. After the story was read, I used a variety of strategies to teach each lesson. Because most of the classes were multiage, I provided choice and paid close attention to the learning styles of the students. There were art activities, simulations and role plays, direct instruction, debates, and cooking opportunities. Family or community members would come and present to the students as cultural informants and resource people. Students were given the opportunity to work alone, in pairs, or in small groups. The most powerful days came when students could connect what they were learning in class to their lives outside school. I would often hear from families that the most engaging conversations at the dinner table were based on what their child had learned in Community Cultures class that day.

A Challenging Topic

Although I taught many lessons as a specialist, there is one nine-week quarter with a group of fifth and sixth graders I will never forget. I met with the teachers before the quarter began, and found that they were both teaching about the Civil War. However, I soon realized that they did not feel comfortable teaching about slavery. Now, I remember when I was in school and the topic of slavery came up, all heads turned toward me in that sixth grade classroom in San Angelo, Texas. Of course because I was black, I had to know all about slavery. I did not want that experience to replay itself for any of my students. I volunteered to teach about slavery since it appeared it was a stress-producing topic for my colleagues. I was also a little disheartened that professionals choosing to teach in a voluntary integration school with a community cultures focus would not see this as an opportunity instead of a challenge, but I also understood that we are all at different places in our intercultural journeys. Previously that summer I had attended a three-week class called "The Teaching of Africa" offered at Yale University. I knew I had some wonderful things to use with the kids and I was excited to begin. At first, I wanted to let families know what we would be talking about for the next nine weeks, so I sent home a letter to families. I know this is a controversial topic for many, and wanted to make sure that if students came home sharing information they had learned in class, they would be prepared. Most importantly, I needed to find out what the kids knew about slavery. I was surprised to discover they did not know a lot, especially my African-American and biracial students. I realized I had to tread lightly, because the last thing I wanted to do was damage. I felt it was important to lay a strong foundation about the continent, which is something many of us did not have the opportunity to learn about in school or in our teacher preparation programs. We began with the history of Africa—kings and queens, contributions in medicine, innovations in farming and irrigation systems. We learned about the vast array of natural resources located on the continent and the scramble then to "acquire" those resources. We learned about European colonialism and American silence as rich cultural beliefs, practices, and languages were stripped away. As we got further along, I started talking about the slave trade: who started it, why it started, and how it was done. I always made certain I left enough time at the end of class to make sure that students had the opportunity to debrief and process the information they learned each day. I actually started talking about slavery with Tom Feelings's (1995) book, *The Middle Passage*. The power of this book is that there are no words, just pictures. I then facilitated a simulation about what happened to the victims once they were captured, until they exited the "door of no return" of the slave forts. The students would lie on the floor of the classroom and learn about "tight packing" versus "loose packing" ships. We talked about lives lost en route to unknown destinations, the language barriers, mistreatment and fear of the victims, who had no idea what was happening to them. The students learned about the sickness that resulted from disease and vomiting caused by the rough seas. Once the slaves arrived at port—South America, the Caribbean, or North America—they were branded and sold at auction to work at plantations that grew sugar cane or cotton. Their identities were reinvented in strange lands with new names, new languages, and new lives. Needless to say, each day generated more questions and, not surprisingly, feelings of empathy. Talk about the power of story and multiple perspectives! So when our discussion of the Civil War came and went, the students had a firm understanding about how and why it happened. However, the students wanted to know more about what happened afterward. What would the future of the freed slaves hold? The quarter ended with the Reconstruction Era and a debate arguing the differing views of Marcus Garvey, Booker T. Washington, and W. E. B. Du Bois. I knew the students were applying all they had learned during that memorable quarter, when I entered the lunch-room and they were still debating their positions at their tables long after our class had ended.

Reflections

I've been out of the classroom for a number of years now, focusing on the professional learning of teachers and district-wide initiatives around equity. I am the supervisor in the Office of Equity and Integration in a first-ring suburb of St. Paul, Minnesota. I think back now to the physical and instructional environment I set up for students in that beautiful Community Cultures class-room and realize adults learn in the same way. They need a safe space to talk about race and other issues. They need to be accepted for where they are and given support to enrich their lived experiences around difference. They need to be able to see difference without judgment and learn that different is just different, not deficient. They need to see through a lens of multiple perspectives, understanding that even if we disagree, we still maintain our own values and beliefs while respecting the rights of others to maintain theirs as well. I still understand I need to tread lightly. To not do damage, shame, or blame, but to take teachers where they are and move them forward to benefit all learners and their achievement. I know I need to give them the theory behind educational equity, and the opportunity for practical application.

In my current position, I often get the opportunity to go to the high school and see some of my former students. Just recently, I ended up in an office waiting to meet with a colleague, when one of my former elementary students saw me through the window and came in. The young man, now a high school senior, started talking about Community Cultures class. "I just remember all of the great books you read to us and all of the things we learned about different cultures. I loved coming to your class." As our conversation continued, I asked about his family, his mom and his older brother, whom I also taught. The most important lesson learned in working with children and adults was building and maintaining relationships.

In no particular order, here are some other lessons learned in my professional journey (so far):

1. **Self-reflect on your practice.** When a lesson doesn't go well, don't immediately blame the students, but ask how your instruction may have affected their learning.

2. **Lean into your discomfort.** We bring all of who we are into our classrooms, including biases and assumptions we may have grown up with. To truly become more culturally competent and racially aware, we must do our own work. We need to purposefully put ourselves in situations where we are the cultural "other," a place where many of our students find themselves on a daily basis in our schools and classrooms. There is no strategy or "quick fix" when it comes to working with historically underserved students. No curriculum or teaching tool will be effective if we have deficit views about students and families. Focusing on how we react and adapt to difference is crucial in seeing students as individuals with differing needs, gifts, and talents.

3. **Know your students and your content, especially when teaching difficult subject matter.** Find out what your students know or don't know about a topic and proceed accordingly. Preview any and all materials before using them with students. Check for dated information, biased language, and multiple perspectives. Through whose lens is the story being told? If you don't know about a particular topic, do some research and ask for help from a cultural informant, community member, or colleague. Finally, inform families about difficult topics you may be discussing with their children. Be clear about why and how you will teach the content. Keeping them in the loop from the beginning can minimize conflicts and problems later on.

Reference

Feelings, T. (1995). *The Middle Passage: White ships/black cargo.* New York: Dial Books.

11

CONVERSATIONS WITH CHILDREN

Discussions About Race and Identity

Cheryl Moore-Thomas and Jennifer Scaturo Watkinson

B y the age of three or four, many children have begun to construct ideas about race and their own racial identity (Araujo & Strasser, 2003; Derman-Sparks & Ramsey, 2011). By the time these same youngsters reach elementary school, their initial reflections on race may start to take root as ideas and frameworks supported by internal theories, familial beliefs and practices, prevalent societal notions, experiences, misconceptions, and even fear. Elementary educators and others committed to the healthy academic, social, and emotional development of children must therefore be committed to creating environments that allow children to appropriately explore and discuss their forming ideas of race and racial identity development. This chapter discusses the racial identity development trajectory of elementary school–aged children and uses a case example to help educators, parents, guardians, and others facilitate meaningful conversations with elementary school–aged children about race.

Race is a powerful political and socioeconomic construct correlated with artificial categorical differences in physical appearance and complex systems of advantage and disadvantage (Brace, 1995; Derman-Sparks & Ramsey, 2011). This correlation can affect an individual's psychological functioning, including one's racial identity development. Moreover, as elementary school–aged children's level of cognitive development increases, they learn the cues and attributes often associated with their own and other group membership (Corenblum, Annis, & Tanaka, 1997) including preferences, beliefs, and dispositions.

Early Understandings of Race

A clear example of this early formation of ideas about race and race identity can be found in the Clark and Clark (1947) doll study. In this groundbreaking work, Clark and Clark showed dolls to black children between the ages of three and seven. The dolls were identical in every way except skin color: one doll was black and the other white. The children were then asked questions to determine racial perception and preference. Data from the study suggested that when asked which they preferred, the majority of the children selected the white doll and attributed positive characteristics to it like *good* and *pretty* while attributing negative characteristics like *bad* and *ugly* to the black doll. The Clarks concluded that at a very young age the children had developed a sense of race, beliefs about race, and a sense of their own identity. It is important to note that the children's racial identity was not formed in isolation, but within a context of societal prejudice, discrimination, marginalization, and segregation. These findings have been corroborated in studies since this seminal work (Aboud & Doyle, 1996; Corenblum, Annis, & Tanaka, 1997), and in a recent study of black and white children that seems to suggest that even today, decades beyond the original Clark and Clark study, children still notice race and assign meaning to it (CNN, 2010).

Given this reality, it is both perplexing and troubling that some individuals who are committed to working with and raising healthy children espouse a color-blind ideology. Those advocating a color-blind ideology profess, "We don't see color. We see children." This particular orientation is not well founded and serves as "a veneer of liberality which covers up continuing racist thought and practice that is often less overt and more disguised" (Feagin, 2000, p. 3). Often, the tragedy of children's early exploration and acknowledgment of race and racial identity is our denial that there is difference and even more frequently, our silence. "Children who have been silenced often enough learn not to talk about race publically. Their questions do not go away, they just go unasked" (Tatum, 1997, p. 36). Children need supportive adults who can help them develop healthy racial attitudes. Indeed, conversations with children that *broach* race or consider the relation of one's race and culture to the manifestation of his or her dispositions, worldviews, and concerns may help support the development of healthy life outcomes (Day-Vines et al., 2007).

Race Constancy

While young children may not yet have developed the cognitive skills to fully process their understandings of race, clearly, as they enter school they are aware of their race and the race of others (Tatum, 1997). Beyond this fundamental awareness of race, children next begin to understand that their race and the race of others is permanent.

Race permanence or race constancy is the understanding that race, unlike height or age, does not change (Dawson, 2007; Tatum, 1997). In a study of eighty children, Semaj (1980) found that between the ages of four and eleven children begin to understand that race is permanent. Similarly, other research has also found that race constancy emerges and begins to develop in childhood (Aboud, 1988; Hirschfeld, 1995; Tatum, 1997). While children at this age may not understand how they got to be black or white or even implications of race (Aboud, 1988), they do begin to understand its permanency.

Racial Socialization

Racial socialization is the process through which parents and guardians give their children racial information that strengthens racial pride and self-esteem, while providing key protective factors that support healthy identity development (Thomas, Speight, & Witherspoon, 2010). Most often this occurs through modeling or casual conversations prompted by children's spontaneous questions about race. At other times, the socialization occurs through more direct means such as deliberate exposure to experiences or readings that urge children to think about their racial culture more deeply. Under ideal circumstances, the racial socialization process often enacted by parents and guardians goes hand in hand with the educative process on diversity and multiculturalism used by educators in schools.

Derman-Sparks and Ramsey (2011) note that it is not enough to teach children to embrace racial and cultural diversity: "[W]e must also help children develop group and individual identities that recognize and resist the false notions of racial superiority and racial entitlement and realize how they can benefit from a society free of systemic and individual racism" (p. 3). Banks (1999) offers educators two approaches that may help children deeply consider issues of multiculturalism, race, and diversity.

Banks's (1999) *Transformation Approach* encourages children to look at concepts and issues from a variety of perspectives. Through this kind of instruction, educators can help children understand race and culture as an integrated element of life. White race worldviews and behaviors no longer mark the normalized standard while overtly or inadvertently subjugating black worldviews and behaviors to the rank of abnormality or "other." The *Social Action Approach* (Banks), a second approach that could be used by educators, extends the orientation of the *Transformation Approach* and moves children to activities and behaviors that strive for social change and justice.

Racial Identity Development

As children mature, they continue their movement through various identity development trajectories. In particular, models of racial identity development describe the process by which individuals come to understand who they are as racial beings (Cross, 1995; Helms, 1995). Determining our racial identity and its meaning on the individual level is not done in isolation. Racial identity development is negotiated through social interactions in various contexts within and outside one's own racial group. The intricate descriptions of statuses, related processing strategies, and schemata of individual racial identity development models are beyond the scope of this chapter; however, three general principles of racial identity development are important for people working with elementary school–aged children to keep in mind.

The first principle is that, although an individual's racial identity development may generally follow a model mentioned previously, each person's racial identity development is distinct. That is, the specific experiences and questions, the internal processing of those experiences and questions, and the personalization of those experiences and questions of race are unique to the individual. Second, the age at which we begin to intensify our questions and experiences of who we are as racial beings often coincides with the age we start to ask questions about other aspects of our identity, including our sexual, religious, and ethnic orientations. Most research suggests this process begins during adolescence (Phinney, 1996; Tatum, 1997). For those working with and raising the elementary school–aged child, however, it is important to realize that it is not unusual for this process to begin for children as young as nine or ten years of age (Tatum, 1997). This may be especially true for children of color who work out their identities in and against a dominant white culture. Third, the sense of racial difference, which is acquired early in life, may serve as a catalyst for preadolescent development of racial identity.

Although it would not be unusual for a white student whose identity is modeled and reinforced by dominant culture to navigate the stages of racial identity much later in life, a black child may start to develop notions of racial identity early because his or her sense of self may not be as clearly and accurately reflected and reinforced by the surrounding dominant culture.

Examples of these basic principles and other discussed concepts of racial identity development are integrated in the following case.

Case Example

During an in-class art activity, Ms. Miller, a third grade teacher at Addison Elementary School, asked her students to draw a picture of themselves as a part of her *All About Me* unit. While walking around the room she noticed Madison's half-finished picture. Madison left her picture to search for a crayon in one of the classroom's crayon bins.

"Madison," said Ms. Miller, "can I help you find a crayon?"

Madison replied, "Yes, I am looking for a crayon that matches my skin."

"Well," Ms. Miller said, "we have brown and black crayons. Maybe one of those colors would work for you?"

Madison said, "But those colors don't match my skin color. I want to find one that does."

Noticing that several of the students had finished their pictures and were preparing to get their things for lunch, Ms. Miller said, "Madison, that brown is a good match. Why don't you just use that color?" Noticing some resistance, Ms. Miller continued, "We are running out of time and I would like for you to get your picture finished before we go to lunch."

Madison said, "But it doesn't look like me."

Ms. Miller said, "I know it isn't perfect, but we don't have time to keep looking. Please go to your seat and finish your work."

Madison went back to her seat and put her head down on her desk. When Ms. Miller went over to her, she noticed that Madison was crying. Not knowing what to do, she asked Madison if she wanted to visit Ms. Langstaff, the school counselor. Madison said that she was fine, dried her eyes and began to color her portrait using the brown crayon.

Later that day, still uncomfortable with Madison's tears, Ms. Miller talked with Ms. Langstaff about Madison, the crayon, and their interaction. Ms. Langstaff noted, "Madison is the only black girl in your class." Ms. Miller had not realized it before, but Madison was the only student of color in her class, and one of only 14 black students in the entire school of 379 students. Getting a little uncomfortable with the direction of the conversation, Ms. Miller assured Ms. Langstaff that she treated everyone in her class equally. Ms. Miller went on to explain that she doesn't see color in her classroom, only children.

Ms. Langstaff asked Ms. Miller to talk about her feelings related to the interaction she had with Madison. Ms. Miller explained that she didn't like how sad Madison got and that it wasn't like her to cry over something as simple as a crayon. Ms. Miller stated that she thinks maybe something is going on at home. Ms. Langstaff listened carefully before speaking and redirecting the conversation. "What meaning did that crayon have for Madison?" asked Ms. Langstaff.

"I don't know," said Ms. Miller, "she just kept saying that she was looking for a color that matched her skin."

"Okay," said Ms. Langstaff, "that was important to her. How did that connect with the assignment you were asking your students to complete?"

"Well, I guess she wanted to have a color crayon that matched how she sees herself," said Ms. Miller. "Maybe not being able to find one made her sad," added Ms. Miller, realizing her mistake.

Ms. Langstaff added, "So it could be possible that Madison was upset because she didn't feel as if any of the colors represented her. From what you have shared, it seems that was very important to Madison. Perhaps not finding a crayon that matched her sense of self may have made her feel left out or sad. Perhaps that significance was not recognized and validated in your interaction."

Ms. Langstaff told Ms. Miller that considering children's racial identity development is a normal part of human development. She explained that to not consider Madison's growth and development as a young black girl would be a disservice to both Madison and the other students in the class. Equal treatment, or giving everyone the same exact thing, is not the same as making sure each student gets what he or she needs, developmentally. Ms. Langstaff noted that as racial beings students should always have their needs considered in a racial context. Madison, she explained, is about the same age as some students are who begin to ask questions about fitting in and otherness. This is especially true for children whose identities are not reflected and supported by the dominant culture. Madison is trying to figure all of this out for herself in a school and community context where she sees few black peers. Although Madison may not yet have the language and abstract reasoning skills to put all she is experiencing into words, she is still trying to make sense of it all. Ms. Langstaff went on to help Ms. Miller think of developmentally appropriate ways she could use the third grade curriculum to create open classroom environments that would allow all of the students to come to more complete understandings of self. The two also decided that Ms. Langstaff would work with the students through a series of classroom guidance lessons on diversity and justice. Using literature that depicts main characters from different races and cultural backgrounds, the lessons would allow for students to ask their own questions about race and identity. To encourage family involvement, Ms. Miller wrote a letter to the parents and guardians of her students explaining the value of multicultural education, even in schools like Addison Elementary where the population is predominantly homogenous.

Implications

The preceding case example suggests many implications for educators and others committed to facilitating meaningful conversations with elementary school-aged children about race. While the paths to these conversations may be varied and must be guided by the unique developmental needs and contexts of the children involved, the following should be considered:

- Engage in constant reflection about your own racial identity development. Strive to understand who you are as a racial being and how your identity shapes your worldview, actions, beliefs, and values. Consider contexts of privilege, marginalization, discrimination, and oppression, and how these may manifest in your environment and the environments of the children whose development you support. Consider how these factors shape your worldview and the ways you may or may not initially recognize and respond to children's questions about race.
- Gain knowledge of racial identity development trajectories and research. Understand concepts of race awareness, constancy, and racial identity development models as they pertain to children. Integrate this knowledge with research-based understandings of children's cognitive and psychosocial development to gain a more complete understanding of children's growth.
- Converse with trusted colleagues and friends about race and racial identity development. Hold honest conversations with others so that you can break adult silence on race and alleviate the discomfort and

resistance against acknowledging race and racial difference. Use these conversations as ways to perception check and enhance your understanding of self and others.

- Commit to including multicultural education in your local school that moves beyond race celebration, to education on race that is transformational and aimed toward social justice (see Banks, 1999; Derman-Sparks & Ramsey, 2011).

- Provide ample space and opportunity for children to ask questions about their race and the race of others. Move from embarrassment and shame to a disposition that respects and honors children's inquisitive nature regarding the world and people around them. Treat each spontaneous interaction as an opportunity to guide children to more authentic and respectful understandings of race and racial identity development.

Conclusion

Many elementary school–aged children have begun to construct ideas about race and their own racial identity (Araujo & Strasser, 2003; Derman-Sparks & Ramsey, 2011). Elementary educators and others committed to the healthy academic, social, and emotional development of children, therefore, have a unique opportunity and responsibility to help young children process their emerging ideas and frameworks of race. Children develop beliefs about race within social contexts and will interpret the events that have occurred within those contexts with or without our guidance. The work, although challenging, reaps benefits. Holding courageous, honest conversations with children about race differences and their own racial identity in the context of the world around them allows children to ultimately more fully embrace themselves and others.

References

Aboud, F. E. (1988). *Children and prejudice.* New York: Blackwell.

Aboud, F. E., & Doyle, A. B. (1996). Does talk of race foster tolerance or prejudice in children? *Canadian Journal of Behavioural Science/Revue canadienne des sciences du comportement, 28*(3), 161–170.

Araujo, L., & Strasser, J. (2003). Confronting prejudice in the early childhood classroom. *Kappa Delta Pi Record, 39,* 178–182.

Banks, J. A. (1999). *An introduction to multicultural education* (2nd ed.). Boston: Allyn & Bacon.

Brace, C. (1995). Race and political correctness. *American Psychologist, 50,* 725–726.

Carter, R. T., Helms, J. E., & Juby, H. L. (2004). The relationship between racism and racial identity for white Americans: A profile analysis. *Journal of Multicultural Counseling and Development, 32,* 2–17.

Clark, K. B., & Clark, M. K. (1947). Racial identification and preference in Negro children. In T. Newcomb & E. Hartley (Eds.), *Readings in social psychology.* New York: Holt.

CNN. (2010). AC360 series: Doll study research. Retrieved from http://ac360.blogs .cnn.com/2010/05/17/ac360-series-doll-study-research/

Corenblum, B., Annis, R. C., & Tanaka, J. S. (1997). Influence of cognitive development, self-competency, and teacher evaluations on the development of children's racial identity. *International Journal of Behavioral Development, 20,* 269–286.

Cross, W. E. (1995). The psychology of nigrescence: Revising the Cross model. In J. Ponterotto, J. Casas, L. Suzuki, & C. Alexander (Eds.), *Handbook of multicultural counseling* (pp. 93–122). Thousand Oaks, CA: Sage.

Dawson, C. A. (2007). Children's use of race in drawing inferences based on their understanding of race constancy. *Masters Theses & Specialist Projects.* Paper 10. Retrieved from http://digitalcommons.wku.edu/theses/10

Day-Vines, N., Wood, S., Grothaus, T., Craigen, L., Holman, A., Dotson-Blake, K., & Douglass, M. (2007). Broaching the subjects of race, ethnicity and culture during the counseling process. *Journal of Counseling and Development, 85,* 401–409.

Derman-Sparks, L., & Ramsey, P. (2011). *What if all the kids are white? Anti-bias multicultural education with young children and families.* New York: Teachers College Press.

Feagin, J. (2000). *Racist America: Roots, current realities, and future reparations.* New York: Routledge.

Helms, J. E. (1995). An update of Helms's white and people of color racial identity models. In J. G. Ponterotto, J. M. Casa, L. A. Suzuki, and C. M. Alexander (Eds.), *Handbook of multicultural counseling* (pp. 181–198). Thousand Oaks, CA: Sage.

Hirschfeld, L. A. (1995). The inheritability of identity: Children's understanding of the cultural biology of race. *Child Development, 66,* 1418–1437.

Phinney. J. S. (1996). When we talk about American ethnic groups, what do we mean? *American Psychologist, 51,* 918–927.

Semaj, L. (1980). The development of racial evaluation and preference: A cognitive approach. *The Journal of Black Psychology, 6*(2), 59–79.

Tatum, B. (1997). *Why are all the black kids sitting together in the cafeteria? And other conversations about race.* New York: Basic Books.

Thomas, A., Speight, S., Witherspoon, K. (2010). Racial socialization, racial identity, and race-related stress of African American parents. *The Family Journal: Counseling and Therapy for Couples and Families, 18*(4), 407–412.

MY · PRESCHOOL EXPERIENCE EXPRESSED IN A MEXICAN PROVERB

La mula no era arisca, la hicieron

Cindy Gomez-Schempp

My Preschool Experience Expressed in a Mexican Proverb:
La mula no era arisca, la hicieron. (The mule isn't jumpy by
nature, they made her that way.)

My most vivid memories of preschool have to do with stories heard while sitting in a circle on shag carpeting, eating Ritz crackers with peanut butter and drinking grape juice from Dixie cups at snack time, and lying down for a nap while someone rubbed my back in a soothing circular motion. Then again, most of my memories from the preschool years are all sensory. By that I mean they lack words. I couldn't speak English at the time, and everyone else at school spoke *only* English.

After I was born in Houston, Texas, in 1970, my parents decided that life in America did not suit them and they returned to Mexico to raise me. I grew up in Mexico City until one day, the economy of Mexico took a nosedive and my father reconsidered his views on living in the United States. We returned to make a life in the United States, this time in Iowa.

The first year of our resettlement in the United States was rough, to say the least. My father worked several jobs around the clock. My mother worked, too, and I was often left to fend for myself with my aunt Lioba's family. My mom's sister, Lioba, had a very *big* family and a very *small* house.

Mom and I complained about the living conditions but there was little we could do. Even though my parents were putting every free moment into work, no bank would lend us the money to buy a home. Undeterred, my father worked nonstop to earn enough for us to pay for a house in full. "Who needs the bank?" he'd say.

In American preschool, I was a marked woman. I quickly realized that without English, I was unable to ask questions or respond to them; I was unable to complain or ask for help. Teachers would shuffle me from one place to another. I was constantly startled, pulling away and crying as adults yanked my arms and shoved me to the next activity; lunch, naptime, snacks, recess. It all became a frightening blur. The kids quickly realized that I didn't understand them. Some of them were annoyed by my seeming stupidity. Others saw my silence as an opportunity. One boy in particular saw me as a dupe. Every time I had a toy, he wanted it. And he took it. He was bigger, stronger, and no one would stop him. I couldn't even tell on him, and he knew it.

I often screamed loudly while he was hijacking my toys, but the teachers always seemed blind to the attacks. Eventually I was forced to take matters into my own hands, literally. The next time the toy-jacker was headed my way I picked up the metal toy truck I was playing with and threw it at his head. I spent the next half hour in tears and punished in a corner. I spent a lot of time in that corner, in the big rocking chair, facing the wall and crying. Eventually, it became comforting to sit there. I didn't have to be confronted by toy-stealing children or arm-yanking teachers. But I was frequently alone and frequently angry.

My parents moved me to a new preschool after that. It didn't help. It wasn't like I was trying to get into trouble. In fact, I steered clear of everyone. But I might as well have been kicking a hornet's nest. In my vulnerable non-English-speaking state, I was a bully magnet. I wasn't even picky with toys. To avoid being bullied I would play with almost anything, even dolls. And I hated dolls.

My grandmother in Mexico gave me dozens of them. My father was always so disappointed with me because she would spend inordinate amounts of pesos on the latest and most expensive dolls and I refused to play with them. They all had amazing leather shoes, some with real hard soles. They had hand-sewn outfits and beautiful accessories like the velvet coat and hand muff on the Russian doll. I took the Russian doll on an adventure that left her shoeless, coatless, and covered in mud.

It wasn't that I was ungrateful. I loved presents from my grandma. But I hated dolls. Cars and boats were my favorite toys—that and animals. Try being the kid at preschool who wants the boys to share the cars with her and doesn't like to play dolls. But I ended up playing with those dolls in the American preschool. The toys I didn't want were the only ones I seemed to be able to get my hands on. Somehow the bullies were not satisfied with my contrition. They just came at me harder. That was one of the central lessons of preschool for me. It wasn't long before even the dolls were yanked from my hands. I remember racing to the toy chest after snack so I could get something decent to play with, anything.

Finally, I snapped under the pressure. No matter what I did, the bully kids would be stronger and snatch whatever toy I managed to grab, right out of my hands. I decided there was nothing to lose but my fear of the bully. I ran for the toy box and grabbed for a big naked doll whose legs were sticking out. I turned around and swung that doll by the legs as hard as I could into the bully.

And here's my most vivid memory of preschool. The head honcho preschool principal came to punish me himself. He took me behind the playhouse and pulled down my pants as I screamed. I didn't understand why he was pulling my pants down, but he did it anyway. He then pulled me over his thighs and held me down while he spanked me on my bare ass.

I was too little to understand what moving to the United States would mean, and my parents were struggling with the new challenges of our new home. And my first memories of preschool began to shape me as a student in American schools. Unfortunately, to this day, my most vivid memory isn't the shag carpeting or the soothing backrub at nap time; it's the spanking and the message of fear it sent about how I would be treated as a Mexican American in school.

Bilingual Education: First and Second Grades Expressed in a Mexican Proverb: *El que no habla, Dios no lo oye.* (If you don't speak up, God can't hear you.)

Even though I could not yet speak English, by the time I was in first grade I was beginning to gain confidence. Jefferson School was not in my district, but Spanish-speaking children of migrant workers were allowed to attend Jefferson for its special bilingual education classes.

I felt normal for the first time in the United States. All the students could speak Spanish, like me. They could talk about their families, their homes, their activities. I began to learn about the town around me and the people in it through the stories of the other Spanish-speaking children. Bullies stopped plaguing me in first grade. Our teacher, Coca Paige, was very loving but strict. Children felt safe with Coca and trusted her with their problems. Even though we all knew Coca was not Mexican like the majority of the students, she was somehow one of us.

Mrs. Paige went to my church, as did most of the children in the classroom. She attended with her white husband, Mr. Robert Paige. He wasn't a real Catholic yet, but he was a teacher, too, and he came to church with her. We all attended mass at the Spanish Catholic service at St. Mary's Church. Coca was from Argentina. At six, I did not realize what the differences were between one Latino and another, so I just thought Mrs. Paige was a very European-looking Spanish-speaking woman. I also noticed she had an odd accent very different from my parents. Even though her Spanish was impeccable, Coca often used weird words I didn't recognize in Spanish.

But Coca, despite our differences, was especially nice to me. Coca was not yet married in the Catholic Church and Robert had to convert to Catholicism and be baptized. A full-grown 200-plus-pound white man was baptized at the front of the all-Mexican congregants in a three-ring, light-blue, rubber kiddie pool. As a child, the single coolest thing I ever saw in church was the baptism of Mr. Paige. I knew then and there that I was going to like him. Coca was more than my first grade teacher; she became my First Communion godmother. Mrs. Paige gave me specialized attention, helping to quickly turn me into a bilingual prodigy. She showered me with bilingual gifts and books so I could continue learning at home.

Learning in Spanish gave me the chance to excel in math and reading while I was learning about American language and culture. Soon I was taking second grade math and language classes in Spanish as a first grader. The second grade teacher, Ms. Stittmatter, was not Latina, but she did speak Spanish fluently. She spoke with a very funny accent and she made strange rhymes and word combinations that sounded silly to my Mexican ears like, "Hola! Hola! Coca-Cola!"

Ms. Stittmatter was patient and kind. Her hilarious renditions of "She'll Be Coming 'Round the Mountain," her colorful pantsuits, and her funny Anglo pronunciations made her all the more endearing. She wanted us all to excel. Ellen Stittmatter and Coca Paige were both teachers who shaped my life. The bilingual education program gave me an advantage to excel in school in my native language, while I learned English gradually. Today, Mexicans in the United States struggle to maintain their rights to "an" education, let alone a bilingual one. In times when states like Arizona are removing Chicano studies in schools and universities, it is imperative that teachers speak up for rights of their students.

Ms. Stittmatter and Mrs. Paige both knew the value of each of their prized bilingual students. I was free from persecution of bullies and white teacher indifference to the bullying I faced. But neither Ellen nor Coca had to fight for the right to teach in Spanish. Today's bilingual and multicultural students are conscripted to assimilate into Americanism. Being "American" nowadays means students are twice removed from their native indigenous roots and their modern-day Mexican roots. Not only are they being stripped of their cultural identity and language identity, they are required to learn and live the culture of Americana.

That was hard for me. Assimilating was something I knew I was expected to do. People expected me to speak English, but wanted to hear me speak Spanish as a parlor trick. I wanted to please my teachers, especially Ms. Stittmatter and Mrs. Paige, who were my friends and the only adult links I had between the white world and my own. Part of my assimilation process involved figuring out what to share about myself and what not. The teachers loved my ability to sing, dance, and speak in Spanish. But when I raised cultural problems, I was treated differently. It was an embarrassment to share the constant troubles that plagued us as non-English-speaking, new-immigrant families.

It was difficult and embarrassing for me to explain why my parents didn't know how to dress me for winter weather or why I didn't have the gloves or boots Midwestern folks were always prepared with. It was even harder to explain our poverty and the resultant grueling work schedule my parents had that kept them from being very involved in my school life. And no one wanted to hear about the cultural differences in discipline for children between whites and Mexicans. The irony for me was that teachers and principals who readily reported concerns of corporal punishment at home to the authorities refused to acknowledge the constant use of wooden paddles to spank us at school and corporal punishment that seemed disproportionately focused on kids of color. White nurses and gym teachers disrobed us and examined us at school, checking in on how our parents disciplined us. White teachers and principals hit us at school. Mr. Lang, our school principal, had "his" and "hers" paddles that hung on the wall beside your head as you sat in his office being interrogated. He was not particularly frightening as people go. He was a very skinny and tall white man with long hair and the best Christmas light display in town. Even though he seemed laid back, we knew that he had the authority to beat our asses if we got out of line. But somehow, my culturally ordained corporal punishment at home was a source of concern for school officials, and confusion and destruction for my family unity.

At a very young age we became intimately aware of the Department of Human Services and their powers to separate families. Many other Mexican and indigenous native families in our community had social workers monitoring their daily lives too. Like many indigenous people before us, our families were separated and our lives dissected by a white societal institution that saw our way of life as barbaric and our parent-child relationships as savage.

As much as I wanted to be the poster child for bilingual education and integration of Mexicans and Americans, I was torn about my identity. On the one hand, I was proud of my heritage; on the other I was ashamed of it. I could tell, even as a first grader, how disgusted whites were with the machismo of Mexican culture, or the perceived subservience of Latina women. At the same time I was fascinated with school, music, and American lifestyles. The struggle, of course, was figuring out the exact amount of Mexican and American I needed to be.

Ultimately, Mrs. Paige adopted a little girl from China but they gave her a Latina name, Lucia. She took my place in Mrs. Paige's life. I remember when Coca brought little Lucia to school. She could write on the chalkboard already and she was only four. She was a prodigy, "like me," I thought. The Paiges remained in my life, albeit at a distance, after that.

The stigma that DHS involvement had in our lives was more profound and more long-lasting than the positive relationship between my family and the Paiges. As good as Mrs. Paige and Ms. Stittmatter were as teachers, they did not teach me the most important lessons I learned in bilingual school. I had to learn those on my own, even though they originated in these early years. This was the first of many life lessons that taught me that learning your language is not enough. Learning and honoring your cultural roots and defining your identity are just as important.

PART FOUR

CLASSROOM DIALOGUES:
MIDDLE AND HIGH SCHOOL

LETTER FROM A HIGH SCHOOL STUDENT #1

Eva Mitchell

Dear Readers (educators, parents, and peers),

In my twelve years of schooling in the Minneapolis Public School District, I was led to believe that the civil rights laws passed in the 1960s had essentially put an end to racial discrimination and inequity in our country. The Martin Luther King, Jr. holiday seemed to celebrate this accomplishment, and class discussions almost always put racial problems in the past. However, by attending a large urban school and living in an increasingly diverse city, it has become clear to me that racial inequity and injustice persist today and perhaps are even intensifying.

When I was a young girl at Lake Harriett School in Minneapolis, you could count on two hands how many people of color there were. There was little intercultural bridging, except with students of color who had been adopted into white families. There were three or four girls who were African-American and they mostly stayed close together. Because I was a basketball player, I had more African-American friends than most of my peers. I would talk with the girls in class, but when I was with my group of white friends, they weren't interested in making the same effort and I felt discouraged.

I never was able to get closer to those girls and often wonder why teachers didn't help us cross the cultural divide. If I saw a situation like that now, I would make more of an effort and be a leader for my friends. Also, when I bridge to another cultural group, I'm not thinking only about the culture. I'm looking for ways that peers of color might be compatible to me or have similar interests. For me, that makes the bridging more authentic.

Being a serious basketball player has brought me into the African-American culture like nothing else. Being one of two white people on an urban basketball team has given me insight into the minority experience. I've been in a gym where I was the only white person. Even in that venue, there is still racial tension that we encounter. With a majority African-American team, there are times when I am not invited to parties depending on who is hosting and the guest list. I know this is because economic and racial barriers separate us. To cross these barriers takes an extra effort on my part. Sometimes I notice myself distancing until I understand better how to create that bridge. In some of the discussions, I can only listen. For instance, when my teammates talk about their plans for how to wear their hair, and the time it takes for braiding, it's new for me and I just take it in. On the flip side, my only other white teammate has been called an "n-word lover" by players on another team. I didn't know until after the game, but I was shocked. That was a big sign to me of the stigmas we still attach to race.

Because of this, the notion that racism is decreasing in our society is something I cannot accept. Because my mother was a cofounder of aMaze, an antibias education program for elementary children,* I was a young person who had learned to challenge my own biases since I can remember. However, bridging cultures is still very difficult for me—nearly impossible without an adult. That is why I have helped to start a student leadership group for interracial awareness.

Most of all, I have learned that adults—parents and teachers—make assumptions about our abilities to build cross-cultural relationships. They think that just because we're together in class, in school, or on the team, that we don't need bridging support. But we do. This support could be in the form of active discussions about race in class or through groups where we practice and learn these skills together. With that extra emotional support, we can go the extra mile.

I'd like adults and friends to know that my intercultural experiences have deeply enriched my life. They have given me the tools to build relationships and to be successful in a diverse world. I will never know what it is like to be a person of color. I see the educational hardships my friends have to face just because they were born with a different color of skin than me. It is important to educate our younger generation about these issues, so that young people like me can acknowledge these issues and learn how to handle them better, especially as our country's demographics are shifting.

---

*See http://childrensliteraturenetwork.org/orgs/orgpages/org_a/amaze.php.

For students in such a diverse school, community, and world, there are not sufficient efforts to discuss racial inequities. We, as students, need teachers and curriculum that explore our fears and hopes about race, and our strong need to create ways to address the issues constructively. It is important that we set a goal for all students, regardless of race, to create opportunities and safety for bridging. Bridging is not easy. We need our teachers and guardians to help start the conversations and build efforts for respect and equity for everyone.

Thanks,
Eva Mitchell
July 2011

14

MIDDLE SCHOOL LESSONS LEAD TO DEEPER INSIGHTS ON RACE AND CLASS

Amy Vatne Bintliff

It is fairly easy to touch on issues of race in the middle school classroom by integrating multicultural curriculum, but if we fail to create a climate in which students can openly dialogue about the issues, if we fail to provide them with the language in which to discuss social inequities, we have only touched the surface. I have found doorways into conversations about race by explicitly teaching elements of human rights education (HRE) and by directly teaching vocabulary such as *oppression* and *stereotyping*. *Human rights education* is defined as all learning that develops the knowledge, skills, and values of human rights (Flowers, 1997). HRE includes teaching *about* human rights, such as providing the history of the rights and information about human rights violations, as well as teaching *for* human rights, which encourages a responsibility for protecting and defending human rights (Flowers, 1997). I first began human rights education work at an alternative high school in the Minneapolis area in 2002 after being trained by The Advocates for Human Rights (www.theadvocatesforhumanrights .org). I have since moved to a middle school in a small Wisconsin town. The middle school contains around 550 students. Ninety percent of the student body is White, with 12% considered socioeconomically disadvantaged. When switching grade levels and geographic locations, I was not sure what to expect in regard to levels of comprehension among my new middle school students. What I found was that my eighth grade students were able to comprehend multiple layers of understanding; began asking complex questions about race, culture, and global conflict; and began exploring advocacy within their own lives.

Deeper Conversations About Race in a Human Rights Persuasive Writing Unit

We were knee-deep in a unit on persuasive writing when students really began dialoguing about race. Prior to the writing unit, I had introduced students to the Universal Declaration of Human Rights (1948) and had directly taught students about oppression theory beginning with folktales and moving into modern forms of oppression. I explained that some stories are ways for oppressed people to give voice to their concerns without being arrested or harmed for expressing their beliefs (Zipes, 2006, p. 7). We then spoke in depth about types of oppression. At first, students spoke of more obvious oppressions, such as sexism, or personal oppressions, such as family rules, but after returning students to the folk tales, they began speaking about socioeconomics as factors leading to oppression. Once we looked at African-American folk tales and discussed their importance to African-American history (Ogunleye, 1997), students then began speaking about racism as a form of oppression. I found that students were at first very hesitant to speak about racism. When I asked, "What are some examples of racism as a form of oppression?" the classroom was first very quiet. One White student finally said, "Well, one of my African-American friends said that the police pull African Americans over more often. Would that work?"

"What do you think?" I asked the class. "How would this be an oppressive act?"

"Well, I think you'd be scared to go anywhere," said Lucy.

"I think you'd also get really angry," said Hugh.

"Fear and anger are both emotions we found in the folk tales, right? I think you are both correct; does anyone want to head to my computer and look up some statistics on this?" I asked. "Any other examples of racism as a form of oppression?"

This time, many hands shot up.

"I think that being judged differently is a form of oppression," said Kristine, an African-American girl.

"Tell me more about what you are thinking," I said.

"Well, sometimes teachers in my old school thought that I was dumb, just because I was Black or couldn't read very well when I was little. They judged me because of what I looked like."

"How was that oppressive for you?"

"They never listened to me. That one story we read talked about being heard. I wasn't ever given the chance to talk like the White kids were."

We continued having rich conversation about oppression in our own lives and in the lives of characters that we were reading about in folk tales. I then began adding stories from current events both locally and globally and we continued exploring evidence of oppression, racism, and human rights violations through these readings. Students were then instructed to choose a human rights or animal rights issue to explore and then write a persuasive essay calling on their classmates to donate time or money to support their issue. As an introduction to their own research, I showed students some websites and articles regarding human rights violations, such as sections of the film *Stolen Childhoods* (2004), a film documenting child labor throughout the world. After watching *Stolen Childhoods,* Penelope wrote:

> This film and my research affected me greatly. Everyday I think of the stupid things I complain about like running eight minutes in gym. But then I see these beautiful children lifting basket after basket of half their body weight, being forced to scavenge through rotting waste to feed themselves. But what really got me were the lies and manipulation. It really makes me feel a strong need to help because I know that I can.

Katherine wrote:

> Before I watched the movie *Stolen Childhoods,* I didn't even know how big of an issue child labor is. Watching all the small children slung over the back of another child out in the hot sun was very sad for me. I have a younger brother and I don't even like to think of him standing out in the sun with pesticides picking coffee beans. Now that I have watched this film I am going to start buying fair trade chocolate and coffee when I have the chance. I think that this movie will affect many of the decisions I make about what I buy for the rest of my life.

Throughout the film, after our research, and after hearing our speeches, we took the time to reflect through journal writing and through discussion in a restorative justice Talking Circle. In Talking Circles, a Talking Piece is used and is passed around the Circle. When a person has the Talking Piece, it is his or her time to speak. When students don't have the Talking Piece, it is their time to listen. This process allows all students to get the chance to share their thoughts or feelings about topics in a safe environment

(Boyes-Watson, 2002; Pranis, 2005; Vatne Bintliff, 2011). Although Circle takes a whole class period, I find the reflection part of the lesson extremely important. I set up questions to guide Circle, such as "What are you thinking and feeling about what you learned?" and "What do you feel needs to be done to help end racism and human rights violations?" As a teacher, I was able to reflect on the experience because my students were exploring the things that they felt and learned. Plus, our whole class was able to support each other when encountering feelings of sadness and anger.

It was after a Circle that I was able to raise more complex questions about race. Many students were working on speeches advocating for an end to the use of child soldiers. Our class watched film clips from the film *Invisible Children* and *PBS Newshour,* and read reports from the United Nations Children's Fund and *Smithsonian Magazine* (Invisible Children, 2004; Li, 2005; Raffaele, 2005; Suarez & Kristof, 2005). documenting the use of child soldiers during the long periods of war in Uganda. In the video clips, hundreds of children became "night commuters" and would walk miles into town to sleep together to avoid being kidnapped and forced into war. After watching the clips, I asked, "Why do you think that the United States didn't fully get involved with this conflict in Uganda?"

"There's no oil," said James.

"True. What else?"

"Maybe we didn't know about it," said one girl.

"Well, we did," I said. "The United Nations knew too. So why didn't the United States do more to end this?"

It was quiet, so I threw out a deeper question. "Do you think race had anything to do with it?"

The students first sat silently with the question. Then one boy said, "Yeah. I mean if all of these kids carrying guns were White kids that looked like us, there's no way that people would just sit by and let that happen."

"What do you all think? Is there truth to this?"

"Yeah, I think so," said Penny. "Could you imagine this happening here? People would never let that happen in our town. I couldn't imagine a bunch of us walking around with machine guns and the rest of the world just standing by."

Invisible Children had actually done a campaign in which US children, many who looked like my students, gathered together and slept in open areas as a sign of protest and support for helping Uganda. The campaign showed poster shots of Ugandan children sleeping and then shots of the US youth, who were mainly White. We looked at the campaign on the projector and then reflected more. Students again insisted that the world would not stand by and watch White children being kidnapped and forced into war. The discussion enabled me to provide some background on US involvement in other African conflicts, such as Somalia and Rwanda. I wanted students to know that the United States had stepped in and attempted to help African nations before, but had been extremely cautious and had made many errors along the way. We read a report from 2004 describing actions that the United States and the United Nations had taken in the Sudan, but students felt that those actions weren't enough (Pan, 2004).

Although our time didn't allow us to delve fully into the complexities of US policy regarding Africa, students began reflecting more on race as a factor. As some students were writing speeches about preventing genocides, they were able to look critically at US actions in Bosnia and Rwanda and wonder, "Why did we help in Eastern Europe, but not in Africa? If race wasn't a factor, what was?" Although most questions remained unanswered, students were beginning to see race as a factor in all policy and decision making regarding human rights. We ended the project with students participating in forms of activism. Whether it was teaching others about fair trade, raising money for an organization, or writing letters to members of Congress, my students were fully engaged and felt empowered through the process.

Engaging More Deeply Through Young Adult Literature

We continued a similar process this year in my seventh grade class with our read-aloud of the novel *Ninth Ward* by Jewell Parker Rhodes (2010). In the novel a young girl named Lanesha must use her intelligence, strength, and courage to keep those close to her alive during Hurricane Katrina and the flood that followed in 2005. My students loved the novel, and the work itself broke down stereotypes as Lanesha was young, poor, and Black, but was also intelligent, loved mathematics, and loved her strong neighborhood. As one student wrote, "I never thought of poor Black girls as being smart. And I always thought of neighborhoods like this as ghetto—full of violence. But Lanesha's neighbors were nice."

Again, arming my students with information on human rights and oppression, I guided students to reflect more deeply on the Hurricane Katrina disaster. We watched news footage from the time, read articles, and watched films. During one of the films, one student asked, "Why did the people coming into rescue others have so many guns?"

"What do all of you think?"

One student sheepishly said, "I think it's because they were going into poor, Black neighborhoods and they expected lots of guns and gangs. That's what I thought of those neighborhoods before we started talking about this."

"How have your thoughts changed?" I asked.

"Well, other than the one video showing looting at Walmart, the Black people were actually helping each other. There were groups of young Black guys that were risking their lives trying to save their neighbors. They were being brave and kind. Those stories weren't in the news as much as the others."

We went on to study the articles that were released by the media, the hysteria surrounding the reports of rapes and murders, the misinformation, and the corrections reported months later (Dwyer & Drew, 2005). We also looked at media coverage of the "looting" and asked why one photograph described a Black man as "looting a grocery store" while a White couple was described as "finding bread and soda from a local grocery store" (Sommers et al., 2006). We read the chapter from President George Bush's autobiography in which he stated that he could only make decisions based on the information that he was given. We could have simply read the book, but we dug deeper to look at how our stereotypes as a nation may have affected our response and actions. One seventh grade student wrote in her journal:

> I think that if reports would have come out in the news like that during a disaster here in the Midwest, someone would have stopped and said, "Really? Guns, violence and rapes?" But because the disaster struck there, in the Ninth Ward, people just believed it all. I didn't know much about Black people and/or inner city people before I started this class, but now I'm going to ask for a lot more facts before just believing a comment or an article.

Another student wrote:

> I think I learned that we sometimes make decisions because of the color of people's skin—not decisions to help or not, but decisions about HOW we help. Maybe we don't ask the right questions when people look different from us.

I continue to be amazed at how deeply young students will go when exploring race. For one thing, my students felt safe and could say exactly what was on their mind. And when what they said may have promoted a stereotype, I encouraged them to dig deeper by asking questions, by showing examples that flipped the stereotype, by giving students new vocabulary to use that enabled them to speak clearly about the topic, by being honest and telling them, "I don't have the answers. I work to unravel my own stereotypes every day."

When we first began the year, a common middle school phrase in our majority White building when anyone brought up race was, "You're a racist." When I asked students why they said it, one student replied, "I thought any time you talked about someone with a different skin color, you were being a racist." Our lessons, and the time we took to dig deeper, have given students the courage to approach the subject rather than shy away, to identify stereotypes more readily, and to question what they read in the media. Middle school students are ready and willing to look deeply at race, connect to their own lives, and begin taking steps toward advocacy. As one of my eighth graders said during a discussion in Circle, "I think people don't think we're capable of being mature about these things. They don't think we care what's going on in the world and that we don't want to know the truth. But we do care and we do think about important stuff all the time." The question is, are we as educators ready to take a risk and facilitate this exploration?

References

The advocates for human rights. Retrieved from http://www.theadvocatesforhuman rights.org/

Boyes-Watson, C. (2002). *The journey of circles at ROCA.* Report on the Period July 2001–June 30, 2002. The Center for Restorative Justice at Suffolk University. Retrieved October 8, 2006, from http://www.pegasuscom.com/PDFs/RocaJourney.pdf

Dwyer, J., & Drew, C. (2005, September 29). After Katrina, crimes of the imagination. *The New York Times.* Retrieved October 12, 2012, from http://www.ny times.com/2005/09/29/world/americas/29iht-katrina.ht ml?_r = 1

Flowers, N. (Ed.). (1997). *Human rights here and now.* University of Minnesota: Human Rights Resource Center. Retrieved August 11, 2010, from http://www1.umn.edu/humanrts/edumat/hreduseries/hereandnow/Intro/acknowledgements.htm

Invisible Children. (2004). People Like You productions. Retrieved from http://www.invisiblechildren.com.

Li, K. (2005). Children bear the brunt of Uganda's 19-year conflict. UNICEF. Retrieved October 4, 2011, from http://www.unicef.org/infobycountry/uganda_25704.html

Pan, E. (2004, September 20). Africa: The Darfur crisis. Council on Foreign Relations. Retrieved November 4, 2012, from http://www.cfr.org/sudan/africa-darfur-crisis/p7714#p2

Pranis, K. (2005). *The little book of circle processes.* Intercourse, PA: Good Books.

Ogunleye, T. (1997). African American folklore: Its role in reconstructing African American history. *Journal of Black Studies, 27*(4), 435–455.

Raffaele, P. (2005, February). Uganda: The horror. *Smithsonian Magazine.* Retrieved October 12, 2012, from http://www.smithsonianmag.com/people-places/uganda .html

Rhodes, J. P. (2010). *Ninth Ward.* New York: Little, Brown Books for Young Readers.

Sommers, S. R., Apfelbaum, E. P., Dukes, K. N., Toosi, N., & Wang, E. J. (2006). Race and media coverage of Hurricane Katrina: Analysis, implications, and future research questions. *Analyses of Social Issues and Public Policy, 6,* 1–17. Retrieved October 12, 2012, from http://ase.tufts.edu/psychology/documents/pubsSommers RaceMedia.pdf

Stolen Childhoods. (2004). Galen Films and Romano Productions. Retrieved from http://www.stolenchildhoods.org/

Suarez, R. (Interviewer), & Kristof, N. (Interviewee). (2005, June 10). Ravaged region. *PBS Newshour.* Retrieved November 4, 2012, from http://www.pbs.org/ newshour/bb/africa/jan-june05/kristof_6–10.html

Universal Declaration of Human Rights. (1948). United Nations. Retrieved September 4, 2011, from www.un.org/en/documents/udhr/index.shtml

Vatne Bintliff, A. (2011). *Re-engaging disconnected youth: Transformative learning through restorative and social justice education.* Adolescent Cultures, School & Society Series. New York: Peter Lang.

Zipes, J. D. (2006). *Fairy tales and the art of subversion.* New York: Routledge.

DISRUPTING SCHOOL

Learning Autobiographies as Queer Curriculum

Jehanne Beaton Zirps

Can we imagine an assignment in which teachers ask students to write in ways that trouble familiar stories? . . . (A)n assignment in which the product is less important than the process? . . . (A)n assignment in which students are helped to resist repeating their own as well as their teachers' knowledges, identities, and practices, and to engage in the discomforting process of signifying knowledges, identities, and practices (which might be possible when rereading one's life through different "lenses")? (Kumashiro, 2002, p. 66)

My motivation for becoming a secondary social studies teacher was combating racism. At twenty-two, I believed the social studies classroom offered a forum, like no other, to work against racism. Twenty years later, I still believe that to be true. I have taught in multiple settings and schools, with literally thousands of students, and central to my social studies curriculum was an antiracist, antioppressive agenda. My curriculum always had an antiracist agenda at its core, regardless of what content area or grade level I taught. On occasion, I have shared examples of my teaching practice with other educators and have been met with stares and silence. I never know how to interpret my peers' reaction. Am I coming across as grandiose and self-congratulatory? Or maybe as though I'm making more of my practice than it really is? My aim in this paper is to sort some of this out by critically examining one assessment task I created and used with my ninth grade social studies students. How might I read my curriculum in light of a framework of antioppressive pedagogy? Where does it fit? And did it serve my students in the way in which I intended it?

It's important to establish context here. I taught for fourteen years, the last four of which I spent in a diverse, urban high school magnet program. Ours was the third "open program" in our district to take shape, created in response to the numbers of students who were being denied entrance into the two other open programs in the city. The district's three open programs were among a district-wide magnet school system that served as a desegregation strategy, in hopes of drawing white and middle-class students into what would be racially isolated high schools, had they taken in only neighborhood kids. Our school's open program less successfully attracted white students; community members and alumni often blamed this failure (and the "changing demographics of the school," a euphemism for poor students of color) on our high school's reputation for violence and gang activity. A significant portion of our students came to us with a case of the sour grapes, feeling like rejects and less-than, not "good enough" to get into one of the more coveted programs on the south side of the city.

Still, we were the "whitest" program in our school, as about one-third of our students identified as European American. Our program also had few East African immigrant students, as many elected the premedical track that also existed in our building. Otherwise, our demographics represented the rest of the school: African American, Latino, Native American, and Hmong. It's difficult to characterize my students as a group. Many were underachievers, bright kids who didn't see the point of school or whose parents forced them into the program against their will. Some had decent grades, but weren't motivated by them. Others were encouraged by a caring middle school teacher to select our program as a way to keep the student from "falling through the cracks." We had a disproportionate number of openly gay students, student artists (although not always recognized by teachers), and students who identified themselves as mixed race. Though some of our students had come from the district's open and Montessori K–8 programs, the majority of the kids had left traditional middle schools before coming to us.

The program assigned me to teach an interdisciplinary course for our ninth graders as a way of supporting their transition into high school. The course sought to help incoming students build community within the program and become acclimated to a different paradigm for learning than their previous schools might have offered. The first major assignment I asked students to complete was a learning autobiography. We spent the first month of school generating reflective writing in response to a series of texts and in support of the learning autobiography assignment. Then students would draft, revise, peer edit, and submit an autobiographical paper that centered on something that had to do with their own learning. I then asked the students to attend parent–teacher conferences with their parent or guardian and we would talk through their learning autobiography. Certainly, the task served as a formative assessment, giving me a sense of my students' writing abilities and their stamina to work through an extended assignment. But even more, it served to give them a platform from which they could reflect on, discuss, and rethink their understanding of school and learning.

Leading up to the actual task, my students read multiple poems and stories connecting to school as a place of learning and as a place of oppression. It may seem odd to spend the initial six weeks of a social studies class discussing and thinking about poetry and short stories, but the format enabled my students to examine their own identities, experiences, and beliefs in a way that traditional high school social studies curriculum rarely does. Kumashiro (2002) writes that poetry "makes explicit, through its unconventionality, many ways in which the story is constructed" (p. 21). In my own experience working with teenagers, free verse and narrative poetry (and, in some cases, selected short stories) frees students from convention and their fear of writing. These forms enable students to find essence in a story, to connect and self-reflect in ways other writing doesn't. During this process I didn't ask my students to "analyze" text in any literary sense. Instead, students talked back to the text. They identified lines or sections that resonated with them, that mirrored their own experiences with teachers and schools, or that challenged them to think about why schools existed the way they did. Students might select a line from Li-young Lee's "Persimmons" and begin their own poem there. When we read O'Brien's short story "The Things They Carried" about the burdens—physical, emotional, and psychological; collective and individual—carried by an American army platoon through the jungles of Vietnam, my students collaboratively crafted their own catalog of "things they carried" to school daily, ranging from the concrete (backpacks and wallets, weapons and makeup) to the abstract (grief for a lost loved one, butterflies of infatuation, or courage to face a bullying peer). Sometimes we illustrated lines from poems or we wrote (but never sent) letters to authors and previous teachers (both in school and out) who denied opportunities or enabled possibilities.

Depending on how I read these texts and the purpose behind my selection of them, I hear Kumashiro's discussion of different antioppressive pedagogies. One reading places this task and supporting curriculum within the framework of *education for the Other* (Kumashiro, 2002, pp. 33–35). Fundamental to the creation of the course itself was an attempt to address the oppression experienced by my students. My selection of texts reinforces a belief that "school is a place where the Other is treated in harmful ways" (Kumashiro, 2002, p. 33). Cisneros's short stories "Eleven" and "Norma," Inada's "Rayford's Song," Northrup's "Ditched," and Slapin's "Two Plus Two" each narrate the silencing of students at the hand of racist, sexist, ignorant, and controlling teachers. Alexie's "Indian Education" catalogues vignettes of being Othered through cutting humor, one stinging snapshot of each grade, K–12. Many of these pieces convey the bitterness and pain, the "hidden injuries" (Kumashiro, 2002, p. 34) that accompany a student's experience with low expectations, stereotypes, and racist assumptions.

Another read of the texts suggests something else. By sharing these texts with my fourteen-year-old students, I intended to "trouble" narratives that said education provided a way "up and out" of poverty and oppression; school guaranteed learning; and teachers were righteous, trustworthy adults who believed in their students. Whose narrative was this? My own? Was I rethinking the normative discourse around school and teachers that I heard at the dinner table, growing up? Or the discourse that circulated among my undergraduate peers as we sat in groups on the floor of our co-ed dormitory in our progressive liberal arts college, debating gradual versus revolutionary change, in all its theoretical glory? Many of the texts I gave my ninth graders presented a very different narrative than the one I understood as a student. Here, in these texts, the narratives read: *Beware: school can crush you. Teachers will shame and silence, exile and ignore. Opportunity is fleeting and conditional; equity is almost nonexistent.* By my tenth year of public school teaching, I had witnessed this alternate narrative, that of School as Oppressor. I had observed and confronted the marginalization, denigration, and silencing of students first hand.

Kumashiro might argue that this reading suggests that my choice of texts falls somewhere between *education about the Other* and *education critical of privileging and Othering.* I viewed myself as an activist teacher (and still do), and recognized the role that school and teachers played in perpetuating oppression and institutional power and norms. I wanted my students to regard school and teachers as such, to critically examine what it meant to be successful in school, to rethink what learning looked like. Yet even as I attempted to establish an antioppressive classroom, I retained my position as expert, the knowing teacher. I selected the texts, determined their sequence with intention. I structured the task and the supporting curriculum so as to provide my students with windows into oppression experienced by others as well as mirrors to see their own experiences with oppression (Styles, 1996). Might such a curricular choice suggest that I thought I understood how my students experienced marginalization through school? Was I essentializing their experiences with oppression? Did I assume that my students didn't already recognize, in some way, school's role in maintaining oppression and the status quo? Did I think they needed me to label their oppression for them?

Kumashiro (2002) cites Miller's critique of teachers' use of autobiography with students, "noting that 'telling one's story' not only presumes a rational development of a singular subject from ignorance to enlightenment, but also privileges the developmental model as *the* story, making other stories unthinkable and untellable" (p. 65). The summative task was for students to craft their own learning autobiography. Their writing could take any form and could center on any experience of learning, in school or out. I framed their learning autobiography as *a* story of their learning. The autobiography did not need to focus on a life-altering experience, something that still shimmered or ached when remembered. It only needed to be about learning, meaningful to them, and written with the understanding that it would be shared with their parents and peers, as well as other team-teachers. Some students modeled their writing using Alexie's "Indian Education" as a model, offering a school story at each grade level. Other students wrote about their experiences with transformative teachers, parents, grandparents, or other adults who had championed their school efforts and helped them to believe in their own ability to achieve. Still others wrote stories that were unexpected. One student wrote of learning to fish and the day he spent with his grandfather on a dock, developing his casting skills, acquiring the language of bait and lure. Another student wrote about how she learned what it meant to be undocumented, opening her piece with a memory of running from the thumping sound of Immigration and Naturalization Service helicopters overhead. And some students shared stories of school as a place of oppression, invisibility, and failure. Whether it be a story of a teacher who denied a female student access to the bathroom because he didn't believe she was menstruating or one that told of a teacher shaming a student for a missed assignment or hiding from peers a student's struggle to read, pain and trauma crystalized on the page.

Thus, a third reading of this assignment suggests that the process of writing their learning autobiography assignments propelled my students and me into a "pedagogy of crisis" (Kumashiro, 2002, pp. 62–63). Kumashiro (2002) writes, "If the unlearning involved in learning . . . leads the student into a state of crisis or paralysis (such as feeling emotionally upset), the student will first need to work through the crisis before being able to act" (p. 48). Moving through poems and stories about school and learning as a ninth grade social studies class, we needed space to be uncomfortable, to discuss what we believed school and teachers should be, and how our experiences measured up against that narrative. This work took time. It required that I rethink my lesson plans, the physical arrangement of my room, and my role as teacher. My classroom needed to encourage conversation between students as they moved through their reactions and resistances to what we read.

Students responded to the discursive part of the learning autobiographies differently; the degree of self-reflection and willingness to trust the process, me, and each other varied by individual student, by the day, and often depending on the text. There were multiple "right" ways for my students to read each text, to write their reflections, and to craft their learning autobiographies. Students could see themselves in multiple texts, cite multiple identities through the various voices from the texts and their peers' writing, and supplement these narratives with their own stories and experiences. And yet, I experienced resistance from some students. Sometimes it manifested as withdrawal from discussion. Other times the resistance was to the paradigm shift itself. A student might turn in what he or she believed I wanted to see; or the student would write the bare minimum just to get it done. And a couple of students simply hated me for it. They sicced their parents on me, challenging my practice in front of my principal. Or they simply shut down. At the time, I rationalized it as distrust in me, as their teacher, and my ability to ensure their emotional and psychological safety in a room of their peers. Looking back, I still gave the final learning autobiography a grade. I still privileged "good writing," as outlined on the rubric that accompanied the assignment. I wish I hadn't, but I still worked and abided by the overarching academic norms that exist in mainstream high schools.

Kumashiro "troubles" his own antioppressive pedagogy, asking if it is "ethical to intentionally and constantly lead a student into crisis" (Kumashiro, 2002, p. 69). My initial response echoes his: to not engage in antioppressive teaching and learning means being complicit in reinforcing the status quo, notions of normativity and power. To not engage in antioppressive teaching is unethical. Yet, even at the time, I knew that my students and I had only 55 minutes together each day. When the bell rang, they headed out into the hallways and toward other classrooms, the majority of which reinforced the oppressive power of School and Teacher, which rendered my students silent, subordinate, and marginal. I also knew they'd be back. Not only back the next day, but the next semester and in subsequent years, as our students stayed with us over the course of four years. I taught some of my students every semester for four years straight as they elected into my semester classes. Thus I viewed our learning autobiography assignment as only a first step, a vehicle through which we could "trouble" school, as a system, and set the stage for years of antioppressive curriculum that continued to examine norms, Othering, privilege, and oppression through multiple societal and historical contexts.

If I returned to a high school social studies classroom tomorrow, I would reinstitute the learning autobiography assignment as the initial assessment for the year. From an academic standpoint, it enabled me to get a better sense of my students as writers and readers, so that I could better tailor future work to their needs. It also offered me a glimpse of how they saw themselves in relation to school, what they believed and trusted, how they'd been harmed and betrayed. All of this offered me context, so that when a student erupted in anger over an injustice, I better understood part of his or her backstory. It also serves as an antioppressive tool. It allows students to trouble the institution they know best, to examine their experiences with school and teachers, challenge the normative narratives, and offer alternative ones. The assignment still needs work; I would need to rethink aspects of it, be that much more intentional about how I framed it. But I think it offers a practical example from which teachers might begin discussion around how to make queer, antioppressive pedagogy come to life in the classroom.

References

Alexie, S. (1994). Indian education. In *The Lone Ranger and Tonto fistfight in heaven* (pp. 171–180). New York: Perennial.
Antler. (1995). Raising my hand. In R. Gordon (Ed.), *Pierced by a ray of sun: Poems about the times we feel alone* (pp. 2–3). New York: HarperCollins.
Ayres, R. (1999). Corporeal. In L. Bosselaar (Ed.), *Outsiders: Poems about rebels, exiles, and renegades* (p. 17). Minneapolis, MN: Milkweed Editions.
Baxter, C. (1985). Gryphon. In *Through the safety net: Stories.* New York: Vintage.
Cisneros, S. (1991). A rice sandwich. In *The house on Mango Street.* New York: Vintage.

Cisneros, S. (1992). Eleven. In *Woman hollering creek: And other stories.* New York: Vintage.

Divakaruni, C. B. (1995). Yuba City school. In R. Gordon (Ed.). *Pierced by a ray of sun: Poems about the times we feel alone* (pp. 80–82). New York: HarperCollins.

Farawell, M. J. (1999). Everything I need to know I learned in kindergarten. In L. Bosselaar (Ed.). *Outsiders: Poems about rebels, exiles, and renegades* (p. 88). Minneapolis, MN: Milkweed Editions.

Haynes, D. (1998). The dozens. In D. Hanes & J. Landsman (Eds.). *Welcome to your life: Writings for the heart of young America* (pp. 70–77). Minneapolis, MN: Milkweed Editions.

Inada, L. F. (1992). Rayford's Song. In *Legends from camp.* Minneapolis, MN: Coffee House Press.

Jones, E. P. (1998). The first day. In H. Rochman & D. Z. McCampbell (Eds.). *Leaving home: 15 distinguished authors explore personal journeys* (pp. 9–17). HarperCollins.

Kenny, M. (1988). They tell me I am lost. In D. Niatum (Ed.). *Harper's anthology of 20th century Native American poetry,* New York: Harper & Row.

Kozol, J. (1996). *Amazing grace: The lives of children and the conscience of a nation* (pp. 38–42). New York: HarperPerennial.

Kumashiro, K. (2002). *Troubling education: Queer activism and antioppressive pedagogy.* New York: RoutledgeFalmer.

Larkin, J. (1986). Genealogy. In *A long sound.* Penobscot, ME: Granite Press.

Lee, L. (1999). Persimmons. In L. Bosselaar (Ed.). *Outsiders: Poems about rebels, exiles, and renegades* (p. 156). Minneapolis, MN: Milkweed Editions.

Lyon, G. E. (1989). Where I'm from. Retrieved from http://www.georgeellalyon.com/where.html

Northrup, J. (1995). Ditched. In R. Gordon (Ed.). *Pierced by a ray of sun: Poems about the times we feel alone* (p. 27). New York: HarperCollins.

O'Brien, T. (1990). *The things they carried* (pp. 1–25). New York: Penguin Group.

———. (1995). On education. In R. Gordon (Ed.). *Pierced by a ray of sun: Poems about the times we feel alone* (pp. 24–25). New York: HarperCollins.

Sanchez, S. (1984). Norma. In *Homegirls and handgrenades.* Avalon.

Slapin, B. (1992). Two plus two or why Indians flunk. In B. Slapin & D. Seale (Eds.). *Through Indian eyes: The Native experience in books for children.* Gabriola Island, British Columbia, Canada: New Society.

Styles, E. (1996). Curriculum as window and mirror. In *National seeking educational equity and diversity project.* Retrieved from http://www.library.wisc.edu/edvrc/docs/public/pdfs/SEEDReadings/CurriculumWindow.pdf

16

LETTER FROM A HIGH SCHOOL STUDENT #2

Bring in Elders, Let Us Talk About These Things

Fardousa Hassan Ahmed

When I was in tenth grade at South High School, in Minneapolis, I learned about a group where students came together to talk about something we don't talk about in class—racism. The group was started by students in my school and was called s.t.a.r.t. (students together against racial tension). At our school, when we discussed racial issues in class, teachers would describe to us the history of African-American people. Yet, because my teachers are not descendants of slaves, I sometimes felt like they did not fully understand how it feels to be an African American or even an immigrant, although they acted as if they knew. And that is the important point: It is not so much what our teachers said, but *how they insisted* on what they knew. Also, these same *teachers* were often more friendly with the white students on a day-to-day basis. I noticed that African-American students weren't given the time to talk about what happened to their families, and so *as a result* they did not feel safe to really talk about this in class. All of this made me want to be part of a group for students to work on these issues together *outside* class.

And it was support from that group that made me want to talk to an African-American leader named Katie Sample. It was really an honor to talk with someone who was active in the civil rights movement. As a Somali student growing up in the United States, I have learned many different views of what America is like. I believe that it is through the type of conversation that Ms. Katie Sample and I had—me as a young Somali student and her as an African-American elder—that we can help people change their perspectives about our country's racial challenges.

There were a couple of things that struck me in our conversation. First, when Ms. Sample was talking about being one of the first Black social workers in our Minneapolis Public Schools, I was inspired and humbled by the risks that she had to take to meet the needs of African-American students. For instance, when one of the boys she was serving was expelled, she stood up for him and helped the school understand the hardships in his life and encouraged and pushed those in the school to act with more compassion. Now I understand more clearly how important it is for our teachers to understand the African-American experience in the United States.

Also, I liked hearing about Ms. Katie Sample's experiences as an African-American student in school. At home, her parents reminded her of the strengths of being African-American. At school, she was teased and even hit just because she was one of the few African-American students. She felt misunderstood, not treated for who she was as a person, but rather bullied for the simple reason that she was different from her peers. She had to work hard day in and day out to help people to see and understand her human qualities—she had to put more effort into all her work.

Ms. Sample's experiences helped me understand that this was harder than it is today, yet I still believe that there's much more work to do. Because I don't take the need for this work for granted, it has inspired me to take a leadership role in our student group in order to help my peers better understand the complicated story about race, immigration, and culture in this country.

I think a lot about Ms. Katie Sample's example. We all need schools to provide more examples of this kind of courage. We also need teachers who are willing to connect with black and brown students, treat them with as much attention as they treat white students, and be comfortable talking about issues of race in the classroom. I would like teachers to know that they have a lot of power over students, because it's their word against ours whenever an issue comes up in the classroom. That advantage that teachers have can also help create positive changes in race relations. I would like teachers to understand that even though we have made progress, it is still a challenge to be a student of color in our schools. I would like teachers to be bold and confident in believing that *all* students will perform well in their classrooms. When teachers really believe that, more students will believe in themselves, and it will make a big difference.

Sincerely,
Fardousa

17

EXPLORING THE INTERSECTION OF AGEISM AND RACISM

Ilsa Govan

In the spring of 2007 I was working in Seattle Public Schools' department of Equity and Race Relations. Given that our mission was to eliminate institutional racism in the district, my job was fairly large in scope. We were constantly trying to figure out how best to spend our limited resources. One area of focus was developing Student Equity Teams in the high schools. This stemmed from the belief that without student voice, efforts "on their behalf" would never be successful. So we were trying to negotiate the line of engaging students, identifying their concerns with equity, and offering them enough information to support their understanding of the social and political context of race relations within the United States. Although we didn't want to come into schools and just tell them what to do, we understood the need for adult support in organizing and having access to adult-dominated spaces within the school district.

It was at this time when the opportunity arose to take a group of twenty high school students to the White Privilege Conference (WPC) in Colorado Springs, Colorado. I expected to gain a few new insights from the conference but was particularly excited about the students having an eye-opening experience. What I didn't realize was how much they would teach me about my own biases.

On the first day of the conference, the youth participated in workshops designed to grow awareness of their own identities, learn what is meant by *white privilege,* and better understand privilege in general. The idea was to provide them with a firm foundation of knowledge, so they could more fully participate in the conference. The youth organizers also assured them they had powerful ideas that needed to be contributed to the conversation. This was done to address issues from the past of youth not speaking up in adult-centered workshops.

In the evening they sat together in a youth-only space and had a caucus where they discussed their perspectives on different areas of privilege and oppression. When I asked what the best part of the conference was, they unanimously agreed it was the caucus. In fact, the caucusing continued in their hotel rooms well into the night, despite the chaperones telling them they needed to get some sleep. They were engaged in real conversations about identity issues and many said they never talked about these concepts, "things that really mattered," as they put it, with their friends or in school. I found it difficult to walk in on a conversation where girls were critically examining their fashion magazines for race and gender stereotypes and tell them they had to go to bed, even when it was close to midnight.

As an elementary school teacher for six years prior to working as an Equity and Race Specialist, I had dreamed of my students having these conversations. I would show them videos and lecture and even have class discussion, but I never really made space for the youth caucus. Believing that my students would get "off-task" if I wasn't there to ask the right questions or carefully monitor them, I actually got in the way of them processing information. I reflected on how many times I asked them questions that had a right answer, rather than letting them explore their own understanding and giving prompts that spurred *them* to ask critical questions.

I have met very few adults who are not interested in learning about their identities. Yet with the youth I had a deep feeling they needed me to steer the conversation. This recognition of my own tendency to dominate the conversation because of my assumptions about their lack of interest was my first big lesson in ageism from the conference.

There is a comfort in being needed by young people, and no one can argue that children do not need adults. At the same time, we need to be reflective about when we are doing for youth what they can do for themselves. When are we "helping" because of what it does for us? Consciously or unconsciously, many of us hold the idea that without a superior leader, one who is White or an adult, young people cannot be successful. It is based in an individual rather than a systems analysis of racial, age, and socioeconomic barriers.

The way we learn to teach from our role models and education programs set us up to be leaders imparting knowledge. No matter how much Freire we may study, it is difficult to differentiate between oppressive assumptions about a person's lack of intelligence and teaching to fill real gaps in knowledge.

As I was observing the conversations at the WPC and talking with the students over dinner one night, I found myself marveling at how smart they were. They had ways of thinking about privilege and oppression that I had never considered, despite spending the past 15 years studying and discussing these issues. This caused me to pause again and reflect on my assumptions.

When I was a teen, I hated adults who underestimated my intelligence. One of my many interests was the history of relations between European Americans and Indigenous people in the United States. So when the 500-year anniversary of Columbus's landing was being marked with protests around Seattle, I decided to skip school to attend an anti–Columbus Day Rally. I remember my physics teacher asking if I really thought that was more important than school. He was not shy about implying he believed I was just looking for an excuse to get out of classes and didn't really understand or care about social justice. The fact was, I understood the issues involved better than he did.

This kind of patronizing attitude was one I ran into often as a youth and was one I consciously tried to counter in my adult life. Yet here I was, marveling at the intelligence of the youth.

And, lest I lie to myself, I have to admit this was not entirely about age. This was a multiracial group of teenagers. In addition to my ageism, I had made race-based assumptions about their intelligence and abilities as well. This became clear to me with one student in particular.

After the first day of workshops and caucusing, one of the students, Lin, came to the chaperones with the complaint that many of the issues facing Asian Americans were not being addressed at the conference. Lin had recently moved to the United States from China and was attending a Seattle high school while her mother was working at the University of Washington. She saw firsthand how new immigrant students were marginalized by the dominant school culture as well as the tension between Asian students as they strove for greater acceptance.

We suggested she share her ideas with the conference organizer, Dr. Eddie Moore, Jr. When she talked to Dr. Moore, he asked if she would be interested in sharing her thoughts with other attendees at the conference. Before I knew it, Lin was on stage before the morning keynote, addressing the audience of approximately 1,000 people. During her four-minute speech she had people laughing, clapping, and cheering. At the end, she received a standing ovation.

I was stunned at her public speaking abilities. She rocked that room in a way I could only dream of. I commented that it must be quite an experience, speaking in front of a large audience like that for the first time. No, Lin assured me, she used to be president of her student body and had given other public speeches like this before.

Again I had to check myself. Because Lin was Chinese and had recently moved to the United States, I had all kinds of stereotypes about her being quiet and complacent. I never imagined she could give a speech like that, much less that she had prior leadership experience.

I have a degree in teaching students who speak English as a second language. I've often talked about how English-speaking Americans tend to underestimate people's intelligence when they are not fluent in English. It was one thing for me to know this was true of others, and another to come face-to-face with my own stereotypes. I wondered in what ways I had subtly communicated lower expectations to my bilingual students in the past. The intersection of my identity as White, adult, teacher combined to assert my internalized superiority (How could she be a better public speaker than me?!) and expect less of her, a Chinese, teenage, student.

As I purposely tried to shift my interactions, I watched the other adult chaperones carefully, noting the very different ways we interacted with the younger people. One of them was always in a teacher mode. He would listen to what they said and then find a way to point out the lesson. He never talked about his own experiences or what he was learning. Another one of the adults seemed distant. He didn't ask questions and only shared his insights when specifically asked. A White female teacher kept talking about how proud she was of the students and all they were learning, thereby taking partial credit for their knowledge. It was only too easy to hide behind the experience of the students and stay in the chaperone role, thus not dealing with our own issues around privilege and oppression.

Understanding my privilege means I recognize some doors will open for me and remain locked for others simply because we were given different keys. It also means that even if my key doesn't work, I have networks in place where I can easily get a new one. What the students need is for me to give them a key that works. Then they can open the door themselves and walk through on their own. By insisting I go through the door first, I'm robbing them of being entitled to be in that room without me, as was the case with the youth caucusing. Ultimately, the rooms should be places where someone with privilege doesn't have to sanction the presence of someone from an oppressed group.

It is not easy to expand beyond our personal interactions and grasp the current and historical extent of White privilege, White supremacy culture, and racial oppression in the United States. People spend years, even lifetimes, trying to unpack our cultural and institutional norms to work toward justice. But what is even more difficult is to act in a way that doesn't perpetuate injustice. Knowing and being are often separate. My experiences with the youth at the WPC showed me that just because I *knew* something about adult privilege didn't mean I thought or acted in ways that countered ageism. If we are going to authentically collaborate with youth to combat racism, we must be constantly vigilant in checking our own behaviors. Adults need to talk with youth and other adults to redefine what intergenerational movements for justice look and feel like.

Since the conference, I've produced a number of videos featuring students from elementary through high school talking about their experiences with ageism and racism in schools. They can name the behaviors of successful teachers and recognize when their voices are marginalized. I've also observed students speaking on panels to rooms full of their teachers or district leaders where they clearly state what needs to change to make schools more equitable. Inevitably, after watching one of these presentations, an adult will come up to me and say, "It is so good to hear the students' perspectives. That was really powerful."

Although I agree we need to be highlighting and listening to these voices on videos and panels, I also wonder why adults aren't already taking the opportunity to listen to the youth they work with every day. Ask your class of students to share their thoughts with you. Invite conversation about the ways privilege and oppression play out in school. Include students on school leadership teams to help make the decisions that ultimately affect them the most.

If we truly want to create equitable schools, adults need to be critically examining the role ageism plays in our everyday interactions and how that intersects with racism and other forms of bias. We should be interrogating our expectations of the capability of youth to engage in work that is meaningful to them and allow them to create youth-centered spaces. We need to be restructuring our ideas of what student engagement means.

COMBATING *HUCK FINN'S* CENSORSHIP

A Step-by-Step Approach to Discussing the N-Word in the Classroom

Justin Grinage

The recent censorship of Mark Twain's classic novel *The Adventures of Huckleberry Finn* has once again brought the controversy surrounding the "n-word" back into America's public consciousness. The announcement that there will be a newly printed version of the novel that replaces the word *nigger*—which is used 219 times in the book—with the word *slave* has rekindled the debate on if, when, or how the n-word should or should not be said or written. The truth is the n-word will never disappear, despite its censorship. Ever since it was first uttered in the early 1600s to its present-day incarnations, the n-word and its multiple meanings and derivatives persist.

Where this publishing decision is most noteworthy and crucial is within the very classrooms where *Huck Finn* is taught to students. Here, educators are confronted with decisions as to how they will approach teaching a text that contains this word. The disappearance of *Huck Finn* from high school English reading lists and the increased appearance on banned book lists, all because of the n-word, no doubt factored into this new reprinting.

I believe that individuals in favor of the censorship are missing the point of why it is important to talk about the word. In fact, Alan Gribben, an Auburn University professor and one of the scholars who were in charge of editing the new censored edition, was quoted in *USA Today* as saying, "All

I'm doing is taking out a tripwire and leaving everything else intact. . . . This novel cannot be made colorblind" (Moore, 2011, para. 6). However, editing the word out of the text does make the novel color-blind. It gives teachers the option to ignore a word that is arguably the most complex and racially charged word in the English language, thus squandering an opportunity to make students aware of the vast historical, political, and social ways the word has been and is still being used. Deleting the word from a novel does not eliminate the word from everyday life. Many students say the word and hear the word on a daily basis, yet have no idea why or how the word has been used in the past.

I believe that teachers can and should critically examine the n-word with their students. Although there is no way to eliminate the uncomfortable feelings that the n-word may conjure for the teacher and students, there is a way to deal with these feelings and increase the class's understanding of the word. Students, through critically analyzing the n-word, will gain a better understanding of a text in which it is used,* while also reaching a cultural and racial comprehension of its historical and modern usages. In this chapter, I provide a step-by-step exploration of how to effectively discuss the n-word.

Step 1: Preparing Yourself and Your Class to Discuss the N-Word

It is important to create an inclusive and trustworthy classroom environment, and this should start, preferably, at the beginning of the school year. An important aspect of creating this environment is having classroom discussions that have set guidelines and expectations. The book *Courageous Conversations about Race: A Field Guide for Achieving Equity in Schools* by Glen Singleton and Curtis Linton (2006) is an excellent resource for establishing guidelines for difficult discussions. The text is typically used as a way to engage educators in productive dialogue around race in schools, but I find that it is just as effective when used with students. Specifically, I use what Singleton and Linton call the "four agreements of courageous conversations." These are stay engaged, experience discomfort, speak your truth, and expect and accept nondisclosure (p. 58). Before our first class discussion, I

---

*I talk about the n-word in my classes at the beginning of our unit on *To Kill a Mockingbird*. However, this step-by-step plan can be used in conjunction with any text that uses the n-word or without a text altogether.

explain these four agreements in detail and we all agree as a class to follow them. As we have more conversations throughout the school year, I repeatedly go over these guidelines and interject them into exchanges when needed. When discussing the n-word, mental and emotional barriers will arise such as nervousness, fear, and resistance. Developing effective classroom discussion procedures and constituting a positive classroom climate go hand-in-hand when decreasing the number of these barriers that you and your students will face when having this discussion.

As a teacher, you will no doubt have a certain amount of anxiety before teaching about the n-word. These feelings may come from the uncertainty of how individual students and the class as a whole will react during discussions. And these feelings may be compounded if you have never felt confident discussing the word in your personal life, let alone inside the classroom. The n-word has become such a taboo subject in recent years that many whites have avoided discussing the word altogether for fear of offending a person of color. There is an added element of uneasiness for white teachers who fear that just by having a conversation about the word with their students, they will be labeled racist or not fit to talk about the word because they are not black. Teachers have to realize that uncomfortable feelings are unavoidable and not let fear overcome their willingness or ability to analyze the word with their students. The most important mental preparation for teaching about the n-word is to acknowledge that both you as a teacher and many of your students will feel varying degrees of discomfort, but this discomfort should not be an impediment to having thoughtful and rich conversations about an otherwise controversial subject. Before we talk about the n-word in class, my students will have already had a couple of class discussions where they have touched on controversial subject matter. It is advantageous to you and your students if you have already experienced nervousness, anxiety, or discomfort together with another topic.

It is also noteworthy to mention that I always give my class at least a week's advance notice that we will be having this discussion. Telling the class in advance allows them to mentally prepare themselves in their own way. Suddenly springing the discussion on them may catch some students off-guard in a very negative manner. The students who may have a negative reaction out of discomfort, nervousness, or even fear, with advance notice will have at least had time to grapple with the thought of having these feelings beforehand and come to class mentally prepared to deal with these emotions.

Step 2: Writing About the N-word

Before any discussions about the n-word occur in my classroom, students must first write about their feelings regarding the word. Not only is it critical for students to process their thinking through writing, but also it gives an opportunity for students who will not talk during the discussion to voice their opinion. I tell them beforehand that they will not be asked or forced to share what they wrote and they can choose whether to put their name on their assignment; I will be the only one to see their writing. (If you are uncomfortable reading their anonymous writing, collecting their writing is optional.) I want my students to be honest, so I make the assignment as nonthreatening and safe as possible.

The writing assignment I provide them with is as follows:

Nigger	Nigga	Gay	Retard

1. What are your feelings regarding these four words?
2. Do you feel it is okay to say any of these words? Explain why or why not.
3. Do you feel it is okay to say some of these words but not others? Explain.
4. How would you feel about saying any of these words in class?
5. Would you be offended if someone read the word or said the word in class during a discussion or while reading aloud? Why or why not?
6. Write any additional comments, questions, concerns, or ideas you have about the words.

My goal is to get them writing about the n-word in relation to other discriminatory slurs, but also to consider the multiple meanings that the word can conjure. I will then highlight some of these critical questions during the classroom discussion. I usually give 15–20 minutes just for students to write silently. (This is with tenth graders; the actual writing time and writing assignment can be adjusted based on grade or skill level.) During this time I do not allow students to ask questions about the words. I want students to pose questions or work out the questions they have through their writing. Any questions that students have can be asked during the discussion portion of the lesson.

Step 3: Understanding the Historical and Modern Usages of the N-Word

Steps 2 and 3 are interchangeable depending on preference. Another necessary step before discussing the n-word is making your students aware of the historical significance of the word, as well as how the word functions in its modern forms. An excellent resource that I use to accomplish this step is the book *Nigger: The Strange Career of a Troublesome Word* by Randall Kennedy (2002). Kennedy meticulously researches the history of the n-word from its early origin to its modern meanings. Not only would I suggest reading this text to build your background knowledge of the n-word, but I also recommend sharing some of the research with your students to increase their understanding of the word.

Here are some research points from the book that I have adapted to use with my students to help shape their comprehension of the word:

Origins of the N-Word

- *Nigger* is derived from the Latin word for the color black, *niger.*
- It originally was not a racial slur, but took on a negative connotation over time.
- From the early 1600s and beyond, *nigger* and other words related to it have been spelled in a variety of different ways: *niggah, nigguh, niggur,* and *niggar.*
- No one knows how *niger* turned into *nigger.*
- At the beginning of the 1800s, *nigger* had become a familiar and frequent insult.
- Throughout the 1800s and 1900s, *nigger* seeped into practically every aspect of American culture, including literature, political debates, cartoons, songs, film, and even nursery rhymes.

The N-Word and Its Multiple Meanings

- Jarvis DeBerry states, "I am not aware of any other word capable of expressing so many contradictory emotions" (Quoted in Kennedy, 2002, p. 29).
- Blacks began to embrace the n-word, and the connotation began to change from a very negative one to a more positive meaning. (One example is comedian Richard Pryor using the word frequently in his comedy act in the 1970s.)

- Today the n-word is embraced by many popular black comedians and hip-hop artists.
- In the black community the n-word is both rejected and embraced. Some blacks use the word as a positive term, while others refuse to say the word at all.
- There is also the distinction between *nigger* and *nigga*. Some blacks believe it is okay to say *nigga,* but not *nigger.*
- The n-word and its multiple meanings raise a lot of perplexing questions.

Generally, I put these in a PowerPoint presentation and have my students take notes on the research as I explain the information. I will also make them aware of Kennedy's book and encourage them to read it. At this point, I still do not answer any questions before we have our discussion. I encourage students to write any questions they have in the margins of their notes. I do this because I want to be able to review the discussion protocols and procedures with my students, as well as set specific guidelines before we talk openly about the word.

Beyond establishing critical historical and modern research surrounding the n-word, it is also effective to share a personal connection with the word as an educator with your class. This can be achieved through telling personal stories about your experiences with the word. I recount to the class stories about myself and my family's personal struggles with the n-word.

Often I find that teachers, specifically white teachers, are hesitant to open up about their experiences with the n-word. Also, teachers sometimes feel that the n-word has not affected them in any way or their stories are not important enough to share with their students. However, if we are going to ask our students to be honest and talk about their experiences with the word, it only makes sense for us, as educators, to speak our truth as well. Everyone in this country has had an encounter with the n-word at some point in his or her life; share a couple of these stories with your students. Moreover, if a colleague or community member has an interesting story concerning the word and they feel comfortable coming into the class to tell it, it could potentially be a powerful experience for your students.

After explaining my personal journey with the n-word, I find that students are a lot less reluctant to speak and more open to disclosing their thoughts and feelings during the class discussion. During the discussion portion, I encourage students to share their own stories and conflicts with the word to the class. Stemming from my story and other stories that students share in class we can start examining and unraveling some of the ideas contained in the long and complicated history of the word.

Step 4: Establishing Expectations and Discussing the N-Word

I have heard the n-word spoken numerous times and in many contexts by white people and people of color alike. One thing that I have never gotten over is whenever the word is stated, especially by white people, a sharp emotion pulses through my body. It is a feeling that is similar to embarrassment, like when a person blushes. But within this sudden sensation, I feel flashes of our country's history of racism and oppression, coupled with impressions of pain and sorrow. Even though it lasts only for an instant, it is a feeling that has not lessened no matter how many times I hear the n-word. I know all too well the emotions that a black student may feel when the word is said out loud.

When structuring the n-word discussion, I am very clear about the reason why we are having this conversation in the first place. We are critically examining the word to have a better understanding of its existence in relation to the text we are reading, but also, we are having a conversation about how to treat the word in class to ensure that everyone is as comfortable as possible. Before we partake in the discussion, I explain to the class that during the discussion the word should only be referred to as "the n-word" when said out loud. I also make the distinction that you should say "the n-word with an er" or "the n-word with an a" if you want to distinguish between nigger and nigga respectively. **At no point during the class discussion does anyone (myself included) say the word *nigger* or *nigga*.** The only actual mention of the word will be in a student's thoughts when they read the word silently, which is unfortunately unavoidable.

It is vital that, before the n-word conversation takes place, you remind your students of the procedures and protocols you have arranged for class discussions. I always thoroughly review the four agreements for courageous conversations, specifically drawing their attention to experiencing discomfort and speaking your truth. I want students to be open and honest about their opinions concerning the word, knowing that they will be uncomfortable; it makes for a much more in-depth discussion if there is a free flow of ideas. To start the discussion I prompt the class to ask any questions stemming from their writing assignment or tell any stories that they have about the n-word and go from there.

Students, often unknowingly, may state a stereotype or racist viewpoint concerning the word. Because many students will be experiencing discomfort, they may get defensive, disengage, or become frustrated. There is no way to know how your class will react. The most important thing to remember as an educator facilitating this discussion is to stay calm and not let your emotions get the best of you. I allow everyone to have his or her own opinion whether I think the student is right or wrong. If a student makes a flat-out racist statement, I do not denounce them right away—even though that may be my first reaction. Instead, I ask them follow-up questions about why they think this way. Usually, they will not be able to come up with any sort of valid argument. This is when I will state my opinion, which allows them to consider another viewpoint. Also, their fellow classmates may speak up to offer an opposing view of the stereotypical or racist statement. At no point do I preach that my stance or viewpoint is right, yet I will make sure to strongly question any opinion that is motivated by bias or stereotypes.

I have always conducted these conversations in a whole-class setting. I would advise against instructing your students to discuss in small groups because you have less control over what students are saying to each other. You may be listening in and offering feedback to one group while another group is arguing over something that one of their group members said. It is difficult to know what all groups are talking about at all times, so you have less control over the direction the conversations are going. It would become more complicated to defuse a tense situation in a small group as opposed to handling that same situation in a large group where all the students can hear each other and the teacher.

The Boiling Pot Metaphor

Although you can never predict what students will ask during the discussion, there are some common questions that are usually posed. Since the n-word is so complex, often there are no easy answers to these questions. To tackle some of these tougher questions, it may be useful for you to explain to students what I call the "boiling pot metaphor." This metaphor involves teaching your students the meaning of and differences between *denotation* and *connotation*. The pot represents the n-word itself or the denotation of the word. When the word was first used back in the early 1600s, the pot's water, the connotation of the n-word, was barely hot. As the word was continually used over centuries to degrade, humiliate, and oppress black people, during slavery and Jim Crow and through the Civil Rights Movement, the water began to slowly simmer, and then boil. Now, whenever this word is said, it carries the historical and emotional temperature of countless repugnant images of white people using the word to oppress black people, sometimes in very gruesome ways. At any point the water, which is already boiling from this historical imagery, can become so hot that it boils over and explodes. Explaining this metaphor to your students illustrates the very sensitive and racially charged complexities that the connotation of the n-word contains. In turn, you can use the metaphor to dissect some of the complicated questions your students may pose.

Frequently Asked Student Questions

How come it is okay to call a white person a *cracker,* but not okay to call a black person the n-word?

This question comes up quite often and it is usually asked by a white student. Whenever a student asks this question, I always respond by inquiring about why he or she feels it is all right to call a white person a *cracker.* They usually respond by stating that black people have called them crackers in the past and sometimes they make fun of other white people by calling them crackers, but that using the word is not that big a deal.

I will tell the student that it is actually not appropriate to call a white person a *cracker* because it is discriminatory language, but at the same time, it does not have the same connotation as the n-word. This is where the boiling pot metaphor proves useful and why it is critical to touch on the history of inequality in this country, as well as describe how blacks were oppressed throughout history and how the n-word was a symbol of this oppression. Because historically blacks were not the oppressors, the word *cracker* does not have as much power behind it, even though it is still inappropriate to say. Therefore, the n-word has much more racial force behind it, because it was used for centuries as a symbol of oppression, whereas *cracker* was not.

Why is it okay to say *gay, retard,* or any other discriminatory word, but not the n-word? Is the n-word worse than other slurs?

Many students are convinced that words such as *gay* and *retard* are not discriminatory, which is the reason why I add this language to the writing assignment. Often students do not believe that saying these words, or any other slur for that matter, is as bad as saying the n-word. By comparing other discriminatory words to the n-word, I illustrate the point that although the n-word contains more connotational weight (or a much higher temperature with more boiling water, if you want to follow the metaphor), it does not mean that it is more hurtful than other slurs. I ask the students to imagine that every time they say the word *gay* or *retard* to describe an object or person, that they actually replace it with the n-word. Students may say that you cannot compare these words with the n-word. However, I urge them to understand that the only difference between the n-word and other slurs is that, historically speaking, it has been around a lot longer than most other discriminatory words in this country. But just because a word has been around longer does not mean it negates or minimizes the hurtfulness of other discriminatory language that is newer. Discriminatory words discriminate equally.

One way this may be contradictory is if you say *gay* or *retard* out loud, but do not say the n-word out loud. Students will call you on this as a reason that the n-word is more hurtful than other words because the class cannot say this word, but can say the other words. If you wanted to drive home the point that one discriminatory word is not worse than another, you could instruct students to not pronounce any discriminatory word out loud, similar to the n-word. In this case they would say the *g-word,* the *r-word,* and so on. Really this comes down to the question of how much speech we should censor, which could be a philosophical conversation you have with your students.

Who can say the n-word and who can't? Is it okay to say the n-word with an "-a" but not an "-er"?

Students are very confused about these two questions because there is no simple answer. I try to focus my explanation on whether it should be said within the school setting. Many of my black students and other students of color say the n-word with an "-a" in the hallways of our school. I tell them that once that word leaves their mouth they have no control over who hears it and who may potentially be offended by it. Whenever I walk down the hall and I hear students saying the n-word, whether it be with an "-er" or an "-a," I am personally offended. Other individuals may be offended when students say this word in the hallway, too; there is no way to tell. Therefore, I clarify that the n-word under any circumstances and in any way, shape, or form, should not be said in the hallways or in the classroom.

Some of my students of color may disagree with my stance and assert that the n-word with an "-a" is a positive term they use with their friends. I then ask the class how many students say the word or hear their friends say the word and have no idea about the history of the word or where the word came from. Most students have not studied the n-word and do not know where it originated. I explain that ultimately, it is up to them to decide whether or not they want to say the word in a positive way with their friends, but to make sure they understand the vast racial history of the word before they use it in their vocabulary. However, I do reiterate that the word should not be used on school property to ensure that no one who may hear it is offended by it. I also communicate to them that in my own personal life I still have friends who say the word in a positive way, but I no longer say the word because I understand the power it has to hurt others.

I usually spend at least two class periods having the n-word discussion. I want to give students the time to ask all their questions and the opportunity to tell their stories. I believe it is critical to spend enough class time discussing the word so students can process their thoughts and ideas. Because the subject can often be so complicated, if we rush through the discussion students may be more confused about the word than they were before. Spend time addressing each and every student's questions and concerns.

Step 5: Postdiscussion Wrap-Up and Reflection

There are a couple of specific options for your students to reflect on what they learned from the n-word discussion. I always have my students reread their initial writing assignment and write a reflection on whether their opinions changed based on our discussion. Also, because the *Huck Finn* censorship occurred around the time my class was analyzing the n-word, I gave my students some articles debating the controversy and we had a Socratic seminar examining the topic. Overall, students are very excited and curious to analyze the n-word, and it often becomes one of the most critical conversations that we have during the year. I find that after we have the discussion we are closer as a class and it is much easier for students to confront other controversial subjects.

Having this discussion is fundamental if you want your students to be more racially literate. Students gain a wider understanding of one of the most racially charged words that we have in the English language. The fact of the matter is that the n-word is not disappearing from speech, regardless of its censorship. Kennedy (2002) asserts, "As *nigger* is more widely disseminated and its complexity is more widely appreciated, censuring its use—even its use as an insult—will become more difficult" (p. 138). What teachers must understand is that the n-word can be critically analyzed without compromising the true integrity of a text. Educators who choose to teach literature that censors the word will miss a momentous opportunity to empower their students by confronting, examining, and discussing this complicated word.

References

Kennedy, R. (2002). *Nigger: The strange career of a troublesome word*. New York: Pantheon Books.

Moore, M. T. (2011, January 6). *Huck Finn* navigating choppy waters. *USA Today*. Retrieved from http://usatoday30.usatoday.com/life/books/2011-01-06-twain06_ST_N.htm?csp = usat.me

Singleton, G. E., & Linton, C. (2006). *Courageous conversations about race: A field guide for achieving equity in schools*. Thousand Oaks, CA: Corwin Press.

19

LETTER FROM A HIGH
SCHOOL STUDENT #3

Carlo Balleria

Dear Reader,
Racial tensions continue to cripple and polarize our society. Despite this reality, we wish to continue to believe in the illusion that we live in a postracial and color-blind society. In our country, and more specifically at my city high school, we continue to make judgments on each other entirely on our perceptions without determining just how accurate these perceptions are. Often, we—students and adults—perceive and interact with each other as if we were confined by masks. This prevents us from perceiving the true qualities and character of fellow students.

I have observed numerous situations with judgment rooted in racial perceptions. One day, I planned to meet a fellow National Honor Society (NHS) officer and a shadowing NHS member from another school in the art room hallway to make a banner for an upcoming event. We were all white males. The purpose of the banner was to thank the school for the generous donations it made during an NHS Penny-for-Patients drive. I arrived later than the other two because I had to discuss an assignment with a teacher. I was still wearing my backpack and had not yet begun to help construct the banner. While the other two began sketching the banner, two African-American male students walked into the hall near us. A hall monitor followed them shortly and asked them for their passes. Neither of them had a pass and the hall monitor escorted them away with nothing more than a glance at the three of us. What I found disturbing about this was that even though I was excused to help make the banner, I was not actively participating and it was equally probable that I was truant as well. Yet the hall monitor did not even question me. It was clear he had assumed the two African Americans were doing something wrong, while I—the white student—must have a reason for being out of class. I was vindicated of all possibility of wrongdoing by the color of my skin. This was not the first time I had been assumed innocent of truancy because of the color of my skin; there were countless other times a hall monitor walked past me in the halls and never asked me for my pass. The reason I remember this one especially was because of the presence of the shadowing NHS member; my school has a strong reputation of tolerance and equality, but for the shadowing NHS member to see this blatant racial profiling exhibited by a staff member of my school was disheartening and frustrating.

The classrooms inside my school are not free from racism. This is exhibited by the demographics of course selection. I prefer to be challenged rather than bored, so I have always opted to take a more rigorous class. I started taking Advanced Placement (AP) and honors classes as they were available to me. I noticed something very interesting when I began attending these more rigorous classes: The demographics of the students in these courses were much less diverse. Now, instead of seeing a fair mixture of racial backgrounds and ethnicities throughout the course of my day, I began to see more and more of my white classmates and less and less of my classmates of different racial backgrounds. This seriously perplexed me; it made no sense why former classmates of mine, who scored as well on any assignment as I did, would pass up a free opportunity to earn college credit. Even now, I do not know the reason why so few of my former classmates were taking these AP classes. One cause could be that my former classmates of different racial backgrounds did not feel encouraged by teachers, counselors, or their own communities to try for these tougher courses. I do believe it was connected directly to institutional racism in our educational system.

Every year, my school's schedule for a couple days is modified because of state standardized testing. We spend the first half of the day testing and then, for the second half of the day, we participate in a workshop hosted by a student-led peer education organization called Stand Up, Speak Out South High (SUSOSH). The purpose of SUSOSH is to raise awareness and facilitate discussion about a variety of social issues, such as racism, sexism, and homophobia. The SUSOSH facilitators usually begin with some sort of activity related to the issue we will be discussing. The first year SUSOSH came to our classrooms was my sophomore year. The subject was racism and the facilitators were in my AP US History class. Both were upperclassmen; one was an energetic white girl who had glasses, a number of dyed streaks in her hair, and an above-average number of piercings in her ears. Her partner was a tall, thin African-American guy who had a quiet demeanor. I believe he was involved in the theater program somehow. I felt that the African American could probably relate to the subject much more than his fellow facilitator. For the introductory activity, the facilitators asked my classmates and me to line up shoulder to shoulder. They read from a list of advantages and asked us to take a step forward if the advantage pertained to us and to take a step back if we did not experience the advantage. Even though the facilitators were there to talk to us about racism, nothing they said directly referred to race; nothing they said explicitly referred to racism. Yet it did not take long for all of us to notice that, yes, indeed, what they were reading was referring to racism. Examples of these advantages included "my parents go on vacations," "no immediate family member has been incarcerated at some time," "my elementary school classrooms had computers," and "I don't know anyone who is on welfare." Each time one of the facilitators spoke, the disparity between me and my classmates from different racial backgrounds and the burdens and privileges we had in our lives became more and more visible. After a few minutes of reading, the facilitators told us to look around the room and see where the rest of our classmates were. When I turned around and saw other white people surrounding me and then saw the distance that separated our group from my classmates of different racial backgrounds a deep sense of guilt set in. I knew some of my classmates during this activity would have to take some steps back, but I never thought so many of them would be my classmates of racial backgrounds different from my white background. If you were to walk into the room and were to guess the activity, you would most likely guess we were dividing ourselves entirely by race and not by the relevance of certain statements to our lives. Realizing the magnitude of this economic disparity between us showed me how race and poverty intertwined and the amount of a head start my privileges gave me. I could easily see we were not all starting from the same place in the competition that makes up school.

Any form of tension between groups is given the opportunity to intensify when there is little interaction or discussion among those groups. This is why daily interaction and discussion is so important in reducing and extinguishing any form of tension. The following is an example of the effect daily interaction can have and how I came to better know a group of students in my school. There is a large population of first- and second-generation African immigrants at my school. I never had much reason to interact with any of them because not many of them were in any of my classes, nor did they live in my neighborhood. I didn't really know much about any of them, except for their stereotypes. However, this changed when I joined my school's cross-country running team. I joined as a junior and was on the lower end of varsity. The next two higher spots were occupied by two east African immigrant students: a junior, Temesgen Fedaku, whom I had known a little about beforehand from the few classes we had shared over the years, and a sophomore, Abdulfatha Sameru, whom I had never met before. I got to know the two of them during my junior year season, but I didn't spend a signifi-cant amount of time with either of them outside practice. Like any high school student I spent time with junior and senior friends from my own circle.

The summer of my senior year was the jumping-off point for a new relationship with these two, and was a time of change for me. We all knew that we would be some of the top runners on varsity for the upcoming cross-country season and did not want to disappoint; we were joined by another east African who had an impressive freshman track season, Mikey Wondimu, and began off-season training shortly after the regular track season's end. The amount of time we spent together on distance runs and the punishment we endured during regular season created a sense of camaraderie. By the end of the cross-country season, I felt as close to these three first- and second-generation east African immigrants as I felt to any of my friends of back-grounds similar to my own. If I had not had these near daily interactions with Temesgen, Abdulfatha, or Mikey, I would never have gotten to know them individually and grown close to them. The false assumptions generated by their stereotypes would have been all I had known. When we act on the false assumptions we make, when we do not look past our own masks, when each of us stays confined within our own perceptions, we are not able to make any connections with others. Any person's experience of life is dimin-ished when he or she is forced to live behind a mask of false assumptions. We must return to Dr. Martin Luther King, Jr.'s wisdom until we get it right; we must lift up these masks to see each other's true "content of charac-ter." To free our society from masking our true selves through false assump-tions, we must take the time to learn the complexities of each person we encounter, without generalizations or expectations based on the color of his or her skin.

In schools it is the administration and the teaching staff's responsibility to help create a culture that promotes fairness and equality. If the prevailing custom of perceiving nothing about an individual but their racial or cultural mask continues, we will never cross racial or cultural or economic boundaries. It is up to schools to be a crucial part in this social justice work. Patterns can be counteracted and progress can be made by supporting groups that facilitate discussion among students on the topic of racism, racial tensions, and racial prejudices. Students should have access to safe environments free from judgment or repercussions to voice their opinions and discuss these topics. There should be groups that meet either weekly or monthly to provide such a forum.

Other than providing a safe environment for discussion, the responsibilities of these groups should include:

Facilitating workshops for individuals to express what they are feeling through art or written word

Organizing awareness campaigns to promote fairness, equality, and tolerance, including outside speakers from their discussion

Facilitating larger mandatory workshops at least biannually to expose individuals who would not voluntarily attend such discussions

Putting into place stringently enforced punishment for any racist action, demonstrating there is no tolerance for racist behavior

Displaying banners and announcements promoting equity

Encouraging participation in all such activities and forums by every teacher, administrator, aide, and student leader

These actions, coupled with the strong socializing effect of school, can be steps toward providing the most effective long-term solution to racial tensions. Harnessing all these elements to promote equality and tolerance can have incredible effects and benefits. When a school takes action against racism, bullying, and harassment of any kind, a great deal of progress can be made.

We need adults to help us. As students, we need fearless teachers willing to go out of their comfort zone if need be, to have tough, fulfilling conversations that can change lives, and ultimately, one by one, can change the country. High school students need schools to go the distance with us. We are ready.

Sincerely,
Carlo Balleria

20

THE MISEDUCATION OF *NIGGER* IN AMERICAN SCHOOLS

Marcellus Davis, Alexander Hines, and Kenneth Turner

In the second season of the popular television show *The Boondocks,* Aaron Gruder and his writing team developed an episode called "The S Word" (spear chucker). The s-word is in replacement of the n-word (nigger) in this parody. It was a parody of an actual event that happened in a Jefferson County High School between a teacher and a student in which the teacher told the student to "sit down, nigga." This episode was exactly like the actual footage that is viewable on YouTube. In the footage, the teacher states that he was just trying to relate with the youth and use the "language they use." He also stated that this pedagogical tactic was what he learned from his district, which the school district quickly denied. The only sane response from this educator's mouth was the question he proposed during his interview: "I don't understand why they use the word, and I need help. I'm trying to understand why this word is used routinely in school."

Recently, we've visited various rural, suburban, and inner-city local high schools in the Minneapolis–St. Paul area and were stunned at what we heard in the hallways. The word *nigger* was being used in multiple ways as a noun, a verb, and an adjective: "My nigga this," "that nigga ain't that," and "nigga, please." Our young people used the word so effortlessly, irresponsibly, carelessly, and with such malice that there became an immediate need for us, as educators, to respond in the true sense of the word *educare,* which means to care for one's education. Thus we researched the word *nigger* and developed a traveling presentation to educate youth, teachers, administrators, and community members about the word's origin.

There was another issue that was even more perplexing than the students' using the word with no regard for the historical context in which the word derived; the issue was that we witnessed multiple educators hearing the word being used repeatedly and not responding in a way we felt was appropriate for the leader of the educational setting or, simply put, as an educator should in this critical teaching situation. We aren't advocating for educators to say, "You shouldn't say that." Youth need more education behind why they shouldn't be using the word in school or as a term of endearment.

This chapter looks at a way to effectively combat and deconstruct the word *nigger* from grades six through twelve. We are aware that there is a host of words (*fag, gay, retard,* and *bitch*) that demand serious attention in our American school systems, and we agree that overall there needs to be a plan to combat all these words, but the focus of this chapter is on the word *nigger.*

This chapter first states the problem, then speaks about the cause, then focuses on solutions, and, lastly, focuses on implementation of the solutions.

The Problem

In many of our American schools the words *nigger, nigga,* and *niggaz* are being used as common language. It's still being used in the old derogatory and demeaning way it's always been used, but it's also being used as a noun ("What up, my nigga?"). It is also suggested as a term of endearment. Some teachers do nothing to combat the usage, but a very few do what schools are designed to do, and that is teach about an issue that plagues schools on a daily basis. There is no curriculum devised that deals with the word *nigger.* This word has so much baggage and lineage in this country that it is irresponsible not to teach about the inappropriateness of its usage in our schools or its ability to degrade another individual.

We don't believe that the word *nigger* being used in our hallways and classrooms is responsible for the high dropout rate, nor do we believe that the word *nigger* is responsible for the achievement gap. We do believe that the failure to provide serious education in support of the eradication of this pejorative, venomous word speaks volumes about the low expectations for our children in many American schools.

There is a developing ideology of what it means to be "a real nigga"; it's never associated with many positives. Being a nigga is being physically tough, a hustler, and someone you don't want to mess with. This romanticization of *nigga* is a misguided phenomenon by the streets, playgrounds, neighborhoods, popular and media culture, some families and communities, and schools. These microsystems, mesosystems, exosystems, and macrosystems all contribute in shaping and molding the identity development of our youth today. Far too often *nigga* is attributed to being Black and inferior, just like it was in 1619. This depiction is not only damaging for the psyche of Black children, it is damaging to all children. In this most critical of times for our youths' individual, social, and moral development, the *nigga* ideology and the acceptance to be identified as a nigga is detrimental for the continual marginalization of a people with a rich history and culture and the unawareness of the African/Black diaspora.

Lastly, American schools help shape society, and society helps shape American schools. Many of today's school hallways function like the scenes from a movie, a music video, a comedy routine, or the streets. In some schools and neighborhoods if you are listening instead of hearing, you can overhear conversations about students' thoughts about their upcoming class, the latest school gossip, whether Chris Brown is really dating Rihanna, and the word *nigga* routinely making its rounds in many of the conversations taking place. The word selection isn't reserved for use solely by male or Black students; this word has been uttered by both genders and many races, nationalities, and creeds in our schools, thus creating a culture that allows popular culture to continue perpetuating myths and stereotypes that are sometimes not addressed, leaving young minds uneducated about the media's lack of normative ethics.

The Cause

This word continues to be an endemic social disorder that has spread like a pandemic flu worldwide with no real educational curriculum that promotes African/Black consciousness or social justice consciousness. From its early conception in Africa, in particular KMT, now Egypt, the word *enger*, pronounced en-ger, which means being made in the image of God, has been mispronounced and misinterpreted through its travels from Africa to the United States. How can *niger*, which is Latin for black, and *negre*, French for black, just to name two, be misconstrued for *nigger* and being inferior?

This word has been part of the socialization of the world through art, school, home, and literature. This socialization has come with no critical understanding of the historical context in which the word was formed. This social disorder has not only plagued our society, but it has invaded our classrooms. School is a place for learning, and our children are not learning about this American White supremacy, but they are learning how to uphold White supremacy and adhere to low expectations from their schools, teachers, administrators, and peers.

The Solution and Implementation

When devising a plan to combat this issue within a school or district, it's imperative to make this an ecologic approach that includes the support of multiple constituencies. The institution leader must be the first person who recognizes that there is a serious issue with this word in the school. She or he will need to assemble a team including teachers, students, a district representative, and parents to combat this issue. It will be very important for the school leader to clearly state why this issue is affecting the learning that happens in the school.

There are two ways to tackle this issue: (a) You can attack the issue of hate language within the school with special emphasis on the words *nigger* and *nigga*; or (b) you can state that this word has become a serious issue within the school, and it's time for some education around the word to help bring understanding to why it will not be tolerated in the school. We suggest that this intentional direct approach be communicated from the very beginning of the school year. It should be stated clearly and emphatically that this language will not be tolerated in this institution that has been dedicated to learning, and that if it is used there will be serious repercussions. The objective is to create a culturally proficient and responsive school that has high expectations for student conduct and performance in and outside the classroom. The importance of understanding the power of the words we choose has to be practiced and learned not only in the home, but in our schools as well.

Teacher professional development must be delivered around the word in order to combat it. What will come out of these professional developments is the deconstructing of fear that keeps many educators in check. This issue involves race and White supremacy. White supremacy has conditioned society to associate *nigger* with Black people in a demeaning and nefarious way that is deleterious to identity development and the marginalization of a Black people. This reality has many educators in check for fear of being called a racist, so professional development around the word *nigger* will not only give historical context of the origin and current-day usage of the word, but will also demand personal reflective self-evaluation of one's issues around race and how it plays a role in one's classroom and school daily. Lastly, teachers will develop strategies that will maintain high expectations of students in and out of the classroom, and plans to build a lifelong command of utilizing language to advance one's life through increasing one's vocabulary and word choice while learning the history and power of words.

The team assembled will determine the strategies and steps in how they will combat and implement lesson plans to educate about this word. The conglomerate team should be able to think this out from multiple perspectives with the array of community members. It will be important to be transparent in the purpose of this the dissemination of the communication should be very common language for the masses, and this objective should be measured to give evidence that this was a corrective tool for the learning community. This team must be tough enough to deal with the outside criticism that will definitely come with the decisions to eradicate hate language from the school setting and educate about the usage of *nigger* in the school environment.

In summary, you will need to get school leadership backing and develop a team consisting of internal and external constituents. Communication must be transparent and use common language that can be easily understood by the masses. You must prepare for outside criticism, routinely state the expectation of the school's learning environment, and evaluate effectiveness.

21

CROSSING THE RACIAL LINE

Making a s.t.a.r.t.

Kate Towle

I get to hear the opinions of my schoolmates of
different races and how they feel about the
impact of race in the schools. I get the chance
to voice my opinion and how strongly I feel
about this subject as a whole. s.t.a.r.t. gives students a chance to actually do something in their
schools that will open up people's eyes and give
[race] the attention it deserves in order for more
students to do better.

—Sadia

A mere fifty-five years ago, in 1957, eight courageous students, supported by their parents and the National Association for the
Advancement of Colored People (NAACP), faced burning acid
sprayed into their eyes, the ropes of lynch mobs, sticks of dynamite, and knives
to fulfill the 1954 Supreme Court ruling that "separate but equal" schools were
still inherently unequal. It was a milestone in the Civil Rights Movement—
the students' extraordinary courage made a powerful statement against segre-
gationist laws that denied African Americans access to educational privileges.

In March 2012, thirty-five students and adults from Farmington, Lake-
ville, and South High Schools in Minneapolis and surrounding suburbs
reenacted the events in Little Rock, Arkansas, for their student bodies as part
of a student leadership concept created by South High students called
s.t.a.r.t. (students together against racial tension). The Little Rock Nine exercise was designed for the s.t.a.r.t. students by African-American leader and

elder Katie Sample. s.t.a.r.t. began in September 2009 as a student-driven effort to develop each other as intercultural leaders through work on identity, cultural bridging, and community action. Two inner-city schools and two suburban districts have begun practicing the model.

In July 2011, the model won a Facing Race Idea Challenge through the St. Paul Foundation—it was selected out of forty-nine models proposed in Minnesota. The South High students who created the initial effort, three of whom have letters included in this book, hosted a table at the National Youth Service-Learning Conference in the spring of 2012 to inform high school peers and teachers how to bring this opportunity into their schools.

The student founders of s.t.a.r.t. were prompted to create their group after rezoning efforts within the Minneapolis Public Schools limited integration funds used for busing in an effort to strengthen neighborhood schools and keep more students in their own communities. South had historically drawn students together across a highly segregated city, from both the southwest area of Minneapolis, having the highest per capita income ($69,000 in 2009) and a majority of white residents; and north Minneapolis, having the lowest per capita income ($36,000) and a minority of white residents. Their school, with one of the city's most diverse populations, would now have to deny busing to students not in its "zone." South students had created friendships from all over the city, and they valued the diversity in which they learned from day to day. They had a burning question as they began to look at the issue of integration with a critical eye: *With such diversity in their school, something that would possibly be compromised, what was the true work of integration? Why didn't students cross cultures outside class often?*

Two young Euro-American women, one a senior and one a sophomore, recruited ten young men and women (three of mixed descent) to talk about something that one of their African-American male friends called "taboo"— the topic of race. "It's one of those touchy subjects," he said. "There's this big aura around race, and it's so hushed about that it's just hard for people to talk because of all the history." The conversation about race, although challenging, was more natural for the white women who were starting the group than for many of their white counterparts. These young women had attended Kwanzaa and other cultural events all their lives and had played with black and brown dolls as they were growing up. Race was a part of their family discussions early on. This is rare. (A 2007 study in the *Journal of Marriage and Family* found that out of 17,000 families with kindergartners, parents of color are about three times more likely to discuss race than white parents; 75% of white parents rarely, if ever, talk about race.) As a parent of one of the founding s.t.a.r.t. students, I promised the group that I would meet with them once a week over lunch to discuss racial equity and to make a plan to bring more students into the dialogue. One of the students' teachers offered his classroom, and as one senior girl with a white mother and an African-American father described it, "I will not forget that my first racial dialogue in high school began with seven others, sitting on the floor of a classroom during lunchtime."

Our first action steps were simple: to encourage a column about race in the student newspaper, to invite speakers and leaders to talk about race, and to read and discuss articles and books that deal constructively with the challenging issues of race and cultural competence. We began small with events that we hoped would have an effect.

Eight of the students talked on a radio show on Martin Luther King, Jr. Day. They stressed the need to be unafraid to have frequent conversations about race and racial issues. One of the girls, whose father is African-American and whose mother is from Sweden, spoke with emotion about the difficulty having her two families understand one another.

"I work in a Scandinavian café, and people question my ability to speak Swedish," she said. "That makes me upset, because I look African-American and no one believes me when I say that I'm Swedish. Then relating with relatives on my African-American side is not always easy either."

She spoke, too, of the challenge of the race discussion: "There's the people who think that there aren't any racial issues anymore and who want to ignore that they are there, and then there are the people who think that anything anyone white says is going to be racist, or [anything] that anyone black says is too. So I think that we need to come to a middle ground, and acknowledge that there are racial tensions, but not everything someone says is meant in a derogatory way."

s.t.a.r.t. students have written about white privilege and cultural stereotypes, how students of color have been encouraged to take less rigorous classes, and how teachers tend to trust only white students to run errands or do jobs for them. s.t.a.r.t. has invited guest speakers to the school, and the students have even facilitated dialogues about race in the community between adults. Two students served on a panel about teaching at the 2011 White Privilege Conference. One student, a white junior, whose letter is featured in this book, took a particular interest in posttraumatic slave syndrome after reading an article I shared from *Essence Magazine* (February 2005), called "Breaking the Chains." He became the group expert on the impact of slavery over many generations, the resilience of the African-American people, and their humanity to those who oppressed them despite the horrors they endured over centuries.

Our small group decided to form an intentional bridge to the Somali and Oromo students within South High, because we had heard that some of the students were struggling to feel accepted in our school. The result of this was that the group doubled. New s.t.a.r.t. students from Ethiopia and Somalia began to share what it was like for them to be at our school, speaking about how they were treated with suspicion not only by fellow students, but by some teachers, who inadvertently raised their voice when speaking to them as if they have difficulty hearing. This caused undue attention to the Somali students and made them self-conscious.

As the students have grown their network, they continue to get challenged as to why they meet to talk about race. A female student from Somalia was told by a white male student that "this discussion is for black students."

"No," she replied, "it's work that we all need to do to learn about ourselves and our true history."

Students tell me that these types of discussions are rarely allowed between students and staff, except perhaps between students and teachers who have fostered cultural affinity groups together. These groups are there to reinforce cultural identity in a predominantly European school system that too readily forces assimilation and discounts cultural assets of students who are not white. Such identity groups and the work they do cannot be underestimated.

However, as the students and I have been invited to bring this work to neighboring districts, we have stumbled on a dynamic that informs our work now and what we see as our work for the future. As we have visited schools outside the urban area, we have been inspired to witness a strong commitment to the mission of s.t.a.r.t. to foster intercultural development between staff and students. At the same time at South, the school from which the idea of s.t.a.r.t. sprang, it has been much harder to pull together students and teachers *across* cultures, and for a good reason. The cultural affinity groups, two of which have names that mean "unity," *Umoja* and *Unidos,* have deep staff support and deep roots in the community. Before s.t.a.r.t., there had not been a group that sought to draw students together across cultures to address equity gaps.

Now the students and I must address how we might act as a convener and leader in bringing students, staff, and parents together across the groups, while supporting their identity-building efforts. It will bring us to a new level of challenge—to urge the conversation about equity and race when our communities are necessarily becoming focused on sustaining their own values and needs.

As we look to the future, we need both aspects of the work: groups that affirm cultural affinity and history and groups that help our students and staff learn the fine art of intercultural bridging. As legislators now debate the importance of integration funding, that work for which the Little Rock Nine and their allies fought so hard, the students—if anyone would ask—are one step ahead. They have learned that crossing racial lines does not just happen because they sit together in a classroom—and they are telling us that the leadership skills involved in bridging cultures requires a safe space for dialogue and action, guided by experienced adults.

The students' reenactment of the Little Rock Nine integration inspired one of the staff, who is African-American, to share how his attorney father talked with him and his siblings each evening in 1957 while the event was occurring. He spoke to the students about how it wasn't enough that Thurgood Marshall, the country's first African-American Supreme Court justice, had successfully litigated *Brown v. Board of Education* in 1954. Justice Marshall had to wait three years to witness and champion the courage of the Little Rock Nine. The staff member spoke of how it touched him to relive that day with student leaders who had chosen to learn about race.

The students responded to his comments with deep affection. "We must remember where we've been," one student said. "How hard it must have been for African-American students to integrate white schools!" another student asserted. Finally, a white student pointed out something many of us were thinking—that our group was more important than she realized, and that it is only through such conversations that we can unlearn the racial tension that is still present in our world.

References

Breaking the chains: Interview with Joy Degruy-Leary, Brenda Wade, and Gail E. Wyatt. (2005, February). *Essence, 35*(10), 150–153.

Brown, T. N., Tanner-Smith, E. E., Lesane-Brown, C. L., & Ezell, M. E. (2007). Child, parent, and situational correlates of familial ethnic/race socialization. *Journal of Marriage and Family, 69*(1), 14–25.

PART FIVE

CONNECTING TO
THE COMMUNITY

22

NOT JUST FOR
A SCHOOL YEAR

Stacy Amaral and Shirley Williams

Why do they come here? What is all this church stuff? How do I fill out the racial profile when it asks me if a student is a "White Hispanic" or a "Black Hispanic"? Why don't they speak English? Why do so many end up in Special Education? Why do so many have to come to school just to enroll one student? Why are there so many last names in one family?

S hirley Williams and Stacy Amaral have worked in collaboration in Worcester, Massachusetts, for the past twenty years. Over this time they have been confronted with questions like these and with situations of resilient students and their families who have to endure the attitudes behind such questions. Both Shirley and Stacy bring strengths and insights, one from a social worker perspective and one from a schoolteacher and school counselor perspective. As a social worker, Shirley worked in a community counseling center in Worcester, and Stacy counseled students in an elementary school in the same city. Because the school and the center share a neighborhood, Stacy and Shirley often worked with the same families. They continue to be friends who count on each other for support, comic relief, and a shoulder to cry on. Shirley is African-American. Stacy identifies as a Puerto Jew or Jew Rican. Their voices intersperse throughout this narrative. Their story emphasizes the importance of community work as it surrounds the school and the inclusion of that community in order to go deeper.

Shirley: In 1994, a wonderful, spirited woman from the local community school just down the block from my office called me regarding two African-American sisters who needed some mental health support to help them function better in their second and third grade classes. This was my first contact with Stacy. I had just graduated from social work school and was a new psychotherapist at one of the oldest child mental health clinics in the country. My role at the agency was to provide services to Black and African-American kids and their families in a culturally supportive way. Stacy asked for a meeting to discuss the possibility of working together to provide counseling as well as a social skills group for kids in her school. We began a journey that has lasted until this day.

Stacy: I was concerned about a student, age twelve, and her sister, age eleven, who were coming late to school almost every day. Not only late but also hungry. Their mother, unable to attend to anything but her own hurt, relied on the eldest to get her sister to class. While the eldest focused on parenting her little sister and herself, the younger girl spent her energy showing us all how angry she was. I knew I had to support the elder sister, to help her find the strength to go on. So I called Shirley.

Shirley: We met with the kids once a week in the school, played games, and discussed healthy ways to express feelings. One day after group, a piece of white paper was left on my desk. I unfolded the note. It read "Dear Ms. Williams Thank you for helping me and my sister at school. I love you." I would see this girl over many years, attending to many adolescent crises when she had to move after her mom became homeless due to substance abuse and then her mom's death. I helped her get her first job and supported her when she had her first child. During these small snapshots of time I learned a lot about the resilience of African-American kids and how they survived in schools.

The connection to Stacy and the coming together of school and community services was the beginning of this long-term link to these young women. We eventually had seven girls in the group. Even though the new school administrator and my own director decided that Black kids should not have a social skills group for themselves alone, we continued to meet anyway. We knew that these girls needed something for just them. Stacy and I became good friends locked in defiance. We were determined to continue to provide support for kids of color.

The lack of any cultural or social justice understanding on the part of the administration would lead to many, many internal and external policies that were not in the best interests of Black children. Over the years, Stacy and I worked together to coordinate services despite this lack of support for our work. She referred kids to the center for individual and family therapy while I suggested that families with kids at her school meet with her. We included anyone important in the child's circle in our meetings. We wholeheartedly believed that work with families was essential to helping kids function well in life. Sometimes we arranged for siblings to enjoy their birthday together, taking them all out for lunch. This was particularly important for those kids who were in foster care. All of them wanted desperately to be connected back home with their parents.

Black kids in my groups or in counseling often felt culturally abandoned after being placed in white foster homes. Some of the social workers and foster parents did not understand the social effect on the children once they were placed in homes outside their culture. For example, I made sure to have hair care products and body lotions available to them. Many school staff and teachers are not aware of the psychological effect of being a Black kid in a strange setting and not having anyone who understands how to care for their hair or skin. In our culture, grooming of the hair is tied to self-esteem. Hair care is a big deal for many Black families.

Through all this, I came to realize that I could always count on Stacy to understand these kinds of needs because she lived in the community. She understood exactly what they were going through each day.

Stacy: Me, I'm a rooted woman. Once planted, I send out shoots that dig in deep. I stake my place and watch my world like some Barrio Empress. Unlike most of my coworkers, I found it to be no problem to live and teach in the same neighborhood. I loved it. Rarely did my neighbors or I step on toes. I knew which families were living on which precipice and this information only helped me to teach. We knew each other's kids and all our ups and downs. I have often felt lucky to have a world that is of one piece and to be available to my neighbors. They are, in turn, available to me.

Even today from my front porch swing I continue to watch the action. At the YMCA, at the park, the bodega, I run into former students. Just this morning Zaida, whom I taught second grade in 1978, caught me up on her graduate studies. Last week Miguel's mother gave me the update on him; we reminisced like two old ladies on a bench in the plaza of Barranquitas. These students weren't just mine for a school year; they have been part of my life for the past forty years and it pleases me to know that I am still part of theirs. I taught all grades in this city from second to eighth and then some high school English as a Second Language classes. One year I taught in Managua. This was soon after the 1972 earthquake. I had fifty girls in a class then.

If I wasn't Maestra, I was "Stacy," "Stacy" at home, and "Stacy" at school. One principal suggested that calling me by my first name showed a lack of respect. I smiled at him. I rarely ran into disrespect. I learned from the best how to turn disrespect around. As I was always the smallest person on any street or in any room I wouldn't have lasted too long if I hadn't learned this. By the time they were in fifth grade, some of my students were as tall as I am.

Dealing with racism is a constant part of my life. I taught at Oxford Street School as part of a vanguard of bilingual teachers. We walked into racism daily, like commuters coming up from the subway in New York's Time Square. No mercy was extended to us and the bright lights of hatred blinked on and off in the most garish of colors. In 1975, my students were part of the influx of families from the mountain towns and cane field villages of Puerto Rico.

These Puerto Rican students were not welcome at this school. In the lounge one day, a teacher said, "Let's put all the Puerto Rican kids on a boat and sink it." This teacher taught third grade. The bilingual staff put our bodies between teachers and students. Boy, did it hurt. Hatred always hurts; it stings and burns. My students didn't need markers on their clothing to identify them. Everyone knew who we were: Bilingual teachers and our students had become linked. We were "they." "Why do they come here?" "Why do they get special classes?" "Why don't they speak English?" The stars who knew all the times tables, the troublemakers, the quiet boy in the corner sucking his thumb, the jump-roping girls, were "they."

When I became a school counselor and was told that I could not run a group just for the African-American girls, I smiled again and called Shirley. "Do you want to run a group with me, Shirl?" This school group would not have happened without Shirley. I am not an African-American woman and could not alone have addressed the needs and feelings of the girls. I brought to them my understandings from the community, my caring, my knowledge of them in school, but Shirley brought her inside wisdom.

I wanted always to live in a shared world. It's the only way I know to really see and to be seen. I think that the first step is to actually see the students and let them see you, to live in their space, shop at the same stores. This can't help but take us all deeper.

I am no longer working as a teacher or a counselor but as an interpreter. It happens that in both my job sites former students' work as my contacts. "Las Vueltas del Mundo,"* as we say.

One day about a year and half ago I was getting into my car to meet Shirley at a workshop. A big hunk of a guy walking two ugly dogs came up to me. If you didn't know him, this young man would look to be a proper thug, tough-looking expression on his face and the gangsta dogs. I soon realized it was Ray. He was a young man Shirley and I had followed from age eight until eighteen, keeping track of him through the neighborhood grapevine. After a hug, I told him that I was just about to leave to meet Shirley and we had been thinking about him and Sean. He told me that he lived nearby and had a child. His brother was going to be released from prison soon and he was hoping that everyone would be okay now.

You have to follow them long distances to make it work. And you have to know the community they come from and have faith they will eventually find stability to make their journey successful.

There are some things we each believe and have to believe in order to work together.

To help students of color we always knew we might have to bend the rules to do what was best for the child. Schools have so many barriers that interfere with a child's progress. And even now we still maintain that accepting risks to our own status to reach students is essential. We are unflinching in our belief in this.

We have found there are things that hinder and things that help the dignity of students in schools. The following unspoken rules and assumptions are barriers to giving students a complete, all-encompassing education:

- Don't talk about differences because all families are the same or should be.
- Parents are always at fault when their child has a problem at school.
- The teacher is always right.
- Pretend that all public schools provide a quality education to any child who wants to learn.
- Lie, if necessary, to parents when a school cannot actually provide services to a special-needs student.
- Do not talk about racism, classism, sexism, or any *-ism*.

---

*The Way the World Turns, meaning how connected we are.

- Blame poverty for failure, assuming schools cannot succeed with poor children.

Such unspoken rules reflect policies, procedures, and customs in many schools. They prevent Black and poor kids from achieving academically.

It has been well documented that people of color have the worst health outcomes in our nation. Racially based inequities lie at the root of the problem. Yet it has become taboo to discuss the needs of Black families and to talk about racism and its effects. This is true even after the election of our first Black president. We are surely not living in a postracial world. We know that Worcester has many wonderful teachers. Yet it is our belief that the desire to blame parents and the retaining of those teachers who do not believe in a child's innate ability to learn are practices at the core of the problem. We have worked with courageous classroom teachers and they are the first to tell us that poor educators can poison the climate for all of those who do care and who do believe in the brilliance of each student who comes before them. We salute these teachers and hope for their sake as well as the sake of the children that teachers who are hurting students can be counseled out with more deliberate speed than is true today.

Some of the principals in the schools in which we worked were well aware that policies of the district were not supportive of parents and often undermined the success of students. And now in a time of test score emphasis, principals are under even more intense pressure to show improvement in the performance of their students, often with their jobs at stake. Thus they find themselves overlooking the individual needs of students, parents, and teachers under their supervision. Also at stake is any creativity in solving problems the way we were often able to do. Schools are more regimented now.

Yet even now there are brave administrators who give a "nod and a wink" to us and to teachers to go on with the work we need to do. And while these courageous individual principals, teachers, and staff are important, we are aware that such single actors are not enough to change the overall need for equity in education in this country. And the schools where principals subscribe to the unwritten rules we have listed hurt many poor and Black and Brown children in great numbers. A true system overhaul is needed.

Finding Hope: What Do We Do?

Shirley: Educators and parents must join together to support grassroots efforts in local communities to increase the voice of parents, students, and community in support of schools.

Educators must be given team time in school in order to share the expertise of key successful teachers, to share best practices, and to understand learning trends. In many ways, schools have not kept up with current trends in child development, not to mention new discoveries in health, science, and technology. We must give teachers the opportunity to use the talents of the best and brightest educators, scientists, artists, and computer technicians in order to learn and share knowledge. They need to be supported in order to explore current proven ways to enhance their practice.

In many school systems, the teachers do not reflect the culture of the students and do not understand the customs and values of families. Students cannot be successful when the school does not value them or their culture as having unique gifts. To help remedy the lack of teachers of color, parent support and engagement are key components to schools' success. Many Black and Brown parents feel intimidated and not welcome at schools. Much of this historical lack of trust comes from the parents' own past traumatic experiences with school systems. To counter this, teachers and staff need to be trained to welcome students, to promote and encourage cultural expression and to make sure all parents feel their presence is wanted and needed.

Stacy: In 1984, ten years before meeting Shirley, I wrote my master's thesis as a handbook called "Pa' la Escuela, Going to School." It was meant to address many of the cultural conflicts and struggles seen with Puerto Rican children newly arrived on the mainland. Although the work was specific to that group, the attitude regarding working with differences could be applied to children of color in general. Among the issues I covered were diverse family expectations of schools, language usage, and general cultural attitudes that often differ from the mainstream white school norms. It was written to address many questions that were coming up in our district, similar to those at the beginning of this chapter. Such a handbook could be developed at the district level in many of our cities and states, and updated regularly.

Cultural and linguistic competency must be instituted as a core standard of knowledge for teachers and not just stand alone as diversity training. Michel Martin, host of *Tell Me More* on National Public Radio, stated that "Diversity training will work when people say 'I GET to go to diversity training' instead of 'I HAVE to go,' when people see it as a way of enhancing their skills and not as a punishment."

Final Thoughts From the Two of Us

Teachers must understand that the family, with both its strengths and weaknesses, is the first teacher. Solutions must include being aware that race does matter. Understanding the interconnection between poor health, educational outcomes, and lack of community resources is basic to understanding the children in our care in school. Hiring bicultural and bilingual staff is not sufficient if the system continues to discriminate by giving subtle and overt messages that staff and students of color are not valued or welcome. This only continues to ensure that the school is another agent of oppression and enforces racist policies.

Although many of the students we worked with graduated from school and moved on to become productive citizens of the community, many did not. Prisons take a significant number of Black and Brown boys and many begin to fail in the third grade. The system breaks down in critical ways for the kids starting this young. There are often few resources to hold them in a safe place. This school-to-prison pipeline must be addressed head on if we are to stop the victimization of Black kids. The two males we worked with (Sean and Ray) fell victim to a hostile environment they did not create. Yet even after this they and others continue to express gratitude for the consistent nurturing school space we attempted to hold for them. In turn we are still grateful for the gift of being part of their resilience in the face of pain, racism, and violence inflicted on them by adults they trusted. We smile when we see them today because they are part of us.

Being the "other" in any situation causes one to feel danger, too often to sense discomfort, to be wary, and overall to carry a heavy load of stress. We have created a bond of trust over the years. Our relationship is a place of safety. Whenever life becomes too much, when the world weighs too heavy, our friendship becomes a room in which to "put down our burdens," as the song says. We don't have to "teach" each other what racism does. We are witnesses to each other's lives. When we hear something absurdly racist, we bring it to our room and look at it. Often we laugh, often we shake our heads, and sometimes we cry.

Teachers deserve such a room, a place of safety. In such a room one could practice talking about race with all kinds of people. In our society we need all the practice we can get without the menace of hierarchies and blame: Who has suffered the most? Whose fault is it? We all need a safe space without the threat of hearing, "We were better off before you came." Teachers deserve a space away from the constant judgment of what is better, prettier, cooler, and of more worth, in order to have open, honest discussions that are sometimes uncomfortable, yet are not shaming.

Not everyone in this social justice work will form strong friendships in the way we have. Yet it is our belief that crossing into unfamiliar territory and making the commitment to stick with tough dialogue is well worth making such an effort both for ourselves and our students. Ultimately this allows us to see the beauty in the others' lives. Because what is there is beauty. Just think about the children in your classes in all their colors and shapes: Beautiful.

23

INTERVIEW WITH MARIANO ESPINOZA, MINNESOTA DREAM ACT MOVEMENT LEADER

Latino Perspectives on Race Equity in Education and Teaching

Jennifer Godinez

The purpose of the national movement for passage of the Development, Relief, and Education for Alien Minors (DREAM) Act is to remove the barriers to higher education that face thousands of immigrant youth who have excelled in US public schools, but lack residency status and have few options for gaining residency status or citizenship status due to broken immigrant laws (Gonzales, 2009). Several states around the nation, however, have passed in-state policy solutions to provide such students access to lower tuition costs for higher education in their respective states (Gonzales, 2009). Minnesota's solution is a "flat-rate tuition policy" that affects a set of Minnesota public colleges in the Minnesota State Colleges and University (MNSCU) system (Minnesota Minority Education Partnership, 2010). Building on the collective movement for higher education rights for immigrant youth in the United States, there are countless community activists, leaders, and educators working in tandem to train youth on their role and right to advocate for policy change that will affect their own lives. Of particular interest to all of us in education should be the unique and powerful lessons taught by community leaders to young people through the trainings for state policy and national policy that would provide greater access to higher education.

The following is an interview with movement leader Mariano Espinoza, who led community members, educators, and youth to advocate for passage of a flat-rate tuition policy in Minnesota affecting thousands of youth and their access to higher education. In this interview, he reflects on the development of education access as a focus of the immigrant rights movement, the pedagogy involved in training youth advocates, and the lessons that all educators can gain from these deeply engaging experiences with Latino, immigrant youth in the United States. Mr. Espinoza also addresses the dynamics of race and culture in education that plays out in this movement— for students and educators.

1. Tell us about how you've played a role in organizing the immigrant community and how you began to learn about the issues around higher education access and undocumented youth in the United States?

Well, it all begins with the 2003 Immigrant Freedom Ride to Washington, DC. One of the focus areas of these Rides was education.

So the Freedom Rides were not just about reforming the immigration system. They included access to education for immigrant youth as well?

Yes, the goal was to connect students to one another from different parts of the country. On the "road" to DC, the students told their stories. So another goal here was to engage these students to tell their stories and gain experience speaking in public. One of the girls who went on the ride from Minnesota spoke out about her experience while in Maryland at a public rally. She breaks out crying, as her parents are listening via phone, and the people in the audience are just overwhelmed by this story. It was a huge, impactful event.

And that was the point—to network one another around these stories. I believe that one of our goals as organizers is to create the space, strategically, for students' stories to be told. On this trip, there were churches, community centers, and eventually the rally at a large university—University of Maryland. The last "stop" was Washington, DC. The young student was ready to speak in DC because of all her experiences along the way. When she was talking in front of legislators, she said, "You think because I eat Mexican food, I am undocumented, but I am not, but I stand here on behalf of my peers who are fighting for their rights."

We identified students like this from Minnesota, so they could be involved in this movement when they returned. We didn't have any formal curriculum planned, we just knew we needed students to continue to push for immigrant youth rights. We knew we wanted to do something institutional, but we weren't sure on details. In 2004, in the legislative session, came the first opportunity to reintroduce the Minnesota DREAM Act (after a 2002 introduction that was done by community members). It was barely at the end of the session when this was introduced. With this group of students and a union organizer who helped us, we began to figure out what to introduce in policy language.

We also needed a school to first "test" to be sure we could find students to organize. We went to a popular Latino charter school in Minneapolis. By the end of 2004, we had a model we were going to use to organize students. We had new board members, some with university experience, so we worked to find a way for university students to be "interns" to go organize high school youth. This was like "the right time and right place"—we brought on additional staff to help develop the curriculum for student training.

2. Tell us about the "DREAM Curriculum," the pedagogy involved in the training of youth to advocate for the Minnesota DREAM Act?

At that time, it was a very diverse group of organizers: public policy experts, staff with a background in popular education, and my background as a community organizer. So we all started to put our own personal experiences into developing a curriculum that explored immigration, race and culture, and the push for new access to higher education public policy. In general, what we were trying to do with curriculum was to start the process of "concientización" consciousness around access to education for immigrant youth. We also wanted to expose the students to engaging in changing policy, or civic engagement, so we created a space for them publicly in order for them to use their talents and influence legislative changes to improve their lives. We trained youth on the use of media for a public campaign. We also taught students how to organize and what an organizing campaign looks like, and we connected them to other schools and other students in situations like theirs. The goal of the curriculum is essentially to build a large movement. One of the components was to do a "Day of Action"—this was our "Day at the Capitol." This is like our "exam." We show our knowledge and tell our stories to media and legislators. This is the day we take collective action. After this process, legislators said they were greatly informed on understanding how students were affected by limited laws on access to higher education and what they could do to make changes to help the community.

Through this curriculum, we also saw a racial integration process— White teachers connected to Latino students. Latino teachers connected to

White teachers. White students and Latino students also came together. It was important to us to always focus on how integration was occurring in the process. There was one school district that had to ask their school board if they could be involved. This was one of those cases where a teacher insisted on doing the curriculum but the district rules dictated that such decisions had to go to their school board. But for those teachers who worked across racial boundaries, there was a lot of learning going on about experiences in education.

I believe that the curriculum is a way to teach something that is not being taught in the public school system. It discusses the history of immigrants in the United States and the realities that Latinos are living in the United States—topics that are often overlooked in the public school curriculum. Once students understood that they could use their experience of race and culture to define their realities in the US education system, we asked students to propose changes they wanted to see happen. The DREAM Act was the first issue, then other issues came up. A student would say, "We are told not to speak Spanish, but this is our language." Because the curriculum asks students to pick a topic they want to see different at their schools, language was often one that came up as well. So, it is evident that since language is based in culture and race, this came up for the students as well.

3. What were the top things they were attracted to in the curriculum? How did race and culture come up in this curriculum?

Discussions about culture, exploitation (resulting from the immigration system and the school system) and the energy to act, their own activism, all appealed to the youth and educators involved in this process. Students often reiterated that they felt very oppressed by the current system. While there are youth who are doing really well, speaking English and fitting in, there are also others who don't know the language well. This curriculum, the process altogether, revealed these realities that are based in racism and cultural clashes within the US education system. When we came in, it was a huge relief to these students in particular. Once these students gained trust with the coaches of the curriculum, they felt more comfortable asking these coaches for help, personal counseling, and so on. The students used the experience to change policy, but more importantly, to find a place for themselves as Latinos in education and in civic action.

The very process of discussing the educational system in the United States, from an immigrant perspective, brings up race and culture in education. As I said before, students stated that due to the Euro-centric approach to mainstream schools, they did not often feel a connection to the educational systems they were a part of. Therefore, this curriculum allowed them to explore what contributions and energy the Latino, immigrant community could make to changing public policy. The community was seen for its assets and contributions to change a policy, rather than a liability to the society.

4. What role did educators play in the process? What do you think educators gained from involvement in this movement?

We didn't know how the education system worked, so we were gaining that understanding in the process. We were learning the system, the district, how the school worked, who would approve the curriculum. This is when we were led to the ESL teachers. I was giving a presentation at a local community center on the DREAM Act. I had several teachers in the audience. This was one of the first times I met teachers. And it was at this meeting that teachers started to organize around "what they could do for their students." Before this, the teachers had not known what they could do for their students. These teachers would come to my trainings and say, "Thank you for coming and letting us know what we can do for our students." Educators were also saying that they felt they were "prohibited" from doing anything for their students. They would say, "What can we do?" I believe these teachers have strong hearts and care—but they didn't know how to make legislative changes. I also think the teachers learned a lot about the real emotional experiences of their students. A lot of these teachers didn't realize that some of their students were experiencing really hard things because of the immigration system and its effect on their parents. I guess we have to ask teachers what they gained; they know best. But it really seemed that they were lost. They are definitely a symbol of how the education system was not serving our students well. Some wanted to change and others could be conforming, figuring that this is what the system is and accepting that reality.

5. Tell us about the outcome of your work with students and educators. What do you think this means now for access to higher education and youth in Minnesota?

In 2007, the state of Minnesota made a legislative change to create one tuition price for all the students, regardless of immigration status or residency status or nationality. MNSCU used to have different categories for prices. At first, we got to one price for seven higher education institutions (two-year and four-year). Now, we have twenty-five of thirty-two institutions that fall under this policy. That is the technical shift and this signifies is a lot.

When you are working in public policy shifts, you want something straightforward and clear to understand—something that can help in general and including those who have been excluded from the system. When I have been asked to speak to students in PhD programs in public policy, they often ask me the question, "What is the goal of good public policy?" I tell them it would be including those outside the system—to make sure they are now included. In this case, we were bringing more access to higher education for more youth, so they can make more contributions financially and socially.

In 2007, we were one of the first movements in the nation that made a greater shift for immigrant youth in an anti-immigrant climate. The governor had specifically targeted the Minnesota DREAM Act in his gubernatorial campaign. So our flat-rate win gave a message to immigrants—youth and families—that we could still make a change to benefit immigrants. It was a huge victory. A movement built from any undocumented community to make a legislative shift of any kind to better their condition is a big win. It could be the first movement historically that made shifts for undocumented youth *by* undocumented youth. Similar to this may be the start of Chicano Studies. This basically showed our community that we can make changes to better our situation in this country. We showed students that they had to be involved, that a movement is formed only by people focused on an idea and vision we share together.

6. What did youth have to say about being involved in the movement? What do you think they gained that was different from what they gained in school?

Students were learning how to make real changes that have an effect on people's lives. They could be in school learning to sell cookies or draw lines on [the] playground. With this curriculum, I believe students really learned what racism looks like—what oppression is, what racism is—because they were reflecting on their own experiences and learning new things on how to combat systemic racism.

Because we don't have enough teachers of color, a goal was to have educators from our background. Even in spaces that are bilingual, bicultural, there are mostly White teachers. These teachers can be a part of it, but, for example, I can't teach White teachers their White culture—in the same way, our students need Latino teachers to assist students.

7. How can we have more honest conversations among educators about race, national origin, and class?

I don't feel that teachers are really prepared to teach. Schools are always talking about integration, but they really don't have a good approach to this. When we see "professional development," it is still White trainers teaching White teachers. One approach is for teachers to begin to "unpack" what they've learned about students of color. Teachers need to address the myths that exist that keep them biased when approaching students of color.

When we look at this problem for a solution, we have to ask what our role is in fixing this problem and what role teachers need to play to make changes. I don't know if teachers are really asking themselves, "What is my role? What do I need to do to assist my students?"

It seems pretty evident from the experience mobilizing and educating immigrant youth around the DREAM Act that teachers play a key role in understanding what issues truly affect their students—and perhaps educating themselves more about those realities. Teachers should not set low expectations for their students, but they personally should broaden their understanding on where they are coming from—and using some of those realities as learning experiences for themselves and their classrooms. We need more bilingual, bicultural teachers in the classroom. Therefore, it seems evident that teachers need to learn Spanish and the culture of our community in order to be more effective with all of our students in public schools.

8. What personal interactions have you had with the US education system as an immigrant parent?

When I think about my role with the schools prior to my involvement, I reflect that I really didn't realize what was going on in that system. I'd get notices with my son and daughter to be involved. I thought I didn't really have a "right" to propose changes in my students' education. We feel, and I think other immigrant families feel, that the educators and the system are like "gods" and we have no voice in what is happening, especially if something is wrong. We just feel bad, we don't think we can challenge what is happening in the system. My daughter was in special education, for example, and I just thought we did something wrong—and it was for language reasons. I just thought, "Okay, we'll just do what the school says we should do." But the special ed marking was a stigma, I realized. The educators didn't know this negotiation that my daughter was making between the "English-speaking" side and "Spanish-speaking" side of her reality.

References

Gonzales, Roberto G. (2009). Young lives on hold: The college dreams of un-documented students. *College Board Advocacy* (pp. 8, 19, 22). Retrieved from http://professionals.collegeboard.com/profdownload/young-lives-on-hold-college-board.pdf

Minnesota Minority Education Partnership. (2010). Policy brief: Access to higher education and Latino undocumented immigrant youth in Minnesota: Removing barriers to develop untapped talent for Minnesota's economic prosperity, p. 3. Retrieved from http://www.mmep.org.

24

THE PINOCCHIO
IN BLACK AMERICA

Ben Mchie

inocchio, a fictional character, was created in 1883. A wooden puppet, he dreams of becoming a real boy. When Pinocchio finds himself in stressful situations, he tells lies, which makes his nose grow. This change affects how Pinocchio looks at life, and how he seeks his dream. Pinocchio has become a metaphor to describe someone who is prone to lying, exaggerating, or fabricating stories. Do some Americans become Pinocchio when talking about race? Yes, and as I move through my own black discomfort to better know who I am, I think about the story of Pinocchio and reacquaint with my soul.

Reflecting on the Black Legacy in America: A Viewpoint

Over one hundred years ago, W. E. B. Du Bois wrote a book titled *The Souls of Black Folk*. Part of the author's reason for writing the book was to impress upon the world the particular experience of being an African American some forty years after the Civil War. First published in 1903, it was reprinted twenty-four times before 1940 alone. Du Bois's book consists of fourteen essays on various topics, from a history of the US government's efforts at Reconstruction to a discussion of the role of religion in the black community. The first three chapters in *The Souls of Black Folk* address historical and political issues.

Du Bois begins the chapter "Of Our Spiritual Strivings" with a provocative question underlying all other questions posed to him: "How does it feel to be a problem?" African Americans in general realize that most of white America still feels that way. We also know that America is not only different from when *The Souls of Black Folk* was published, but much of African America is better off, as well. However, in Minnesota, to take one state as an example, the poster children for welfare are black, brown, and red. Soul searching about all this means digging deeper. It is the antithesis of living with a Pinocchio view of life.

Racial Integration, Desegregation, and Assimilation in America

Du Bois makes a profound statement about the "double consciousness" of being black in a white world. This phrase and its description hit me hard when I read *Souls* as a teenager. The term originated from an 1897 *Atlantic Monthly* article written by Du Bois titled "Strivings of the Negro People." In a later collection of essays, it was republished and slightly edited under the title "Of Our Spiritual Strivings" and thus became part of *Souls.* Du Bois argued that being black meant being deprived of a "true self-consciousness." I interpret that to mean blacks often perceive themselves and one another through the generalized contempt of white America. This deep psychological fact of our lives means that when laws changed, it was not enough. We had to deal with psyches damaged by centuries of abuse.

Desegregation is largely a legal matter, integration largely a social one. One result of the Civil Rights Movement of the 1960s and 1970s was that the white status quo in the United States by law had to allow blacks physical access into nearly all aspects of public life. This included higher education, private and public jobs, home ownership, and more. Many African Americans seized these new opportunities for upward mobility by trying to provide security for their families. Many of us were under the assumption that "we had arrived" and the doors were open to a utopian coexistence with white America. Yet reviewing history shows no heyday of brotherhood between blacks and whites.

How much of integration by black America was a rejection of blackness and favoring whiteness?

- How much of our perception of blackness was tied to class and money?
- How much of our perception of ourselves is tied to whites' perception of us, as Du Bois describes?

- Did suburban life change how we see our communities that many left behind?

Where Does Whiteness Fit In to Talking About Race?

Whiteness in America is the template of how to be a normal American. This is a distraction to blacks who are descendants of slaves. In recent years, nationally, there has been effort devoted to revealing, attacking, and dismantling "white privilege." Regarding this effort, what do white people want blacks to do while they figure themselves and their color out? Whiteness is still the sun of America's solar system and all other colors revolve around it. Every day, whiteness plays out in situations to which the rest of us react. It is especially prevalent in today's media and in how information is disseminated. Whiteness is the filter through which we have judged ourselves from the Middle Passage to this very day. I am convinced that this lens of color is why many African Americans neglect one another.

Black Accomplishments and Situations That Still Haunt America

In *The Souls of Black Folk* Du Bois goes further to elaborate on "double consciousness" as:

> a world that yields him no true self-consciousness, but only lets him see himself through the revelation of the other world. It is a peculiar sensation, this double-consciousness, this sense of always looking at one's self through the eyes of others, of measuring one's soul by the tape of a world that looks on in amused contempt and pity. One ever feels his two-ness—an American, a Negro; two warring souls, two thoughts, two un-reconciled strivings; two warring ideals in one dark body, whose dogged strength alone keeps it from being torn asunder. (Du Bois, 1903, p. 47)

Double consciousness, according to Du Bois, means a "sense of always looking at one's self through the eyes of others" (1903, p. 45). Du Bois views the history of the American Negro as the history of this strife, this longing to attain self-conscious manhood or womanhood, to merge this double self into a single better and truer self. The African-American twenty-first-century path to social, fiscal, and philosophical status is clear. Using Du Bois's book as a benchmark, the last one hundred years have seen us move from being hunted down and lynched to being elected as the 44th president of the United States. Financially, we own a spending power that is the 11th largest in the world and consistently influence many of the societal exports of what American culture represents. Many art forms and medical breakthroughs have our inventive stamp.

At the same time we own a murder rate within our communities that is quadruple that of the lynchings of the Ku Klux Klan during Jim Crow segregation. African Americans have 2.4 times the infant mortality rate of non-Hispanic whites and are four times as likely to die as infants as a result of complications related to low birth weight as compared with non-Hispanic white infants. We are in general homophobic and are the least likely group to get and stay married as an expression of family. Greeting us through the maze of these realities and the distortions of the black experience in American media is what we see in the mirror.

I am convinced that as victims of racism, like any victim, we still have to look at what we are responsible for. And understanding internalized racism is part of that work, part of what is our responsibility. One example of internalized racism is our preference of doing business with someone or for something that is not produced by a black business. It has been said by some that nepotism is the cousin of racism. To go out of your way to spend time in the house of your oppressor says a lot about what and who is important to you. Internal racism slows down our recognition and acceptance of us by us. Going deeper requires uncovering the many lies about blacks that society tells. More importantly, we must unearth the lies about us as a group that *we* are responsible for; this is where Pinocchio lives within each of us. Understanding internal racism helps us recognize and love each other more.

African Americans are *not* pathological, but the cracks that citizens can fall through are deeper for us. We have all doubted our black humanity in the face of white values and perceptions of us, even if for only a moment.

We must acknowledge that white European slave trade to the Americas was done with some cooperation from black African leaders from the fifteenth through the nineteenth century. It is also a fact that the "Willie Lynch Speech" has never been proven to have occurred. Lynch was a white slave owner who in 1712 supposedly gave a speech on the banks of the James River to American slave owners on how to psychologically control their African slaves. Fighting with each other about these things keeps us bound in the status quo.

Through understanding ourselves, we more honestly witness our blackness and potential as citizens of the world. Dr. Joy DeGruy Leary's theory and book *Post Traumatic Slave Syndrome: America's Legacy of Enduring Injury and Healing* is a valuable resource for going deeper about race in this way. Posttraumatic slave syndrome is a theory that explains the etiology of many of the adaptive survival behaviors in African-American communities throughout the United States and the diaspora. Internal racism is a mirror and white racism is a window, both obscuring the truth for today's black pride. We must use books like DeGruy's to cross the difficult to address the potential Pinocchios in black America.

Racial Wellness: The Opportunity Before Us!

Du Bois saw the prevalence of racism and figured out that sometimes people were themselves responsible for their mistreatment by others. Double consciousness lets African Americans see themselves through the revelation of the other world. Their behavior is distorted through others' negative image of their race. Because of the bombardment of these images, African Americans can feel low self-esteem. Du Bois saw the color line as a scale that divides all people, each from the other, and leaves people prejudiced and stereotyped. Surrounding this phenomenon is often a code of silence among whites: this code is to remain silent about facing racism at all.

The multimedia industry is a large communication tool. It is also dedicated to sales through advertising, branding, and public relations at the expense of anything or anyone. Their small or large screens trivialize pain and tantalize our senses regardless of age. Many of the producers and writers of the material (music included) are black and should be credited or blamed for what they create. As consumers, we would be naive if we did not pay attention to the media "sales pitch."

The experience of consuming mass media goes deeper than whether an image, suggestion, or symbol of a black person is used to sell something. The most targeted audience of advertising is still the white consumer. Research suggests that popular, positive portrayals of blacks are marketable because they affirm white consumers' self-concept as nonracist. As the perception is portrayed as positive, it deceptively affirms racism's end. White consumers' positive responses to programs like *The Cosby Show* or constant situation comedies is a form of enlightened racism whereby white consumers' fears of seeming racist are comforted with the symbols of such programs. Television in particular trivializes most anything it creates. Often on TV, producers, directors, writers, and others add recorded laughing to enhance the antics and words the actors use, and a false sense of reality is created. Many of the post–affirmative action black consumers tend to respond more and more in the same fashion to the same content. Constant buffoonery presented often enough can hide the world many blacks live in that is not comedic. Our nose continues to grow as more of us prefer to be entertained while calling it "enlightened."

From miscegenation to the white American obsession with President Obama's birth certificate, the issue of race mixing is a matrix of its own. I am one of the many African Americans with European blood in past generations; I have navigated these waters for over sixty years. And like many Americans who are descendants of slaves, my black blood meant inferiority. I truly empathize with African Americans who have parents who are both black and another color. But until I see the six o'clock news describe someone the police are looking for as biracial, I won't bet my mortgage on this country being able to blend the two with respect.

The Benefits of Talking About Race

African Americans born after 1980 have many advantages that their predecessors did not. All people are also left with the task of finding that sweet spot of blackness in America left undone. Through racial solidarity, our young and old must talk more about defining and acting out what it means to be proud to be black in the twenty-first century. If Du Bois could speak from his grave, he might ask some of the following questions derived from his writing of double consciousness:

- How can African Americans connect better with our black brothers and sisters who are here from the continent as immigrants?
- What can we do about this "fake," "geek," "lame," "acting-white" peer pressure put on some of our youth in our schools?
- What can we do about the skin color issue in black America?
- Where do the whites who are parents of black children go for more visibility in black America?
- What does the next generation of the African-American community want?
- Can white people, even the most sincere, and even after their work on white privilege, live outside their comfort zone in relation to race and to the black contributions to life in this country?

Years ago, signs (literally) of public racism were visible and ominous. *Talking about race* meant a different type of support or opposition. Yet even during these struggles, many blacks openly resisted the voter registration drives of the Freedom Riders and thought Dr. King and others were stirring the pot too much. This was a very public and open struggle among us.

Today, talking about race to work on our situation seems to be more of an internal and spiritual puzzle requiring new ways to remember who we are, who we were. The bugaboo of racism that Crispus Attucks, Marcus Garvey, Mary Bethune, Malcolm X, and Rosa Parks encountered was different from today. Yet today's form of racism requires a similar attitude of perseverance even now. An example of such perseverance could be to defy the media's constant patronizing and misuse of black images. Can we be more aware and sensitive to how it sells our image back to us and how we often sell our image back to ourselves, particularly through music and music videos? Yes! With the many outlets for disseminating information on cable, the Internet, satellite, and radio, we can use this media to educate and inform.

My experience may help make my point. I have a deep love for jazz music, its purity and its black roots. In a 2011 interview with Grammy-winning jazz trumpeter Terence Blanchard, I asked him why he thought the black community did not support jazz as much as it could. His reply was:

> I think for some in our community, they have allowed others to define who we are and when jazz is not a part of that then our community does not participate. But those who are enlightened, who know more of our history are very responsive toward us. When I hear a young person say jazz is old people's music, it tells me how much that person has allowed external sources to shape their vision; you can't do that, you have to seek things out for yourself then if you don't like it—cool. (Black support of jazz, 2011, n.p.)

Beyond how damn good it sounds, I am proud of the strength and resilience of jazz. Yet so much of what we kept and whom we maintained has its purity tested for control by the dominant American white culture. Without vibrant and consistent media exploration of all of this—the music, the history, the defiance, the innovation—many will continue to be entertained, rarely informed, and often unaware of the rich literary and cultural history we possess.

Finally, what can talking about race mean in present-day black communities? Parents can make black heritage a daily part of life for their children and scale back on television, DVDs, downloads, Internet, and music in the home or car. Truth be told, our families must interact more without media. A recent Kaiser Family Foundation study shows that black and Hispanic kids consume four and a half more hours of media every day than do their white counterparts—investing a startling total of more than ninety hours a week on television, video games, social networking, and other distractions. Talking about race means reading to your children from birth each day, beginning them on a lifetime journey through the thousands of resources of black literature. And when they are able, it means reading *with* them every day until they are at least five years old. This is an issue that African Americans can explore more.

By reading more, we preserve and teach about our race for the future (the questions come naturally).

We close any K–12 achievement gap: When you read and comprehend well, you can understand anything and become anything.

Where does this chapter's title have relevance? Pinocchio's character is a metaphor, a symbol, another way for black people in America to see one another without distortion or misinformation or self-deception. It is a way to explore one way I have viewed our (my) community. African Americans are not perfect and I am as guilty as the next person of being late in exploring race; part of my journey is writing this chapter. Over time I am able to critique myself through black America as a community and critique black America through my own imperfections. With Du Bois guiding me, my nose gets shorter all the time.

References

Black support of jazz, Terence Blanchard [video]. (2011). *African American Registry.* Retrieved from http://www.aaregistry.org/videos/view/black-support-jazz-terence-blanchard

Center for Educational Research and Innovation. (2010). *Educating teachers for diversity: Meeting the challenge.* Paris: Organisation for Economic Co-operation and Development.

DeGruy Leary, J. (2005). *Post traumatic slave syndrome: America's legacy of enduring injury and recovery.*

Du Bois, W. E. B. (1903). *The souls of black folk.* Chicago: A. C. McClury & Co.

Minority Report Card, Professor Ellen Wartella, Northwestern University, 2010.

PART SIX

DIGGING DEEPER
IN THE ARTS

HIP-HOP AND CONVERSATION

Jennifer Skoglund

In this chapter, I address the possibilities, concerns, and logistics of using hip-hop as an entry point for student learning in various disciplines.

Thoughtful educators are aware of the importance of crafting learning experiences that will relate to their students' life experiences to engage them in the learning and help them make connections. However, experiences and conversations throughout my career have led me to believe that although hip-hop has permeated American culture, it is missing from many classrooms.

As a future music educator attending college during some of the most important moments in hip-hop history in the late 1990s, I knew the genre would have a home in my classroom. To this day it is still a work in progress, but I hope some of the following tips will help educators who are considering using the genre in their classroom.

I have taught classroom music since the year 2000 in an urban school district. The school I currently teach at is composed of primarily African-American prekindergarten through eighth grade students who qualify for free and reduced lunch.

I never make assumptions about the musical preferences of my students. However, the majority of my students continue to cite hip-hop as their favorite style. For example, 100% of students surveyed for my thesis study completed in 2010 selected "like" or "strongly like" when asked about the hip-hop musical genre (Skoglund, 2010, p. 133). I have found that students across the grade levels are consumers of the genre. Although I have not formally surveyed primary students, I have discovered through conversation and observation that even the younger ones have been exposed to hip-hop. I have heard students spontaneously reciting lyrics and have noticed them performing popular dance moves during a classroom movement activity.

Hip-hop, understandably because of its controversial nature, is not a genre that commonly receives a place in the music curriculum. In fact, the bridging of "school music" and the music that students consume outside school has been a challenge to music teachers since the invention of the radio. However, the absence of hip-hop in so many classrooms contradicts writers in the field of urban education, who stress the importance of knowing your students and providing them with a relevant, engaging curriculum.

Many teachers have asked me how to manage the content and language in a genre that is often inappropriate for children. Frankly, they are right to be concerned. Hip-hop lyrics often include references to drugs and alcohol, sex, violence, crime, the exploitation of women, gangs, and materialism. And it is that way for a reason. To be considered authentic and increase one's reputation, the hip-hop artist must tell the gritty story of life on the streets, however shocking it may seem to mainstream society. The music is a way to tell the story of the violence, drugs, and police brutality on the streets, while the artist portrays himself or herself as ruthless and tough. So how does an educator include hip-hop in the classroom while protecting students and without offending families and colleagues? Furthermore, what educational value is there in studying the genre? First, I explain some of the procedures I use, and then I discuss some of the many uses for the hip-hop genre, including ways it can help your students "go deeper."

I am not claiming to have all the answers, and the way I manage the integration of the genre is not right for all school populations or settings. Most importantly, I do not recommend using the genre unless you are willing to do the research. Often the lyrics go by so fast it is hard to catch every controversial item just by listening. I have also noticed that students tend to defend their music and consider it appropriate for the classroom despite the amount of questionable language or content present. Rosenbaum and Prinsky first discussed student perceptions of controversial content in music in 1987 with their study seeking student ratings of songs based on the following offensive material: drugs and alcohol use, sex, the occult, and violence (Rosenbaum & Prinsky, 1987, pp. 387–388). Their research findings state that students enjoy music for the "beat" and are unaware of or have a shallow interpretation of the controversial content in the lyrics (pp. 387–388).

In addition to the hip-hop music I have in my curriculum to satisfy various music and dance standards and objectives, I welcome student requests. Early in my career students would bring in CDs to be played in class; however, with the ever-changing technologies I find this happening less and less. I make it very clear to students that I need at least an overnight to look over the request. Many of the websites I rely on to read song lyrics are blocked on my district's network (rightly so because of the controversial content in the lyrics) and I have to look them up at home. I spend a lot of time reading lyrics, listening to tracks, and viewing and learning dances on the Internet and at a hip-hop dance class. I will not purchase the track unless I can find within it a valuable musical or movement concept to teach; I do not buy every song my students like just because they like it. When I cannot use a song, I make sure to explain to the student the reason that the song cannot be used in school, citing examples. Students, especially teenagers, tend to strongly associate themselves with their choice of music, and it may even coincide with a lifestyle. I don't ever want the student to feel rejected because his or her song choice was.

Because I teach in a school that contains grade levels from prekindergarten through eighth grade, I have different standards for songs used with various age levels, in the classroom and in performances. For my elementary classes, I only choose repertoire that is 100% clean. For middle school classes I choose repertoire differently based on their development and content that I can use as a teachable moment. Because many of our elementary students attend school performances, I will not allow any swearing or inappropriate content in performance repertoire. I encourage my middle school students choreographing dances for performances and talent shows to do their own research, and go through the process of programming a show themselves. Don't let the label "clean version" fool you! They may have cut out the language, but the content remains. You may need to look up slang words to make sure you know the interpretation as well. In some cases I have used instrumental versions, which are becoming increasingly available on music purchasing sites. I have also created mixes, when there is a section that needs to be cut out and combined with another song to extend the length. This is a time-consuming process, but well worth it knowing that quality and appropriate music has been selected for my students. It is critical that the teacher stays consistent, and also communicates the policy to other educators at their site. Of course there are times when popular music is used differently without such restrictions in place, such as a school dance or a classroom party. The high school setting or a middle school that does not have the elementary grades may also have different standards. Educators need to find the right policies for their school community.

Lyric study can be done with middle school students to accomplish objectives in various classroom settings. In my classroom I have had students journal while listening to and reading the lyrics of songs that address social issues such as racial tensions, gangs, violence, drugs, pregnancy, or dropping out of school. Some of the selections I have used recently include Black Eyed Peas' "Where Is the Love?" and "One Tribe," City High's "City High Anthem," Sean McGee's "My Story," will.i.am's "It's a New Day," Common's "Changes," and "We Are the World 25 for Haiti." My students have opened up about adults who have given up on them, people they can count on when life gets rough, racial injustices, and how hard it is to do the right thing. Not only can lyric study focus on social issues, but also language concepts such as rhyme, simile and metaphor, and storytelling. The possibilities for educators in the language arts and other subjects are endless. Students can also write their own raps either on a learning topic or to assist in memorization for any course. Resources such as Flocabulary are now available for classroom teachers wanting to incorporate hip-hop.

Other uses include teaching the genre itself. Every year, I teach the history of African-American music to my students, culminating in the history of hip-hop. The elementary students do a genre each week, following the timeline with activities including genre-specific dances, writing their own twelve-bar blues song, and imitating some well-known sampled hip-hop drum beats. Middle school students get more in depth, placing the genres in historical context as well as performing increasingly complex musical tasks.

For arts teachers, music and movement concepts can be taught through the genre of hip-hop. My students write choreography, arrange dances, and learn the elements of dance. Musically, I am constantly discovering various rhythmic patterns and ostinati from hip-hop tracks to teach and improvise around, and musical forms to analyze. I have also found material useful in teaching the augmentation and diminution of the beat. Students could sing the lyrical tracks, which sometimes might consist of only the refrain, or rap the spoken word sections alone or in a group. My students have also written their own raps and instrumental accompaniments as a musical composition task. I have used hip-hop in many performances, with students dancing, rapping, singing, and playing instruments.

The advice I would give is to start where you are. Study the hip-hop music you have heard before and look for curriculum connections. If you are a classroom teacher, collaborate with the music teacher at your school. Get song ideas from lists and awards such as the playlist of your local radio station, Grammy award winners, the *Billboard* charts, and, most importantly, your students. Look up the lyrics and just start reading. Music teachers, listen to the music for rhythmic or melodic content you are teaching in your classroom, just as you would do in any other repertoire search. Yes, controversial content is prevalent. You need to determine whether the song is valuable enough to work around cuts and instrumental versions, or whether to keep looking. Use the instrumental version and rewrite the lyrics. Or have the students rewrite the lyrics. Songs that focus on social justice issues will most likely be cleaner than other repertoire. As I stated earlier, working with this genre is not an easy process. Each individual educator needs to determine if the genre is worth pursuing in his or her classroom setting. The reward will be increased engagement and deeper conversations with your students!

References

Rosenbaum, J. L., & Prinsky, L. E. (1987, June). "Lee-rics or lyrics: Teenage impressions of rock 'n' roll. *Youth and Society,* 18: 384–397.

Skoglund, J. L. (2010). The influence of hip-hop culture on the classroom behavior of urban middle school students (Unpublished master's dissertation). University of St. Thomas, St. Paul, MN.

"I KNOW MY BROTHER AND HE IS GOOD"

Using Photography to Engage Youth in Discussions of School and Race

Kristien Zenkov, Marriam Ewaida, Megan R. Lynch, Athene Bell, James Harmon, and Anthony Pellegrino

"My Life"

This is a picture of a gun. It is black and 57 inches long. . . . The gun reminds me of my dream and goal, which is to become an air force officer. . . . I want to protect the United States because there are a lot of bad people in the world and we need to stop them. For example, I want to help stop illegal immigrants from coming to the United States. . . . Even though I am originally from Panama and came to the United States three years ago, I still want to serve the United States. . . . Reading and writing are my protection, just like the gun. When I read and write, I gain the knowledge and feel smarter than other people. I am no longer ignorant, but I know more information. The purpose of reading and writing is to protect me, like the gun, against ignorant people and bad thoughts.

—Delonte

D elonte was practically a poster child for the complex and even seemingly incongruent demographics of the increasingly racially diverse young people in the urban and ex-urban Midwestern and Washington, DC–area classrooms and communities where we work as English and social studies teachers and teacher educators. He was a recent immigrant to the United States, but he did not come from one of the homes most Americans believe are common among these recent arrivals. His family was well educated and he was very much a *legal* immigrant from Panama, which meant that he was both Black and of Latino origin—again, not a racial or ethnic combination that most people in the United States are accustomed to seeing.

Delonte was also aware of the immigration controversies in the United States, and his professional goal was to help ensure that future "illegal" immigrants would not so easily enter his adopted country. This unwitting complexity—and even these seemingly contradictory notions about race and racism—represent some of the most important ideas about how we might address such issues. Delonte did not volunteer these insights into the realities and complexities of race through a standard lesson in one of our English language arts class, however. It was only when we appealed to "photovoice" methods that began with young adults' photographs that Delonte and many of his peers grew as writers, engaged as productive students, and provided these poignant insights into the realities of race and racism in our schools and communities.

Contexts

We are middle and high school language arts and social studies teachers and teacher educators working in mid-Atlantic US ex-urban communities that have experienced considerable demographic changes in the past decade. The population of one of our school districts has shifted from 5% to almost 40% English for Speakers of Other Languages (ESOL) students in just the last ten years. These diverse families are arriving from as close as our major city's inner-ring suburbs and as far away as Guatemala, El Salvador, Sri Lanka, and many other nations. In our settings the high school dropout—or "push out"—rates have remained above 50% for better than three decades. While researchers have recognized factors that appear as early as sixth grade (e.g., low attendance, lack of motivation, and failing grades) and identified young adolescents who may drop out of school (Lan & Lanthier, 2003), we are troubled by the fact that the voices of these struggling students are often silent in the debates about schools and our instructional practices.

Seeking perspectives of students through various expressions may serve to bring about more inclusive pedagogies attentive to issues of social justice (Lynch & Baker, 2005). Sister Joan Chitister asserted that "if it is not in the language, it is not in the mind; and if it is not in the mind, it cannot be in the social structure" (Wisconsin Public Radio, 2005). Fortunately, in an effort to understand diverse youths' perspectives on school and engage them in meaningful writing activities, some researchers are considering students' perspectives on school (Beuschel, 2008; Easton & Condon, 2009; Lynch & Baker, 2005; Rodgers, 2006). Yet such inquiries are still occurring too infrequently and fail to utilize the media with which our students are most proficient as research tools (Cook-Sather, 2009; Mann, 2011; Zenkov & Harmon, 2009). Moreover, with the knowledge about the extent to which literacy development plays a role in adolescents' decisions to drop out of school (Alvermann & Strickland, 2004; Morrell & Duncan-Andrade, 2006; Smyth, 2007), opportunities exist to engage students in relevant literacy activities grounded in their experiences. With our project we appealed to current concepts of literacy for a more responsive framework and set of texts to engage these often aliterate (i.e., they *can* read and write but are choosing *not* to do so) and detached youth (Kist, 2005; Lankshear & Knobel, 2006). Literacy in this millennium incorporates "texts" with which many of our diverse students are most familiar, including digital and visual forms (Christenbury, Bomer, & Smagorinsky, 2009; Clark, 2005; Moje, 2008).

Multimodal methods and photo elicitation techniques have been applied to examinations of young adolescents' and young adults' perspectives of school (Doda & Knowles, 2008; Harper, 2005). These visually oriented processes reveal that image-based tools motivate students to develop an awareness of and share—through complex writings and presentations—personal insights related to their school experiences (Marquez-Zenkov & Harmon, 2007; Raggl & Schratz, 2004). These perspectives on diverse adolescents' school experiences and literacies led us to the tools of this photovoice project, through which we hoped to help our students consider their relationships to school—to inform themselves, us, each other, and our broader communities about these connections (Clark, 1999; Hibbing & Rankin-Erickson, 2003; Streng et al., 2004).

Our Project

So we have wondered what we—middle and high school teachers and teacher educators working with more and more racially and ethnically diverse students—might do to stem the tide of students accepting this almost unavoidable school failure fate. This question has driven our teaching and research efforts as we have used this photo elicitation project (the "Through Students' Eyes" project, www.throughstudentseyes.org) to explore our students' perspectives on school. We now believe that *asking* youth about school, rather than merely *telling* them about its importance, might empower them to find new reasons to show up for and care about our English classes, while developing some of the very literacy skills on which we know they must focus.

Approximately 200 students used digital photographs and related reflections to illustrate and describe the purposes of school, the supports for their engagement and achievement in school, and the obstacles to their school success. With support from local foundations and our schools and universities, the project supplied students with cameras with which they took pictures for four months to over a year to answer three questions:

1. What are the purposes of school?
2. What helps you to succeed in school?
3. What gets in the way of your school success?

Using visual and qualitative analysis methods, we have reflected weekly on these activities and on students' work (Kress, 2006; Pole, 2004; Rose, 2006). In these young adults' visual and written responses to the project's questions we also discovered important insights into their perspectives on race and the race-related challenges they were facing in and out of our classrooms. In their photographs and reflections these youth depicted and described how the everyday racism in these settings makes many young people reluctant to come to school, as more US communities threaten to deport "illegal" immigrants, and the adults in these young people's lives fear drawing the attention of local authorities through school attendance records.

Based on these youths' images and writings, we now know a number of things about what race means in our increasingly diverse schools and what racism looks like in our classrooms and communities. We also understand better how we might engage students in discussions of race and racism and how to best address their concerns with the existence of racism. We also have ideas about how to be better teachers in schools that are increasingly filled with youth who don't look like us and with whom we share neither a first language nor developmental experiences.

Youths' Perspectives on Race, Racism, and School

These lessons—which we illustrate and depict with examples of our students' pictures and reflections—include the idea that we should explicitly *ask* students about race and allow them to answer these questions with tools with which they are proficient, and even ones that require all of us—teachers and youth—to step outside our traditional school curricula and practices. These young people have repeatedly emphasized that we need to be aware that racism happens most often *outside* where we meet them, and it occurs in some disturbingly subtle ways. And, finally, we know now that perhaps our best way to learn about these issues of race and racism is to explicitly and often turn to these young people themselves for these insights.

Ask Students About Race—By NOT Asking and by Using Tools With Which They Are Proficient

The issues of race with which our students deal frequently appear in their interactions with us—the teachers and other caring adults in their school lives. But these are concerns that our students are not frequently able to name because they are not given the opportunity to do so, because these are concerns that seem too sensitive to identify, and because they are not provided with the tools to share these worries. But when we take a much more humble stance toward our students—when we dare to learn from them by *asking* about their lives, rather than explicitly inquiring about these issues—they are much more willing and able to identify these realities.

When she produced the following photograph and paragraph, Alycia was in our sophomore English class—one of the 90% or so of our students who were African-American. She presented us with persistent management "challenges," relishing any opportunity to be the center of attention. Her pictures were consistently eye-popping and her writing was often painfully honest.

"Clogged"

This picture makes me think of all the struggles that get in the way of me succeeding. For example . . . I had a Catholic schoolteacher for sixth grade who blamed me when she lost her baby. How can you tell a sixth grade student that it's their fault for having a miscarriage?

> The drain is clogged and that could be representative of all the stuff that holds me down but the basketball is there to remind me that I still need to get up and do what I need to do in order to succeed.
>
> —Alycia

Although she often distracted the class with what we thought was just a teenage sense of drama, it turned out that behind these behaviors was a young woman who had experienced a great deal of pain at the hands of the men in her life. The reproach from Alycia's middle school teacher might seem extreme, but we encountered not just her difficult experiences but also numerous other examples of what most people would consider complicated relationships between youth and teachers. Although we are not sure that the hurtful and even damning assumptions this teacher made about Alycia were rooted in their racial differences, Alycia believed this to be the case, and this perception has deeply affected her nonetheless.

What seems most important in this lesson is that we did *not* begin by asking our students about race issues: we just inquired about their school lives and they frequently named race-related concerns as primary. What is perhaps just as important is that the means through which we made these inquiries were not the usual writing-based activities. The use of these other media—with which neither we nor our students were proficient, as *classroom* tools—seemed to put us and our students on a more even learning and teaching level. We did not know what our students would say and show in response to these questions, *if* they would engage, and if they and we and our colleagues and students' families would see this project as a waste of time.

Racial Tensions Most Often Happen in Our Presence but Beyond Our Purview

The everyday nature of the racial tensions our students feel was disturbing to us, especially because we count ourselves as aware teachers who regularly greet and interact with students during and between classes and before and after school. These tensions were all the more troubling because our schools are places where demographic shifts have been occurring for at least a decade. Although the adults in our school *appear* to be responding to these changes, Juan's photograph and writing made us wonder just how accurate our perceptions were:

> "Guns and Racism in the United States"
>
> Guns make me unsuccessful in and out of school. For example, if my parents knew that I had a gun, they would kick me out of the house or they would send me to the correctional center until I am

eighteen or more. . . . My parents told me that if I do go to the correctional center, they would send me back to El Salvador. Guns are bad because they might hurt innocent people. . . . Also, I am scared of getting into fights with other kids in the school, because some of them are racist towards Hispanic students. One time my friends and I were walking in the hallway and a group of kids approached us. They said, "Get the @#$% out of America, you stupid Hispanics!" . . . I think teachers need to talk about these issues with students.

—Juan

Juan was an eighth grader in a language arts class for English language learners when we introduced him to our photo elicitation project. He was a bright young man who playfully engaged with us. Sadly, he often struggled to find reasons to positively participate in school and to demonstrate the English proficiency he needed to be successful in school and beyond. But when we appealed to these "photovoice" methods, he not only was able to grow as a writer and student, but he provided poignant insights into the realities of race and racism.

Again, it seems important to note that the method of our project—beginning by *not* asking about race and using multimedia tools with which our students were more comfortable—facilitated Juan's revelations about the existence of the racial tensions in our school. But the greatest insight we have drawn from his and numerous other youths' reflections and images is that we cannot assume that we are present when these conflicts arise. And we cannot assume that because a community has a *history* of integrating different-looking and different-speaking students that it is doing so *positively.* Perhaps what our students have taught us through their pictures and writings is that we might help them to resolve the racial tensions they encounter by explicitly looking for their existence in the places we might *least* expect racism to occur.

Race Issues Affect Our Students in the Most Subtle Ways

Our project has also taught us that once we are open to *seeing* these racial tensions and factors in other spaces in our schools, we might discover that the most insidious forms of racism may be those that are the most subtle. And the fact that these are unintended actually does little to help our students to be aware of how to address these. With the following image of books his family brought with them from his home country of Sri Lanka, Chathuranga described the unique ways that English posed a problem for him in school:

"My Name Is Short"

What makes me unsuccessful in school is language. . . . My name has caused me many problems in America. In Sri Lanka, my name is short and everyone can pronounce it. However, in America, my name is long and difficult to pronounce so nobody can say it correctly. When I do an assignment for class, I have to make sure there is a space provided for my name. . . . Sometimes I cannot understand what Americans are talking about because there are a lot of differences between American English and British English. . . . English is hard and can make me unsuccessful in school.

—Chathuranga

Every interaction we had with Chathuranga suggested that he was fluent in a very formal, British colonial version of English. It was a language that we could make sense of, but that was quite different from the form of this language that was utilized by his teachers and peers. He had already come to understand that his school-related English activities were much more about his ability to navigate expectations—even the directions teachers give or the spaces provided on an assessment for his name. These were more foreign to him than the English language, and he saw these as tied to race issues, and

to his teachers' lack of consideration for young people who didn't look or talk like them.

It is vital for us to acknowledge that racism represents something far *different* from those intentional acts. As teachers attempting to serve increasingly racially diverse populations, modern-day lynchings are not our primary concern. The examples of racism that our students identify are the systems and traditions that marginalize them. A favorite responsive teacher mantra is that "There's no such thing as a stupid question," but what happens when our students do not even feel like they have the language to ask questions? When racism is that sinister?

Closing Thoughts

Finally, when we step back from our years of working with an increasingly diverse population of students, we are left with the key insight that, even as well-intentioned, veteran teachers, ultimately we are not the best sources of either the nature of or the solutions to the racial challenges our students are facing. In fact, the most important effort we might make to consider and respond to these racial tensions is to very intentionally allow our students to play these expert roles, not just on what is meant by "racism," but about what constitutes effective schools and teaching.

Even those of us who are open to the evolutions of our classroom demographics can be dangerously shortsighted when it comes to these issues, to racial realities that we simply have never had to *live*. Assuming that our good intentions are enough may be one of the most limiting factors in our abilities to actually *do* good. We now believe that any effort to make our pedagogical practices and schools in general relevant to our racially diverse students' cultures must involve *them* in the definition of what is relevant. Perhaps the ultimate relevance of school is, in fact, a *process* of determining such pertinence, with our students as the guides.

Sadly, it is not only us—as White teachers—who are prone to making negative assumptions about these youths' capacities as positive, contributing students or members of communities. Sometimes their own families have both inaccurate and critical perspectives on these young people, their siblings, and their peers. Although he was practically mute in our eighth grade language arts class, Fernando was a diligent student who, it turned out, was more than occasionally impeded in school by the damaging conjectures made by the adults in his own family. His reflection, which accompanied an image of his brother, poignantly illustrated just why we might continue to ask our students about school and race:

.   "I Know My Brother and He Is Good"

> One thing that makes me unsuccessful is my mom. . . . She thinks my brother is a gangster but he is not. She always tells him, "Luis, don't talk to those guys." She always asks me if Luis is involved with gangsters. She worries about him. My mom worrying also make me worry about him. I know my brother and he is good. . . . When my mom asks me questions, I cannot concentrate on my homework. In class, I am thinking about my brother and who he talks to.
>
> —Fernando

Perhaps if we asked *all* of our racially diverse students about school and allowed them to use visual and other media with which they are more comfortable to answer these questions, we—their teachers and the other caring adults in their lives—would appreciate where and how racism occurs and the effects it is having. And perhaps if we allowed—*required*, even—them to be the experts on their lives, our schools, our pedagogies and curricula, and on these issues of race and racism, we would better *know* them and know that they are "good."

References

Alvermann, D. E., & Strickland, D. S. (2004). *Bridging the literacy achievement gap: Grades 4–12*. New York: Teachers College Press.

Beuschel, A. C. (2008). *Listening to students about learning*. A Report from the Carnegie Foundation for the Advancement of Teaching. Strengthening Pre-Collegiate Education in Community Colleges. Stanford, CA: The Carnegie Foundation for the Advancement of Teaching.

Christenbury, L., Bomer, R., & Smagorinsky, P. (Eds.). (2009). *Handbook of adolescent literacy research*. New York: Guilford Press.

Clark, C. D. (1999). The autodriven interview: A photographic viewfinder into children's experiences. *Visual Sociology, 14,* 39–50.

Clark, K. (2005). Educational settings and the use of technology to promote the multicultural development of children. In Clark, K. (2008). Educational settings and the use of technology to promote the multicultural development of children. In G. Berry, M. Ellis, & J. Asamen (Eds.), *Handbook of child development, multiculturalism, and media* (pp. 411–418). Newbury Park, CA: Sage.

Cook-Sather, A. (2009). *Learning from the student's perspective: A methods sourcebook for effective teaching*. Boulder, CO: Paradigm Publishers.

Doda, N. & Knowles, T. (2008). Listening to the voices of young adolescents. *Middle School Journal, 39*(3), 26–33.

Easton, L., & Condon, D. (2009). A school-wide model for student voice in curriculum development and teacher preparation. In A. Cook-Sather (Ed.), *Learning from the student's perspective: A secondary methods sourcebook for effective teaching*. Boulder, CO: Paradigm Press.

Harper, D. (2005). What's new visually? In N. K. Denzin & Y. S. Lincoln (Eds.), *The Sage handbook of qualitative research* (3rd ed., pp. 747–762). Thousand Oaks, CA: Sage.

Hibbing, A. N., & Rankin-Erickson, J. L. (2003). A picture is worth a thousand words: Using visual images to improve comprehension for middle school struggling readers. *The Reading Teacher, 56*(8), 758–770.

Kist, W. (2005). *New literacies in action: Teaching and learning in multiple media*. New York: Teachers College Press.

Kress, G. (2006). *Reading images: The grammar of visual design*. New York: Routledge.

Lan, W., & Lanthier, R. (2003). Changes in students' academic performance and perceptions of school before dropping out of schools. *Journal of Education for Students Placed at Risk, 8*(3), 309–332.

Lankshear, C., & Knobel, M. (2006). *New literacies: Everyday practices and classroom learning* (2nd ed.). Maidenhead, UK: Open University Press.

Lynch, K., & Baker, J. (2005). Equality in education: An equality of condition perspective. *Theory and Research in Education, 3*(2), 131–164.

Mann, M. (2011). Helping students express their passion. *Learning & Leading with Technology, 38*(6), 10–15.

Marquez-Zenkov, K., & Harmon, J. (2007). Seeing English in the city: Using photography to understand students' literacy relationships. *English Journal, 96*(6), 24–30.

Moje, E. B. (2008). The complex world of adolescent literacy: Myths, motivations, and mysteries. *Harvard Educational Review, 78*(1), 107–154.

Morrell, E., & Duncan-Andrade, J. (2006). Popular culture and critical media pedagogy in secondary literacy classrooms. *International Journal of Learning, 12.*

Pole, C. (Ed). (2004). *Seeing is believing? Approaches to visual research (Volume 7).* New York: Elsevier.

Raggl, A., & Schratz, M. (2004). Using visuals to release pupil's voices: Emotional pathways to enhancing thinking and reflecting on learning. In C. Pole (Ed.), *Seeing is believing? Approaches to visual research* (Volume 7; pp. 147–162). New York: Elsevier.

Rodgers, C. (2006). Attending to student voice: The role of descriptive feedback in learning and teaching. *Curriculum Inquiry, 36*(2), 209–237.

Rose, G. (2006). *Visual methodologies: An introduction to the interpretation of visual materials.* Thousand Oaks, CA: Sage.

Smyth, J. (2007). Toward the pedagogically engaged school: Listening to student voice as a positive response to disengagement and "dropping out"? In D. Thiessen & A. Cook-Sather (Eds.), *International handbook of student experience in elementary and secondary school* (pp. 635–658). Dordrecht, The Netherlands: Springer.

Streng, J. M., Rhodes, S. D., Ayala, G. X., Eng., E., Arceo, R., & Phipps, S. (2004). *Realidad Latina*: Latino adolescents, their school, and a university use photovoice to examine and address the influence of immigration. *Journal of Interprofessional Care, 18*(4), 403–415.

Wisconsin Public Radio. (2005, April 5). *Here on earth: Women in the Catholic Church* [Audio podcast]. Retrieved from http://www.wpr.org/hereonearth/

Zenkov, K., & Harmon, J. (2009). Picturing a writing process: Using photovoice to learn how to teach writing to urban youth. *Journal of Adolescent and Adult Literacy, 52*(7), 575–584.

27

LOOKING AT RACE

Adding Images to the Conversation

Adam Levner

History shows that images have the power to change the nature and substance of difficult conversations. The discomfort inherent in talking about sensitive or controversial topics leads people to find ways, consciously or not, to shift their attention to something safer. The heart of a challenging matter is often avoided by verbally dancing around the edges, speaking in platitudes, and hunkering down in familiar trenches.

Visual images can play a critical role in shifting the altitude of a conversation from 30,000 feet up to ground level; from theories to real, substantive questions about practical implications and consequences. While images now can be manipulated easily and convincingly by anyone with a computer or even a smartphone, people assume that the stories depicted by images are accurate and objective. The faith that we instinctively place in the truth of what our eyes perceive makes it a much more difficult task to keep debates at an abstract or academic level.

The topic of race exemplifies an issue to which most people would prefer to turn a blind eye. It also exemplifies an issue where visual images succeeded in forcing society to look and to confront, even if only to a limited extent. Images have been necessary, and at times sufficient, to focus the conversation on the true role that race plays at both personal and systemic levels.

During decades of racial segregation in the United States, many people, particularly in the North, were easily able to ignore, disbelieve, or deny segregation's severity and even its very existence. The effectiveness of the Civil Rights Movement in creating the awareness and outrage necessary to end legalized segregation and disenfranchisement depended greatly on the use of visual images. Speaking to Spider Martin, a prominent photojournalist during the Civil Rights Movement, Reverend Martin Luther King, Jr. stated, "Spider, we could have marched, we could have protested forever, but if it weren't for guys like you, it would have been for nothing. The whole world saw your pictures. That's why the Voting Rights Act was passed." (Selma to Montgomery, n.d.)

Although today's images focusing on the topic of race might not depict stories as dramatic as peaceful marchers being attacked with fire hoses and dogs or well-dressed students being arrested for sitting at a lunch counter, they can still isolate powerful elements of the discussion. Images can highlight examples of the continued challenges posed by race—high school students sitting in racially self-segregated groups in the cafeteria, AP classes with only white students and remedial classes with only students of color, neighborhoods illustrating the still-close relationship between race and socioeconomic status—as well as counterexamples that illustrate progress that has occurred despite the challenges.

There are numerous efforts across the country to document issues affecting underserved communities, including the role of race in our society. One example is the work of Critical Exposure, a Washington, DC–based nonprofit that teaches low-income youth how to use the power of photography and their own voices to create real change in their schools and communities. Participating students have used cameras to express their perspectives on issues of social justice that directly affect their lives. Their work attests to the influence that visual images can have on both the public and policymakers and the influence of young people's perspectives in particular.

In some cases, the students' work has directly confronted the topic of race. More often, the students have focused on concrete issues that exemplify the inequities and injustices they face daily and that have their roots in racially and socioeconomically biased systems that the students are only beginning to consciously examine.

The following are a few of the thousands of photographs and pieces of writing that Critical Exposure students have created. Some of the photographs are explicitly about race—several were taken in Albuquerque, New Mexico, as part of a project in which students documented what they perceived to be the legacy of two court cases intended to promote racial equity in education, *Brown v. Board of Education* and *Mendez v. Westminster*. Other photos simply illustrate current conditions that exist in many schools serving low-income children of color. Taken together, the students' work tells a small piece of the story about the continued role of race in our society and helps to illuminate the possible contributions that visual images can make to our efforts to deepen the conversation about race.

ALTERCATION
Christian, Eleventh Grade, Washington, DC

"There has been a huge altercation involving anywhere from fifteen to thirty youth. The police line and frisk them, some are even arrested."

HAZARD
Levi, Tenth Grade, Washington, DC

"This is a picture of my Spanish class. The condition of classrooms makes kids leave. The reason the kids leave is because the ceiling gives out a really bad odor that makes most students who come to class leave. When it rains the water starts to spill over from the buckets."

UNTITLED
Manuel, Tenth Grade, Washington, DC

"Being an immigrant and not knowing English is the most horrible thing, because a lot of people take advantage of those people who don't know English. Some people feel like they don't know how to do anything, because other people tell them that they are ignorant. In our countries, there is a lot of poverty and the majority of people come to this country because it is called 'the country of opportunities.' But because of the discrimination in this country, many immigrants go back to their countries.

"One of the things that is affecting the schools in the District of Columbia is discrimination. Many of the African-American students say that they are better than the Latino students. However, I believe that in this world we are all equal, no matter the race, the culture, or the language. Many students, especially Latinos, stop going to school because of the discrimination. I have seen many cases in which other students and even teachers have discriminated against students. This makes me feel disappointed because our teachers are in the school to teach us and not to discriminate. This also makes me feel disappointed because we are all humans. We all have skills, we are all intelligent, but overall, we all have feelings. I would like to not have discrimination or racism in this world and that we all treat each other the same way."

BROKEN FENCE
Fatimah, Albuquerque, New Mexico

"This picture is of a broken fence in the back of my school. I felt that this fence meant something to me. Because the fence appears to be broken, I felt that the fence represented and symbolized the promises desired from the *Brown* and *Mendez* cases. While they appeared to be fixed on the surface, if you look deeper or beyond the surface there is still much to be changed and fixed. We cannot continue to just attempt to mend those problems of which the cases fought for. We have come a long way, but we still have further to go."

STUDENT HANDS
Andreina, Albuquerque, New Mexico

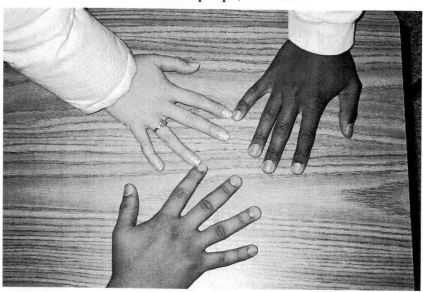

"This picture shows how *Brown's* dream was fulfilled and how we of all colors come together."

SEPARATE TABLES
Randa, Twelfth Grade, Albuquerque, New Mexico

"These pictures were taken of a photography class. It shows how students are separate—there are tables for white students and other ones for African-American students. They don't interact together in class!"

OUT OF ORDER
Ken, Eleventh Grade, Sto-Rox School District, Western Pennsylvania

"I took this photo to depict the state of despair that parts of our school are in. I hope that when others view 'Out of Order,' it makes them think about how we feel when surrounded by visuals like the broken urinal. Although we are used to visuals such as this in our school, they affect our thoughts daily. We, the students of Sto-Rox High School, feel as though we do not deserve better. Therefore, we are less inclined to strive for better."

CLOCK
Khalid, Washington, DC

"This photo depicts a broken clock in a classroom. It shows how time is lost and how simple things are broken, [and how] a simple thing can affect us in such a [big] way."

BROKEN WINDOW
Ian, Tenth Grade, Baltimore, Maryland

"This window has been broken for months."

CROWDING AT THE BACK DOOR
Jacquan, Eleventh Grade, Washington, DC

"It's an issue of dignity to have a school of mostly African-American and Hispanic students walk through the back door of a school."

Reference

Selma to Montgomery: A march for the right to vote. *The Spider Martin Civil Rights Collection.* Retrieved from http://spidermartin.com/archive/about.html

28

OUTSIDE THE BUBBLE

Rachel Rycerz

The most profound dialogue on race and racism I experienced as a teacher came unexpectedly. I was administering a reading test from a prescribed curriculum—I had noted that the article was on "Sagging," and my first thought was "Good—a subject my students will be interested in," as many students in my essentially 100% African-American school adopted that style. I honestly didn't give it much more thought, or really read the article thoroughly. I would be correcting their ten multiple-choice question tests soon enough, and the curriculum didn't really call for going any deeper.

Standardized test prep wasn't how I first came into teaching, or most specifically how I came to School of the Arts, a neighborhood school on the South Side of Chicago. I loved the focus of integrating the arts into all subjects, being part of a small school where there was a real opportunity to form community, and our principal's belief in using one's strengths to overcome weaknesses. These same points led School Redesign Network at Stanford University to recognize School of the Arts in a documentary and case study in 2005, my first year there.

One of the ways of building on the strengths of our particular community was recognizing the value of African-American heritage, through filling the school with images of student-painted African-American art, honoring the founders of the school with a mural, and an African-American studies class taught junior year. We held an African festival every year. As a teacher who didn't reflect the majority culture at the school, I was also encouraged to bring my own strengths and passion to the classroom. For me, those were poetry, drama, and going beyond filling in the "right" bubbles, encouraging students to taking a seat at the table as participant, interpreter, and critic.

So when one of my students came up to me and told me she thought the article on sagging was racist in the way that it was framed and the assumptions that it made, and she didn't want to take the test, I hadn't expected her reaction, but saw it as an opportunity.

I told my student that if she didn't want to take the test, she could instead write a letter to the author of the text about why she found the article offensive. I extended the offer to other students in the class; they could write comments if they wished in addition to taking the test, or write a letter in place of it. Two students each chose to write letters; many other students went ahead and took the test and added comments.

Because we were in the pilot program of the Instructional Development System (IDS) Kaplan curriculum as part of High School Transformation, I had actually met the author of the textbook and knew we could make contact with her. I brought the letters and the compiled comments to the next IDS meeting, where I spoke to the author and gave her my students' responses. She wrote a letter back to my students, addressing their concerns, apologizing, and letting them know that the following year the text would be changed based on their feedback.

I was thrilled to get the response, and for my students to get the response. I was even more thrilled with what came next.

Our school had an academic fair coming up. I shared the response letter with the two students who wrote the initial letters, and asked if they would like to design a project around the experience. They ended up designing a survey using the Likert scale (from strongly disagree to strongly agree) to be given to all the freshmen at the school on their response to the article, and then to the author's response letter. They asked whether the students thought that the original article was racist, and whether they thought the author was racist after they read her response letter. The two students who wrote the original letters then analyzed the responses and presented them at the academic fair, including to a representative from "downtown."

Most importantly, the students had an experience of expressing themselves and having their voices heard—and in defining themselves outside the "bubble" of standardized testing.

Before School of the Arts adapted the Kaplan IDS, standardized testing was specifically *not* the way we defined success. We were looking for a "deep literacy," for students to be able to interact in meaningful ways with literature and make it part of their lives. I played a part in that definition—inspired by my student teaching experience in an AP Comp Lit class at a magnet school in Chicago, in which my mentor teacher told our students that the purpose of the class was not to score a 4 or 5 on the AP test, but to meaningfully interact with powerful literature—and that test scores were a by-product, not the goal. I felt our students at the School of the Arts deserved nothing less.

One program that helped make literature a meaningful part of my students' lives was Poetry Out Loud. The program provides materials and judging criteria to support students memorizing and reciting published poetry, which can be used from the classroom level all the way up to a national competition. For my freshman students, I pulled from the Poetry Out Loud Anthology all the poems by African-American poets, to expose and familiarize the students with the authors. Each student chose a poem to memorize and recite, and the students used the criteria to help critique and improve the performance of their classmates. The students became intimately familiar with the poem they had chosen, and also became familiar with others through listening to the recitations. We went beyond that—for Open House night, I put out a selection of poems, from the anthology and beyond, and invited parents or guardians and the student each choose to one poem that was important to them, and write a paragraph of why they selected it. I then took a picture of them together and created a poster of their poem, responses, and picture. The posters were placed around the school. My fourth year there, for the African-American History assembly, not only students but adults from the school as well, including the principal and the dean of discipline, recited poetry in front of the school. The students, familiar with the poems from each freshman class's exposure over the years, responded with wild enthusiasm.

Familiarity and comfort with poetry gave it relevance and meaning to my students in different contexts as well. In the 2008 presidential primaries, my students compared Barack Obama's definition of *hope* from his speech announcing his run for presidency with Emily Dickinson's in the poem "Hope is a thing with Feathers." It also gave them a context for the poem Maya Angelou wrote for candidate Hillary Clinton, a variation on her poem "Still I Rise" titled "State Package for Hillary Clinton."

The Goodman Arts in Education program also immeasurably enriched my students' lives. The program provided scripts, study guides, and play tickets for students as well as further support for teachers for a series of plays over a season. The first image that I remember is sitting on the floor in a circle with my kids, talking about *A Christmas Carol,* specifically about the Ghosts of Christmas Past and Christmas Future. I remember asking my students what from their pasts had made a difference in who they were today, and several of them really opened up. One student talked about her mother going to jail, while the other students listened attentively and supportively. Later we talked about the Ghost of Christmas Future and who the students wanted to be. At the end, one of the students said "We love you, Miss Hoover." That didn't come from going through standard exercises or following an IDS. It came from creating community and sharing experiences together that helped to build trust and helped the students connect their lives to both literature and to each other, giving a bigger framework.

Sometimes connecting to that larger framework was painful, as when we delved into *The Ballad of Emmett Till*, the story of a fourteen-year-old African-American boy who was kidnapped and lynched because he was accused of whistling at a white woman. Tensions came to the forefront, including students whistling at me during class and repeating my first name under their breath, seeing how far they could push the limits. Ultimately confronting the work of art and the issues that it brought up together gave students a chance to go deeper in responding to the effect of racism in history and in their own lives.

Knowing test scores were our weak point, our principal chose to have us join the High School Transformation program—the point of which was to raise student achievement as measured through test scores—in the first year of implementation, with the hope of protecting our school politically. Unfortunately, when School of the Arts adopted a defined curriculum, we moved away from using our strengths to overcome weaknesses. The reading "coach" for our school thought it was not worthwhile for our students to be involved in the Goodman program, because studying the scripts would cut down time following the scripted curriculum. Fortunately my principal backed me up on that issue, and we stayed in the program for the rest of my time at the school, but other things began to fall by the wayside. As the IDS spread from ninth grade to both ninth and tenth, then adding eleventh, art teachers from School of the Arts lost their jobs. The African-American History class was cut. And this last year, the school itself was phased out.

A brand-new building was built, and teachers and students were prepared to move into it until, at a teacher meeting teeming with District Office security guards, it was announced that a new magnet school with students selected by test scores would be moved in. School of the Arts would be combined with another small school, move into an old building across the street, and stop taking in new students. The principals and teachers from the schools that were combining could apply for jobs at the combined, shrinking school. Students who came to a school with the motto "We are stars with a purpose—let it shine!" would lose the support and community that had been formed.

I came to the school because I believed in what it stood for. I believe that having the opportunity to have a supportive community that integrated the arts helped the students bring who they were to the table and find new ways to create dialogue not only with each other, but with the world, and find a way to navigate and create their paths in it. I hope that my former students bring the experiences that we shared forward as they go on.

My great-uncle, Ernest Oppman, as perhaps the only white student at Howard University back in the 1940s, participated in an early round of lunch-counter sit-ins. The police told him that he could leave, but he said, "You arrest my friends, you arrest me." He was bailed out of jail by Thurgood Marshall, who told him, "I appreciate what you are doing, but you will never understand what it is to be black." That made my uncle angry; shortly afterward, on the bus on the way home from a date with his well-off girlfriend, he realized that Thurgood Marshall would not have been allowed into the restaurant where he, a poor—but white—graduate student had just eaten. And he realized that Thurgood Marshall was right; civil rights was a cause that my uncle could pick up, but he did not have to live with discrimination every day because of the color of his skin.

As teachers, I believe that our role is not only to educate, but to empower. One of the ways my school sought to empower students was to recognize and value their African-American heritage. As a white teacher, I could support that, but not represent that—and Thurgood Marshall's words to my uncle still resonated. I could learn African-American history and read the works of African-American poets, but I would never walk down the street as a young African-American man or woman. And one of the things that I learned is that I needed to recognize that, but not be intimidated or feel invalidated because of it; just as I believed in what my students had within them and to offer the world, I needed to believe in what I had to offer them, beyond administering a prescribed curriculum. We are a gift to each other. In a world where more and more people are "connected" through electronic devices and get their information only from sources that reinforce what they already believe, being present to and learning from the person in front of you is radical.

Don't be afraid to invite students to speak from their experience, even or especially if it challenges the text you are reading or your own worldview. Setting up parameters from the beginning where students know their contributions are valued and they are expected to give—and receive—respect will make a difference in and beyond the classroom.

PART SEVEN

IMPLICATIONS FOR TEACHER EDUCATION

29

TALKING ABOUT RACE

A Story From a Teacher Educator

Ok-Hee Lee

Talking about race isn't something many people feel comfortable or safe to engage in for an array of reasons, especially when the dialogue takes place publicly or if they are part of diverse nations like the United States, Canada, and others. Frankly, it is hard for me to do so as well because I am talking about my own personal story, not about racial phenomena observed in the society; I have a sense of unease from sharing my personal journey with racial issues mainly because of the uncertain emotional responses my story will evoke from others, particularly those about whom I deeply care and for whom I feel respect including colleagues, students, and friends. Nonetheless, I still choose to take the risk and candidly share my journey from the beginning point of lacking a racial identity to the current point of teaching multicultural education to future teachers in a predominantly white university. I decided to share my story for the following reasons: First, I clearly see the need for people to open up and engage in dialogue around one of the most avoided topics of all time, race and its attendant issues, because the more we avoid, the further we lag behind in building social justice for everybody. Second, by sharing my private, untold stories with others, I am inviting them to do the same or at least listen to different perspectives diverse individuals bring to the discourse of race and social justice. Finally, I would like to reflect on my personal journey so far in relation to racial issues and social justice and think about the journey ahead of me. I will start with how I became conscious about my racial identity and issues related to race.

How I Was Awakened to My Racial Identity, Racial Issues, and Social Justice

Born and growing up in Korea where diversity in race was almost nonexistent, the topic of race wasn't significant to me. Seldom was race brought up in any form of public or nonpublic discourse, whether it was a political arena, debate in the media, or academic discourse, except for brief coverage on racism and racial relations during high school social studies class as a social phenomenon often observed in distant countries where many different racial groups cohabitate. Because of the insignificance of racial identity to the people in Korea, race had never been a significant identifier with which I consciously associated. Relatively privileged socially, economically, and academically, the notion of privilege was an unknown territory to me. However, my move to the United States to pursue a doctoral degree in education changed my entire association with the concept of race and issues around it, transforming my concept of race from that of a minor significance to a profound meaning that pertains to my life as a teacher educator as well as a person. How did that happen?

Being the only person who had a different skin color, a different mother tongue, and a different religion from everyone else in the classrooms of fifteen to twenty people when I was a graduate student at Indiana State University, I was slowly awakened to my racial identity, a part of me of which I wasn't fully aware before. I am not implying it in any negative sense; I am just identifying the time I took a first step in discovering my new identity that I almost forgot I had. The sense of being different and of being a minority became clearer and clearer as I encountered more culture shocks while interacting with people inside and outside the university. For example, one of the cultural differences I initially noticed was that in America people were more direct in their expressions compared with people in Korea. When Koreans are offered a favor or a treat, they often say "no" to it the first time just to show modesty even if they would like to accept the favor or the treat. Therefore, it is typical that Korean people prompt a second offer if not a third or even more. However, here in America, the first "no" meant no, nothing else. I learned I needed to be more direct in my expressions.

Along with the sense of being different, I came to understand what it means to be a minority bit by bit. As an international student who came from a non–English speaking country, I always had to study much harder than most of my American peers because it took significantly longer for me to finish the same amount of reading assignments. There were often moments when I didn't understand either my instructor or my peers due to the way they spoke (either too fast or mumbling) or to the vocabulary they were using (either slang or words that I didn't know or couldn't remember the meaning). I didn't complain, nor was I discouraged by the situation as I anticipated the challenge and was ready to take it. Although I took my challenge for granted, the struggle I went through taught me an invaluable lesson that I might not have learned had I not left Korean soil. That is, for the first time in my life, I truly began to realize the power of privilege. Regardless of how I took the challenge, it was true that my peers were privileged because their native language was English. Having had many privileges myself in Korea, not only was I blind about how privileged I was, but also I was ignorant about the life underprivileged people endure. The challenge from the language barrier was tough to tolerate even when I deliberately chose to take it. Then what about people who didn't choose to be in the position of the underprivileged? With such a question, I began to develop more critical perspectives on differences in power between and among people and grew to empathize with people without privileges. In retrospect, it was around that time the seed inside me to work toward social justice was planted.

Outside the university, in the meantime, there were numerous incidents in which I seem to have been treated differently because of the way I looked. I was shouted at by people in a car passing by who yelled, "Go back to China" or "Dirty Chinks" on the streets; was asked to show my identification when using my credit card although people in front of me were not asked to do the same; and had to wait much longer to be waited on in restaurants than other people, just to name a few. A more frightening experience came when a member of a neo-Nazi organization shot a Korean international student, just like me, to death solely out of racial hatred in Bloomington, Indiana, the town where I lived and went to school. Such upsetting experiences made me more alert and sensitive to the ways people treated me. As some people say, like many other minority people I developed a sixth sense for racial bias. More importantly, those experiences taught me how intimately my race was connected to my existence in the United States.

Drawn by my anger toward the hatred embedded in racial discrimination, the prejudicial behaviors of certain people, and the desire to change the status quo, I was already eager to explore racial issues in greater depth by the time I got into my doctoral program at Indiana University in Bloomington, Indiana. Fortunately, many courses I took while in my doctoral program fulfilled my strong appetite for more knowledge on racial issues and further assisted me to understand those issues in much broader social, political, economical, and historical contexts. Reading such authors as Michael Apple, Henry Giroux, Peter McLaren, and others, I began to realize how microscopic my perception of racial relations had been and came to an understanding of how racism is pervasive throughout the society even with the rhetoric of racial equality and equal opportunity, how power relations in society are reproduced through hegemony, how schools serve as one of the major apparatuses in the power–class reproduction process, and how institutional racism disenfranchises certain groups of people and thus perpetuates the status quo. As a person in the field of education, the roles that schools play in racial relations was one of the most important aspects in the realm of racial relations, and thus I was naturally drawn to the ideas of critical pedagogy and began aspiring to be a critical pedagogue myself. Equipped with the knowledge and theoretical lens to use and the desire to become a change agent, I was excited about my new opportunity when I left Bloomington, Indiana, to teach at Minnesota State University Moorhead (MSUM) as a teacher educator about a decade ago.

My Struggle With Teaching Multicultural Education as a Teacher Educator

If asked to summarize my experiences to instill critical pedagogy in my students through multicultural education for the last ten years at MSUM, I have to say, even with some triumphant moments here and there, it has been a constant struggle walking the fine line between not imposing my perspectives on students versus trying to help them unpack their preconceived notions about false racial equality in the United States. It has always been tricky to pinpoint where the fine line lies; I don't want to push too hard so as to provoke resistance from students, but at the same time I want to push hard enough for them to embrace new perspectives. Also there has been always a sense of doubt on my part, not knowing whether my students respond to the topic the way they do because of my teaching style, my race, a combination of both, or neither, especially when I sense strong resistance from the students toward the topic of multicultural education. Those intricate elements of teaching are hard to tease out even with such devices as middle- and end-of-semester course evaluations along with other forms of evaluations. Thus overall it has been a lonely journey trying to walk the fine line with many unanswered questions and yet it has been a fulfilling journey as well, fueled by a constant stream of sense of hope from the students I taught.

MSUM is a mid-sized college located in northwest Minnesota where the population is predominantly white. Throughout my ten years of teaching experience in the Teacher Education program, I had only a handful of non-white students, nonwhite students mainly being Native Americans. Students in the courses I teach every semester have been consistently homogeneous: 90%–100% white, female students from middle to low-middle class, many from small towns in either Minnesota or North Dakota where diversity is rare. Therefore, their exposure to diversity is usually minimal, and naturally racial issues are rather a distant topic to the majority of them without much relevance.*

The courses in which I have addressed multicultural education content since I began to teach at MSUM are one early childhood methodology course and one curriculum course for special education majors, both being upper-level undergraduate courses. Due to the nature of the courses placing a main focus on the teaching methodology and curriculum, respectively, the amount of time I could devote to multicultural education issues was limited to only three or four seventy-five-minute class sessions, which was far shorter than I wished. With such a limited amount of time, it was more challenging to delve into the topic in greater depth, let alone help the students adopt critical pedagogy. Therefore, there is a greater chance, I believe, that my experiences might have been different from what I would have had if I had taught a course that could tackle multicultural issues the entire semester.

Considering my students' limited experiences with diversity and their socioeconomic backgrounds, it was not surprising to me that many of them were not really engaged with the discourse of race and social justice issues, even though it still shouldn't be the case given the many years they spent in schools. For many students, I was the first nonwhite teacher they ever had. Therefore, I find it always difficult to initiate and invite them into class discussions about racial and cultural issues, paying special attention to the ways in which schools serve to reproduce the unequal power relations and what they as teachers should do to rectify the situation. I often start with discussions about what culture is and have them look at their own cultural values and customs to reflect on not only what their norms are but also on

---

*I am referring to undergraduate students only here. The attitude of students in my graduate-level Socio-Cultural Foundations of Education course was very different from the undergraduate students' attitudes. As current teachers and administrators, many of them already had worked with diverse students and were eager to explore the issue in greater depth and find better ways to meet those students' needs.

the role of culture in shaping who they are as people before they start thinking about other cultures. There are times that students are deeply engaged in thinking about their own culture and make comments about how strange it is that they did not think about their own cultural values and heritage before. Then it becomes easy to get into the discussion of why Euro-Americans lack cultural awareness and how it reflects the privileges that they have, but are unaware of, just as they don't appreciate air very much because they are surrounded by it all the time. After such discussions, I have them think about what role culture plays in schools, how institutional racism plays into schooling, what teachers can do to change the status quo, and how to meet the needs of diverse students.

One of the most distressful times is when students seem to automatically shut down and don't want to invest their energy and time to think about the issues once I utter the word *culture*. Typically such reaction to the topic turns the entire class into an uncomfortable silence and there seems to emerge a racial line between my students and me, leaving me the sole member of a minority group who wants them to be engaged in the discourse of multicultural education. I fight back the silence and try to share some of my personal stories including my own biases so as not to give any false impression that I present myself as bias free. I try to stress that I am not there to foster a sense of guilt within them. Also I try to share some of the incidents of discrimination I experienced against my race and ask them if they had any experiences in which they were treated differently based on their gender or disability, if not race, to help them empathize with the feeling of isolation or unfair treatment. Students seem to soften their guard a little bit when confronted by real stories from real people. Then there are times students regard my stories as a class issue rather than a racial issue, as evidenced in their statements like, "If the person knew you were a college professor, he or she would not have treated you differently." Many of the students seem to think that inequality is only the perception of minority people because in America anyone can achieve their highest potential if they work hard enough, so if someone was unsuccessful in school or later in life, it is his or her fault, not anyone else's or the society's. It clearly showcases how the belief in meritocracy in society is translated into blaming the victims. My argument against the fallacy of self-help ideology doesn't always work in helping them rethink, let alone change, their ideas. I want to push more in those situations, but sometimes I move on, wishing there would be more times and resonating voices throughout their entire teacher preparation process, not just mine.

When I face resistance from students, many questions rush through my mind. I sometimes wonder if it will make a difference when my white colleagues challenge the students to look at the issue from the perspectives I hold instead of me doing it. Will it make our students less resistant? Can they be more open and express their ideas more freely, perhaps with less worry about inadvertently offending a member of a minority group, a member of which happens to be their instructor? Or is it better for faculty from a minority background to do it because they bring their own experiences and stories to share? After asking those questions, I tend to come to the same conclusion: It should be done by both, by everyone, not a few, regardless of one's racial, ethnic, religious, or socioeconomic status. We need more concerted efforts.

Also I often wonder what makes some students more open to different perspectives than theirs and what makes other students more closed. I wonder if critical thinking skills make any difference. Students who are willing to tackle complicated ideas and issues and look at those issues from multiple perspectives always seem to be willing to actively explore the issues of race and social justice. If our PreK–12 school system did a better job in focusing more on problem solving and developing critical thinking skills, I wonder if my students would be better prepared to grapple with the issues of race and schooling even if they have not been exposed to diversity before.

My Journey Ahead

As mentioned before, it has been a challenge for me to help my students embrace critical perspectives on racial issues and the concept of critical pedagogy, but it wasn't a challenge that has left me with a sense of despair. When I see my students' eyes brighten when we discuss multicultural issues, I see hope and that gives me the energy to continue my work. Also other people who exert the same effort with me to bring changes to the status quo always invigorate me and give me confidence in what I am doing. For example, Rudenstine reminds me how patient I should be in carrying out my responsibilities as a critical pedagogue:

> We know that close association among people from different backgrounds can lead to episodes of tension, and that common understandings often emerge only slowly and with considerable effort, if at all. Yet we need to remember that the character of American society, from its very beginnings,

has been shaped by our collective willingness to carry forward an unprece-dented experiment in diversity, the benefits of which have seldom come without friction and strain. (Rudenstine, 1996, p. B1)

I am glad for the opportunity to reflect on my journey so far with the issues of race and social justice and share it with the readers of this book. My story is nothing special, but writing it and sharing it with others have given me time and space to look back at my experiences and think about the rest of my journey. I wish others would have the same opportunity and join the club talking about race.

Reference

Rudenstine, N. L. (1996, April 19). Why a diverse student body is so important. *Chronicle of Higher Education,* p. B1.

30

CROSS-RACE MENTORING IN TEACHER EDUCATION

Black Teacher Educators Supporting White Pre-Service Teachers

Valerie Hill-Jackson and Omah Williams

It seems appropriate to begin this chapter by debunking the myth of the word *race*. *Race* is a term of invention, only a few centuries old, and yet it remains a chief source of major social boundaries in America. Race is not an observation founded in science, but a construct created and maintained by members of society. The prevailing and false definition of *race* is based merely on physical differences or attributes (such as skin color, hair texture, and facial features) between groups (Kottak & Kozaitis, 2012). However, all human beings share nearly identical DNA—we are a collective and therefore exist as one species (i.e., one race). The authors thought it responsible to share this fact validated through scholarship. The word *races* has inaccurately been used as a default term among those who lack scientific sophistication and by those who seek to further distinguish ethnic groups into different species. In the spirit of accuracy, this chapter should be titled "Cross-Ethnic" or "Cross-Cultural Mentoring," and *not* "Cross-Race Mentoring." Cross-cultural mentoring occurs between "mentors and protégés who differ on the basis of race, ethnicity, gender, sexual orientation, disability, religion, socioeconomic class, or other group memberships associated with power in organizations" (Ragins, 2007, p. 282), whereas cross-race mentoring focuses on the singular dimension of race (Scandura & Mezias, 2010). Since racism is a real outcome from the imagined conception of "race," we sometimes use the terms *race* and *ethnicity* interchangeably to pay homage to the field of race studies. But we digress—perhaps this conversation on the absurdity of the word *race* should be tabled for another discussion.

The White racial frame is a precondition for racism in which power and dominance are conferred to White citizens based on skin color, Whites hold a negative conception and lack of appreciation for people of color, and Whites embrace a positive understanding of White people and White traditions or norms (Feagin, 2006). Mentoring is a complicated practice in society and, akin to racism, presupposes an inherent power structure in which the mentor and protégé participate. The superior, more experienced professional provides direction to the novice (Scandura & Mezias, 2010). Black teacher educators (BTEs) who serve as mentors to White pre-service teachers (WPTs) are consequently caught in a dilemma: Society has created the burden and expectation of Black racial inferiority and powerlessness, but the mentor's position carries with it the weight of presumed authority. The result is a Black mentoring role that is, upon further scrutiny, counterintuitive to the distribution of racial power in American society and its institutions. Quality mentors have been extensively documented as persons with the ability to build trusting relationships and act as an advocate, guide, friend, supporter, and role model (Pitton, 2006, p. 1). This essay posits that an effective cross-ethnic mentor must possess these qualities *while* consciously working to transgress cultural boundaries.

The conceptual framework for appreciating this chapter is located at the nexus of W. E. B. Du Bois's (1903/2003) double consciousness theory and McIntosh's (1988) White privilege argument, as well as Johnson-Bailey and Cervero's (2004) illuminating ideas on the negotiation of power within the mentoring dyad. The relationship between BTEs and WPTs can be negatively affected because of society's overt and covert discriminatory attitudes—further obscuring the "hierarchically prescribed mentor/protégé relationship" (Johnson-Bailey & Cervero, 2004, p. 15). The mentoring literature is replete with cultural studies across gender, language, age, and ethnic differentials. But deliberations on ethnicity, in which Black professionals are in the advantaged position of mentor, are rarely addressed. Conversations on mentoring across ethnicity are often collapsed within discourses in which White faculty members help support peers or students of color. Consequently this chapter begins by unveiling the power dynamic that often exists when BTEs mentor WPTs. This chapter then discusses the K–12 incentive for understanding why BTEs can be indispensable mentors in supporting

White teachers in training is exposed. Finally, this chapter concludes with four strategies for mentoring across ethnic divides.

Mentoring and Power

The vision of the university mentor conjures up images of the aging White male professor, spectacles tipped at his nose, at the ready to impart wisdom among hungry students. Astute observers note that the function of the mentor in higher education is most often occupied by White male scholars, and this reality carries with it certain unexamined themes related to race. In cross-race (ethnic) mentoring:

> What should be a simple matter of negotiations between two persons becomes arbitration between historical legacies, contemporary racial tensions and societal protocols. Cross-cultural mentoring relationships are affiliations that exist between unequals who are conducting their relationship on a hostile American stage with a societal script contrived to undermine the success of the partnership. (Johnson-Bailey & Cervero, 2004, p. 11)

The rapport between mentor and protégé is fragile in the field of teacher education, where trusting relationships are the cornerstone for professional and instructional growth of novice teachers. The mandate of trust in the mentor-protégé relationship becomes even more tenuous in cross-ethnic mentoring, where invisible walls, erected between society's diverse cultural groups, undermine the sacred bond (Bowman, Kite, Branscombe, & Williams, 1999). This tension represents Black mentors' long-standing record of oppression, which deviates from WPTs' experiences as unconscious heirs to power in a race-conscious society (McIntosh, 1988).

The Double-Conscious Black Mentor

To better understand the relationship between BTEs and WPTs one must note the contradictory experiences of faculty and instructors in higher education who are both academics (typically respected and trusted) and Black (typically discounted and suspect). "We are in positions that make us less powerful as a result of our identity statuses and at the same time more powerful as a result of our faculty positions" (Murrell & Tangri, 1999, p. 213). Johnson-Bailey and Cervero (2004) lament:

Race and racial group membership are defining markers in our world. Consequently these signs of membership and exclusion are powerful forces in the academy. When assessing the experiences of blacks in the academy, the literature overwhelmingly asserts that black faculty are routinely viewed as interlopers and are rejected as rightful participants. . . . The academic lives of black faculty are marred with racist incidents, isolation or benign indifference. (p. 13)

Cross-ethnic mentoring for female faculty of color is, at best, a challenging enterprise due to a history steeped in Black victimization and White supremacy. Additionally, Black mentors in higher education experience "*double consciousness* which allows them to see the world from the white and black perspective" (Du Bois, 1903/2003, as cited in Johnson-Bailey & Cervero, 2004, p. 17; emphasis added). They are astutely aware of their own identity status and the perceptions of them held by novices as well. Harris-Perry (2011) in·*Sister Citizen: Shame, Stereotypes, and Black Women in America* echoes Hill Collins (2000), as both isolate the negative stereotypes that have inaccurately defined Black women as hypersexed, Mammy, or angry. Black female mentors must intentionally act against these prevailing beliefs while simultaneously providing trust, encouragement, support, and guidance to their White protégés.

White Pre-Service Teachers and Their Invisible Knapsacks

By contrast, WPTs enjoy the benefit of living in a society with a singular consciousness of self. In other words, their identity is defined by their own perceptions and not by the views of others (Marx, 2004). "Many, perhaps most, . . . white students in the U.S. think that racism doesn't affect them because they are not people of color; they do not see 'whiteness' as a racial identity" (McIntosh, 1988, p. 15). Normalcy in the minds of some White people is based in White beliefs, actions, and privileges; all that is non-White is characterized as deficient and exotic (McIntosh, 1988). When asked, WPTs will say they have no culture (Marx, 2004); American is their culture.

Being an American, for some White people, is the luxury of unexamined and undetectable social, economic, and political entitlements. McIntosh (1988, 1989) refers to these privileges as "unearned assets which [Whites] can count on cashing in each day, but about which [they are] 'meant' to remain oblivious" (McIntosh, 1988, p. 1). These assets are housed in an invisible knapsack, unknowingly worn by White people. Applicable examples from McIntosh's list of privileges include being a part of a culture that "gives little fear about ignoring the perspectives and powers of people of other races" (McIntosh, 1988, p. 7), and "[remaining] oblivious to the language and customs of persons of color who constitute the world's majority without feeling in [White] culture any penalty for such oblivion" (p. 8). Consequently, WPTs may consciously or unconsciously empower or disenfranchise others as predicated upon their belief systems, which align with mainstream norms. If WPTs fail to understand they have such power, they unwittingly perpetuate marginalization of the powerless.

In mentoring relationships, often WPTs assume White privilege. This phenomenon runs counter to the expectation that the superior, more experienced professional (BTE) provides feedback, advocacy, and counsel to the novice (WPT). Instances of White privilege in mentoring include occasions in which BTEs are unfairly reprimanded by their administrators, without investigations or inquiries, solely because of the displeasure of WPTs; not trusted (by administrators and WPTs) in their motivation to support WPTs; disregarded due to their perceived lack of knowledge, credentials, or experience; disrespected by WPTs, in communication and action; and evaded by WPTs who seek mentoring relationships elsewhere. When these actions occur, WPTs—and the administration that supports their actions—preserve the marginalization of BTEs. Moreover, when WPTs are not challenged to rethink or acknowledge their invisible advantage, "silence and denials surrounding privilege" (McIntosh, 1988, p. 18) act as political tools. Without guided introspection, WPTs unconsciously learn how to maintain the status quo, keeping the "thinking about equality or equity incomplete" (McIntosh, 1988, p. 18). WPTs need opportunities to challenge White privilege and the potential harmful effects in their future classrooms.

WPTs, Diverse Learners, and the Moral Imperative

America's teachers—past, present, and future—are principally White, female, and middle class, and most have lived culturally encapsulated lives; their places of worship, communities, and schools look similar to their White ethnic background. Meanwhile, schools are struggling to meet the academic demands of diverse learners. In 2007, Hill-Jackson, Sewell, and Waters warned:

> By the year 2010, 40 percent of learners in classrooms will be children of color, while the teaching population will remain around 85 percent white and female. . . . How, then, are teacher education programs addressing

the need to prepare White pre-service teachers (WPTs) for multicultural classrooms? (p. 175)

Given the rising diversity among the K–12 student population, there is a moral imperative to provide a culturally competent teacher in every classroom in America. White educators can have an opportunity to affect the achievement and learning outcomes of diverse K–12 learners due to their huge demographic presence in the field. Culturally responsive teaching is a framework for classroom instruction that leverages high academic achievement from K–12 students of color (Gay, 2000, 2002).

Taylor (2010) connects the importance of increasing student achievement of diverse learners by training WPTs in culturally responsive teaching. He cites research linking cultural discontinuity between schools and homes as a contributing factor to student failure. Emphasizing the need to close the cultural gap between home and school, WPT training should include culturally competent teaching practices. While Taylor (2010) lists a few culturally competent classroom practices, he emphasizes the importance of allowing WPTs to reflect about their culture, value systems, and biases toward others. Failing to allow WPTs to explore their beliefs encourages erroneous application of instructional and classroom discipline practices on diverse learners (Howard, 2003). WPT training in culturally responsive teaching allows positive support of the academic achievement of diverse learners (Gay, 2002; Howard, 2003) and requires WPTs to consider and use culturally based background knowledge of their students to illustrate examples, demonstrations, and concepts.

Additionally, diverse K–12 students learn best from teachers who embrace a social justice ideology. Villegas (2007) clarifies *social justice* as "a broad approach to education that aims to have all students reach high levels of learning and to prepare them all for active and full participation in a democracy" (p. 372). The research confirms that when diverse students feel culturally welcomed and affirmed in their classrooms, academic gains are made in all subject areas (Darling-Hammond, French, & Garcia-Lopez, 2002; Gay, 2002; Ladson-Billings, 2006, 2009; Marshall, 2002; Nieto, 2003).

Diversity training via cross-ethnic mentoring can help WPTs become culturally competent. Cross-ethnic mentoring between BTEs and WPTs offers a value-added component to teacher preparation programs because teacher educators and mentors "control the gates of social reproduction" (as quoted by Johnson-Bailey & Cervero, 2004, p. 16, from Margolis & Romero, 2001, p. 82). In other words, how a teacher is trained to think and behave is reflected in her classroom and therefore affects the ways in which social structures are reproduced. Buchner (2007) connects cross-cultural mentoring to diversity training by stating, "interaction of this nature has been found to change our thinking about others more than studying cultural differences or just talking about intolerance" (p. 223). Cross-cultural mentoring may help novice teachers unlearn bias, connect on deeper levels, and rouse culturally based talents. Similarly, when BTEs mentor WPTs, BTEs can nurture social justice, model cultural competency, and promote the assets of their culture. The relationship becomes the platform for interactions, discussions, and reflections needed for WPTs to develop culturally competent dispositions. Once WPTs develop dispositions for cultural competence, they can become more receptive to learning strategies that will increase the academic achievement of K–12 students of color. Accordingly, BTEs can be a conduit for the cultural growth of WPTs if they are given the strategies for effective cross-ethnic mentoring.

Recommendation: Supporting Cross-Ethnic Mentoring

The suggestions for cross-ethnic mentoring have been articulated in support of White mentors and novices of color, but there is a paucity of mentoring solutions for Black university mentors who desire to champion White students. Black faculty members may be unwilling or unsuccessful mentors at the university level if they lack the skills to nurture cross-ethnic relationships. If mentors of color are given the tools for supporting White students, then more positive relationships can be promoted between them. The strategies we suggest for university mentors of color who are interested in enhancing their capacity to mentor White students include (1) encouraging private critical reflection, (2) exhibiting and modeling empathy, (3) staying alert to communication styles, and (4) identifying and nurturing protégés with a disposition for social justice.

1. *Encourage WPTs' private critical reflection.* Critical reflection allows individuals to recover and examine personal histories and background circumstances that shape their ideas, actions, and influence on society (Kemmis, 1985). BTEs can encourage WPTs to critically reflect for the development of inclusive ideas that influence positive actions in the classroom (Howard, 2003). WPTs are unaware of the affect of White privilege; they must learn to look beyond White privilege to consider the cultural circumstances of others (McIntosh,

1988, 1989). As WPTs realize their unearned social power, they may react in anger, guilt, or complete denial (Hill-Jackson, 2007; Taylor, 2010). Having WPTs conduct private critical reflections strives to minimize these reactions so WPTs will be apt to accept whiteness and the responsibility of becoming culturally competent (Howard, 2003). BTEs may encourage private critical reflection through the following techniques: journaling, rhetorical questioning, discussion of articles or incidences in popular culture, the sharing of personal stories, and the inclusion of anonymous answer collection techniques (e.g., classroom response systems and online classroom suites). The use of these techniques privatizes critical reflection, allowing BTEs to help WPTs "hold up a mirror" for self-discovery and private introspection. Public forms of critical reflection may only exacerbate White privilege, causing WPTs to feel attacked or personally threatened.

2. *Exhibit and model empathy.* BTEs should exhibit and model empathy to facilitate students' understanding about culture. Researchers describe empathy in cross-cultural relationships as being "able to think and/or to act from another cultural perspective" (Bennett, 1986, as cited in McAllister and Irvine, 2000, p. 16). WPT reflection on White entitlements and the possibility of relinquishing the social construct of power can be an agonizing, guilt- and anger-filled process. BTEs who exhibit and model empathy teach WPTs nonjudgmental behavior patterns and how to value difference. Examples of exhibiting empathy toward WPTs include welcoming and engaging conversations about race without showing anger or discomfort (Johnson-Bailey & Cervero, 2004), framing race-based conversations within White cultural perspectives (Bennett, 1986), highlighting the individuality of each WPT (Johnson-Bailey & Cervero, 2004), and emphasizing values that cross cultural boundaries (e.g., American values such as democracy, competition, or self-preservation, and American exceptionalism) (Gay, 2000). Empathy recognizes differences without judgment. Empathy also cultivates an atmosphere of trust in the growth for the mentoring relationship. When BTEs exhibit empathy during cross-race mentoring, they model how WPTs should acknowledge and value differences.

3. *Stay alert to communication styles.* A chief principle of basic pedagogy is to "meet learners where they are." It is important for BTEs to take the time to think beyond their actions, but seriously contemplate verbal exchanges with WPTs. It is essential to remember that

WPTs bring certain images of otherness to their teacher training experience, so exchanges must counteract their preconceived ideas and stereotypes about persons of color. Conversations should respect a genteel tone and temperament because passionate communication styles may be misinterpreted by WPTs as aggressive and confrontational. Although many BTEs may find this approach to be a compromise to their cultural identity, the more conscious BTE understands that true relationships and growth for our protégés happen only when we meet them where they are, and not insist that they meet us where we are.

4. *Identify and cultivate WPTs with social justice ideologies.* Twenty-first-century schools are occupied by an entirely White teaching force while the student population is predominantly made up of diverse students. Darling-Hammond, Wise, and Klein (1997) propose that the changing demographics is prompting a new mandate in education, and:

> This new mission for education requires substantially more knowledge and radically different skills for teachers. . . . If all children are to be effectively taught, teachers must be prepared to address the substantial diversity in experiences children bring with them to school—the wide range of languages, cultures, exceptionalities, learning styles, talents, and intelligences that in turn requires an equally rich and varied repertoire of teaching strategies. (p. 2)

Given this demographic mandate, White teachers must learn to "reach across the racial divide . . . with a high degree of comfort and sincerity" (Johnson-Bailey & Cervero, 2004, pp. 9–10). Teachers in the twenty-first century must also have progressive dispositions about all types of differences and embrace a social justice ideology to be effective teachers for their K–12 learners. No longer can White teachers deny White privilege, "unearned race advantage and conferred dominance" (McIntosh, 1988, p. 15). BTEs have a unique position in teacher training programs; they can detect WPTs with a propensity for social justice ideology. BTEs can use cross-cultural mentoring to dissuade a disregard for cultural differences and nurture the talent and interests of WPTs through such activities as sharing critical knowledge about people of color; presenting at local and national conferences; involving undergraduates in research; sharing culturally responsive literature, curricula, and ideas; and supporting graduate school ambitions. These WPTs may become more effective educators with a broad range of experiences, attitudes, and strategies to support their future diverse K–12 learners.

Summary

When BTEs mentor WPTs they are obligated to reconcile the precepts of racism with the noble goals of mentoring. Cross-ethnic mentoring can positively affect WPTs who, in turn, affect the academic outcomes of their future diverse students. WPTs need to become culturally competent and increase their training in culturally responsive pedagogy to ensure the academic achievement of an increasingly diverse K–12 student population as there is no loftier moral imperative. Several strategies may be used by BTEs to encourage WPTs to develop cultural competency that buttresses student achievement. The authors suggest (1) encouraging WPTs' private critical reflection, (2) exhibiting and modeling empathy, (3) staying alert to communication styles, and (4) identifying and nurturing protégés with a disposition for social justice. The BTE–WPT mentoring dyad can be a powerful site for diversity training, helping novice teachers hone their cultural competence skills and expand their social justice lens.

References

Bennett, M. J. (1986). A developmental approach to training for intercultural sensitivity. *International Journal of Intercultural Relations, 10,* 179–196.

Bowman, S. R., Kite, M. E., Branscombe, N. R., & Williams, S. (1999). Developmental relationships of Black Americans in the academy. In A. J. Murrell, F. J. Crosby, & R. J. Ely (Eds.), *Mentoring dilemmas: Developmental relationships within multicultural organizations* (pp. 21–46). Mahwah, NJ: Lawrence Erlbaum Associates.

Buchner, R. D. (2007). *Building cultural intelligence (CQ): Nine megaskills.* Upper Saddle River, NJ: Pearson Education, Inc.

Darling-Hammond, L., French, J., Garcia-Lopez, S. P. (Eds.) (2002). *Learning to teach for social justice.* New York: Teachers College Press.

Darling-Hammond, L., Wise, A. E., & Klein, S. P. (1997). *A license to teach: Building a profession for 21st century schooling.* Boulder, CO: Westview.

Du Bois, W. E. B. (2003). *The souls of black folk.* New York: Barnes & Noble Books. (Original work published in 1903.)

Feagin, J. R. (2006). *Systemic racism: A theory of oppression.* New York: Routledge.

Gay, G. (2000). *Culturally responsive teaching: Theory, research, and practice.* New York: Teachers College Press.

Gay, G. (2002). Preparing for culturally responsive teaching. *Journal of Teacher Education, 53*(2), 106–116.

Harris-Perry, M. V. (2011). *Sister citizen: Shame, stereotypes, and Black women in America. For colored girls who've considered politics when being strong isn't enough.* New Haven, CT: Yale University Press.

Hill Collins, P. (2000). *Black feminist thought: Knowledge, consciousness, and the politics of empowerment.* New York: Routledge.

Hill-Jackson, V. (2007). Wrestling whiteness: Three stages of shifting multicultural education perspectives among white pre-service teachers. *Multicultural Perspectives, 9*(2), 29–35.

Hill-Jackson, V., Sewell, K. L., & Waters, C. (2007). Having our say about multicultural education. *Kappa Delta Pi Record, 43*(4), 174–181.

Howard, T. C. (2003). Culturally relevant pedagogy: Ingredients for critical teacher reflection. *Theory into Practice, 42*(3), 195–202.

Johnson-Bailey, J., & Cervero, R. M. (2004). Mentoring in Black and White: The intricacies of cross-cultural mentoring. *Mentoring and Tutoring, 12*(1), 7–22.

Kemmis, S. (1985). Action research and the politics of reflection. In D. Boud, R. Keogh, & D. Walker (Eds.), *Reflection: Turning experience into learning* (pp. 139–163). London: Kogan Page.

Kottak, C. P., & Kozaitis, K. A. (2012). *On being different: Diversity and multiculturalism in the North American mainstream* (4th ed.). New York: McGraw-Hill.

Ladson-Billings, G. (2006). Yes, but how do we do it? Practicing culturally relevant pedagogy. In J. Landsman & C. W. Lewis (Eds.), *White teachers/Diverse classrooms: A guide to building inclusive schools, promoting high expectations, and eliminating racism* (pp. 29–42). Sterling, VA: Stylus.

Ladson-Billings, G. (2009). *The dreamkeepers: Successful teachers of African American children* (2nd ed.). San Francisco: Jossey-Bass.

Margolis, E., & Romero, M. (2001). In the image and likeness: How mentoring functions in the hidden curriculum. In E. Margolis (Ed.), *The hidden curriculum in higher education* (pp. 79–96). New York: Routledge.

Marshall, P. L. (2002). *Cultural diversity in our schools.* Belmont, CA: Wadsworth Group.

Marx, S. (2004). Regarding whiteness: Exploring and intervening in the effects of white racism in teacher education. *Equity and Excellence in Education, 37*, 31–43.

McAllister, G., & Irvine, J. J. (2000). Cross cultural competency and multicultural teacher education. *Review of Educational Research, 70*(1), 3–24.

McIntosh, P. (1988). *White privilege and male privilege: A personal account of coming to see correspondences through the work in women's studies. Working Paper No. 189.* Wellesley, MA: Peggy McIntosh.

McIntosh, P. (1989, July/August). White privilege: Unpacking the invisible knapsack. *Peace and Freedom,* 10–12.

Murrell, J. J., & Tangri, S. S. (1999). Mentoring at the margin. In A. J. Murrell, F. J. Crosby, & R. J. Ely (Eds.), *Mentoring dilemmas: Developmental relationships within multicultural organizations* (pp. 211–224). Manwah, NJ: Lawrence Erlbaum Associates.

Nieto, S. (2003). *Affirming diversity: The sociopolitical context of multicultural education* (4th ed.). White Plains, NY: Allyn & Bacon.

Pitton, D. E. (2006). *Mentoring novice teachers: Fostering a dialogue process* (2nd ed.). Thousand Oaks, CA: Corwin Press.

Ragins, B. R. (2007). Diversity and workplace mentoring relationships: A review and positive social capital approach. In T. D. Allen & L. T. Eby (Eds.), *The Blackwell handbook of mentoring: A multiple perspectives approach* (pp. 281–300). Malden, MA: Blackwell Publishing.

Scandura, T. A., & Mezias, J. (2010). Assessing the state of cross cultural mentoring research. *Management Faculty Articles and Papers.* Miami, FL: University of Miami. Retrieved from http://scholarlyrepository.miami.edu/management_articles/1

Taylor, R. (2010). The role of teacher education programs in creating culturally competent teachers: A moral imperative for ensuring the academic success of diverse student populations. *Multicultural Education, 17*(3), 24–28.

Villegas, A. M. (2007). Dispositions in teacher education. *Journal of Teacher Education, 58*(5), 370–380.

REFLECTIONS ON TEACHING AND LEARNING ABOUT ANTIRACISM

Sue Peterson and Tracy Clark

Teaching the Antiracism: Theories and Foundations course was both a challenging and rewarding experience for the instructors. The course introduced students to a theoretical framework of antiracism and its applications. The required texts included Tatum's (1997) *Why Are All the Black Kids Sitting Together in the Cafeteria?* and Loewen's (2007) *Lies My Teacher Told Me: Everything Your American History Textbook Got Wrong*. A supplemental reading packet was also provided. Students explored the cultural and social aspects of racism and learned to use an antiracism framework in which to develop strategies to help dismantle racism as a form of oppression on both individual and systemic levels. Students discussed the concepts of disparity, privilege, and socialization as they relate to power. In addition, the constructs of prejudice, discrimination, oppression, institutional transformation and change, and social justice for personal and institutional analysis were studied.

Teaching this course was a wonderful opportunity to expose students to antiracism content, but the general demographics of the region did result in some limitations, one being that the majority of the students enrolled in the course were White (94%) and had limited experiences interacting with people of color. In addition, approximately 60% of the students indicated that this course was the first one they had ever taken that focused on antiracism or one that even included antiracism material. As one student indicated at the end of the course, "As I think about my racial identity now, I find it very interesting and a little sad. Before this class I had never thought of myself as White, even though being White has affected me for my entire life. . . . I am still learning and becoming aware of how White privilege affects my life and how racism affects everyone." In spite of the limitations, the majority of students commented on how the class helped them "view the world a bit differently."

In designing the course, it was strongly recommended by the university's antiracism team that the course be taught by one person of color and one White person to include both perspectives. Thus instructors were able to role model cross-cultural communication, collaboration, and mutual support for one another. In addition, although not necessary to the pedagogical approach of the course, in this instance both instructors were female.

Based on the instructors' antiracism training, it was determined that some of the critical areas for student learning outcomes include:

- Developing a sense of social identity, particularly identity related to race and culture
- Applying models of racial identity development
- Defining and differentiating between prejudice, discrimination, and oppression, and various forms of racism including individual, institutional, and cultural racism
- Examining the concept of power and its role in the structure, dynamics, and perpetuation of racism
- Critiquing racism as a system of oppression and its effect on one's self and others personally and systemically
- Analyzing the concepts of White privilege and Whiteness and their manifestations at the personal, cultural, institutional, and systemic levels in US society

The course used a seminar-style format that created an engaging learning environment, which promoted trust building among the students. This format was also useful in encouraging greater involvement of students in identifying barriers to talking honestly about course concepts. It was critical to initiate this type of discussion on the first day of class to gain a baseline of how students were thinking and feeling about these topics. It was also important to divide students into smaller discussion groups to provide them with an element of safety, particularly for students who have never really openly talked about race and who may have concerns about inadvertently offending someone or being judged. These discussions were the precursor to discussing the ground rules for course processes.

Because the instructors realized the potential emotional effect that these types of discussions can have, it was imperative to enlist the students' input in establishing basic ground rules for the class and their thoughts and ideas about these basic assumptions. Students came up with most of the general ground rules; however, it was also important to incorporate rules such as confidentiality, keeping an open mind to new information regardless of whether one agrees, suspending judgment, and practicing respectful communication. Maintaining the ground rules helped create a safe environment, which contributed to honest discussions, especially once students learned to trust that the rules were consistently "enforced" by both the instructors and themselves. Daily reminders of the rules as a point-of-process also helped to manage class dynamics effectively.

The instructors also proposed four primary assumptions of the course's content, which provided a foundation to begin open and honest discourse on racism:

- Race matters.
- Racism is not just a Black and White issue.
- Everyone has knowledge about race and are experts in their own way.
- Racism hurts everyone, not just people of color.

Instructors reassured students that it would be normal to feel a sense of discomfort and that emotions might surface during some of the discussions as they explore, deconstruct, and consider new information. It was helpful to discuss ways in which to navigate these potentially difficult class discussions in which students might feel angry or experience other painful feelings related to racism and White guilt. Having instructors representing two different races allowed students to identify with one or the other when grappling with emotional reactions to racism and White privilege.

An important pedagogical approach included the role of the instructors as facilitators rather than only lecturers. The instructors used a variety of facilitation processes for small and large group discussions, such as guided reflective journaling, in-class short writing assignments, and student facilitation of reading materials. Throughout the semester students reflected on concepts such as power, privilege, disparity, oppression, and racism. In reading students' journals, it was interesting to note how students engaged in understanding their own and others' social locations and the complexities of cross-cultural relationships, particularly in relation to their own racial identity development. Some student comments follow:

> [This course] has given me ways to talk about my racial identity and how to try to begin to conceive how people of color observe the world. . . . This class was also really the first time I realized how being White played out in my life and helped me get to where I am now even though that still hurts.

> This semester I began to feel differently about who I was, and what being a part of the White culture meant. . . . Learning about racism from the inside out has caused me to question who I am as a person, asking myself what should my duty and quest be to help end racial prejudice?

> Makes me wonder why conversations about race have never been told to me in school before.

> [Prior to this course] I went along with my days thinking that I wasn't participating in a broken system, but I was and it is a behemoth system that has an almost insurmountable fracture right down its center, with Whites and individuals who pass for White on one side and literally everybody else on the other side.

> Looking at the world through an antiracist lens has affected my life profoundly and I want to be able to continue to gain insight and knowledge that I will be able to pass on to my children, friends, and family.

The lack of racial diversity in class created opportunities and challenges in teaching and learning the antiracist content. For White students, this lack of diversity created a level of safety for them to be more candid and honest in their discussions that may not have existed if more people of color had been present. Although the homogeneity increased the likelihood of honest sharing and critical discourse during small group activities, there was potential for the discussion turning into "White bonding" experiences. Because students of color were underrepresented, those students did not experience the same level of safety in the classroom as White students. Therefore, the instructors encouraged participation from students of color, but were cognizant of safety factors and the risk of tokenization. This homogeneity did not allow opportunities for students to hear more diverse experiences, which was unfortunate because many of the White students had little prior exposure to racial diversity. Because of the noticeable lack of racial difference in the class, the skill to effectively engage in cross-cultural dialogue around race was not as fully developed as it could have been had there been more students of color present. However, there were opportunities within the classroom for individuals to learn how to become allies and provide support to one another, especially for students of color. Another challenge that emerged with the racial demographic of the course was teaching students the appropriate use of culturally competent language when discussing people of color. Students' use of words like "colored" or viewing differences as "weird" presented routinely in class. Students who were aware of this inappropriate use of language relied heavily on the instructors to mediate and rectify this vernacular. White guilt was an underlying constant throughout the course for students. Most students experienced some form of it to a greater or lesser degree. White guilt manifested among students as displaced anger at the instructors for suggesting that students had White privilege, being angry at the "atrocities" done to cultures of color, and being angry and frustrated that they didn't know how to undo it and the "unfairness" of it all. Some students experienced multiple forms of White guilt over the duration of a semester, but as one student commented, "the first and most important step to developing an antiracist identity is accepting the inequality among races. Whites must accept that racial oppression exists and that Whites continue to perpetuate it, both consciously and unconsciously." The instructors encouraged students to become aware of the feelings associated with White guilt, but stressed the futility of remaining stuck in those emotions. Although it was important to help White students manage their White guilt, it was very important not to ignore feelings experienced by students of color who equally needed to feel supported in expressing their hurt, anger, or other emotions that might have arisen as a result of their life experiences.

It is not unusual to experience some fears and anxiety related to teaching an antiracism course. Reflecting on the planning and teaching of this particular course, the instructors agree that it was helpful that they shared similar teaching philosophies and ideological understandings of racism. This increased the comfort and confidence in providing support for each other. Additionally, in teaching this type of course, it was beneficial for the instructors to critically reflect on their own social locations, racial identity development, and the type of support needed in teaching the course and to discuss these areas with one another.

Coteaching this course allowed the instructors to debrief with one another after class sessions, which was one of the most significant benefits. Although both instructors had similar experiences in the classroom, it was found upon reflection that each person's social location allowed her to perceive and see things through her unique lens that the other may not have grasped. Additionally, coteaching allowed for one instructor to pick up on dimensions of classroom dynamics that the other may not have realized while lecturing.

Because racial identity development is a process, both instructors and students had the potential to be emotionally "triggered" by media content, assigned readings, class discussion, and emotional reactions from others. Not only did instructors have to continually assess where they were in their own racial identity development, but they also had to understand the stages in which individual students might be, and the influence these stages might have on the class as a whole. Assessing from a developmental standpoint helps to understand that "triggers" need not be viewed as personal attacks, but as learning opportunities to recognize how racial identity should not be ignored in cross-racial relationships. The instructors gained a deeper personal understanding of their own racial identity development. Having to navigate "triggers," both interpersonally and intrapersonally, assisted in advancing their own antiracist skills.

It was rewarding for instructors to see their students experience "a-ha" moments. In this particular course, it was exciting to see those moments when students grew past resistance and defensiveness and began to see themselves in relation to racism in an unprecedented way as their racial identity development evolved. Students talked about how this class changed the way they "listen to others and see how people act." One student commented, "I know myself better and I have grown as a person, which has really had a positive impact on my life." Another stated, "This class, without a doubt, has had more impact on my life than any other class. The lessons that I have learned about being antiracist will affect the rest of my life."

Teaching this antiracism class required instructors to break typical cultural norms of not talking about racism and White privilege, and to have the expectation that their students do the same. Having genuine conversations about racial dynamics can broaden personal worldviews, which can affect how individuals interact with individuals and institutions. As we recognize the changes within a global society, it is imperative to expose students to a course such as this. It is a challenge to teach content that potentially confronts students' deeply imbedded belief systems, but it is a rewarding and effective method to develop the skills needed to engage in meaningful antiracist actions.

References

Loewen, J. W. (2007). *Lies my teacher told me: Everything your American history textbook got wrong.* New York: New Press.

Tatum, B. (1997). *Why are all the black kids sitting together in the cafeteria?* New York: Basic Books.

32

PREPARING NATIVITYMIGUEL TEACHERS TO WORK WITH CHILDREN OF COLOR FROM HIGH-POVERTY ENVIRONMENTS

L. Mickey Fenzel and Melodie Wyttenbach

NativityMiguel middle schools have received high praise for their effectiveness in meeting the educational, social, and spiritual needs of urban children of color placed at risk (Fenzel, 2009; Fenzel & Monteith, 2008; Podsiadlo & Philliber, 2003). With over sixty schools across the United States, the NativityMiguel Network seeks to break "the cycle of poverty through education" (NativityMiguel Network of Schools, 2009). Like so many urban schools where the vast majority of students are from underserved minority groups, most of the teachers are middle and upper middle class and White. This configuration can potentially place students further at risk for obtaining an education that fails to relate to their cultural backgrounds and to provide them with the skills needed for success in higher education and tomorrow's workplace.

In this paper, we examine ways in which administrators and teachers in NativityMiguel middle schools take part in conversations about race, culture, and poverty to better prepare teachers to engage their students in a high-quality educational experience that is culturally relevant. These conversations are central to the preparation and professional development of the teachers for these schools that will help them educate and care for their students.

NativityMiguel schools face a situation common in many urban schools for students placed at risk in which most of their teachers are White and most of their students either African-American or Latina/o (Fenzel, 2009; NativityMiguel Network of Schools, 2011). Such racial and cultural differences between students and teachers suggest that teachers (and administrators) need to receive considerable preparation and mentoring to meet the educational needs of their students. As researchers (Conner, 2010; Delpit, 2006) have pointed out, White teacher candidates often harbor deficiency views of urban children of color that affect their teaching practices.

The task of preparing teachers for work in high-poverty, high-minority schools is often made more difficult by the lack of awareness that many White teachers have of their own status and privilege, together with the resistance they have to examining these issues (Locke, 2005; Mueller & O'Connor, 2007). As some research (Bales & Safford, 2011) has shown, many candidates enter urban teacher preparation programs with little awareness of the social and political structures that affect urban children's access to good-quality education and often think that children and their caregivers need only to work harder to extricate themselves from economic poverty. However, to become culturally competent and effective educators of children who are members of underserved or oppressed groups, middle-class and upper middle-class White teacher candidates, as well as those who are not White, must have an understanding of their privileged status and the social justice issues that accompany it (Allen & Rossatto, 2009).

A possible means of expanding beginning teachers' awareness is to include issues of bias, discrimination, institutional racism, power, and White privilege as topics for critical examination in their pre-service and professional development programs. As is suggested by critical race theory, these teachers must be challenged to view the world from the lens of cultures other than their own to examine critically what Delpit (1995/2006) has termed the *culture of power* and assumptions about White as normative (McIntosh, 1998). In addition, it is essential for beginning teachers to become knowledgeable of the cultures of the families and children at their school and to understand that, even for a small school, diverse perspectives exist within the community served by the school (Bales & Safford, 2011).

The Present Study

Data for the study reported here come from personal interviews and electronic communications conducted or facilitated by each of the authors independently. In all, interviews and other input were obtained from thirteen

participants, twelve of whom were administrators and one a teacher, representing eleven NativityMiguel schools. Questions addressed to the interviewees focused on how teachers are prepared to provide culturally relevant
instruction and interact effectively with students and parents, the assumptions about the students and areas of resistance that teachers—especially
White teachers—bring and how they are addressed, and the nature of the
materials that are used to facilitate the conversations about race, culture, and
poverty.

Recent data on the NativityMiguel schools (NativityMiguel Network of
Schools, 2009), which number approximately sixty across the United States
with a mean enrollment of seventy-one students, shows that 52% of students
are identified as African-American and 39% as Latina/o. In addition, 87% of
students qualify for the federal free and reduced meals program. With respect
to teachers, 76% self-identify as Caucasian or White, 15% as African-American
or Black, and 6% as Latino/a. Nine of the eleven participants in the present
study are White and nine are women.

Among the over 400 teachers in the schools, 48% are fully certified and
22% are first- or second-year full-time *volunteer*, or intern, teachers—recent
college graduates who commit to a minimum of two years of teaching in
their schools. Although most of the volunteer teachers have had prior community service experience in urban settings, most have had very little if any
classroom teaching experience. These data suggest that many teachers in
NativityMiguel schools have lacked the preemployment preparation to be
effective teachers of their students. (A further analysis of the effects of having
a large number of volunteer teachers on the education of students in Nativity-
Miguel schools can be found elsewhere [Fenzel & Flippen, 2006].)

Findings

New Teacher Misunderstandings and Assumptions

A number of the administrators interviewed indicated that some inexperienced teachers arrive with some misconceptions of the students that need to
be addressed. Most common among these misconceptions is the notion that
most of the students are deficient in their academic aptitude. One principal
reported, for example, that she has heard teachers make comments to students such as, "You are very articulate," indicating an expectation that students at the school are deficient in their expressive language skills and being
"articulate" represented an exception to the rule. Other teachers hold

the perceptions that most of the children are troublemakers who are disrespectful and rude. Administrators also reported that in several cases, new and inexperienced teachers project a disposition of needing to "save" the children from their current life circumstances and trajectories. Certainly, this is more likely to be the case when teachers hold deficiency perceptions of the children.

Also among inexperienced teachers' initial dispositions is their perception that they know how to teach urban children, believing that their students would learn as they did in school. They also often tend to infer motivations of a lack of care or desire to achieve for some student behaviors, such as failing to complete home assignments, when difficult home situations of which they are unaware may be the main reasons. Often, teachers want to hold the parents responsible for any challenges that students present.

Pre-Service Workshops and Professional Development

Administrators at all NativityMiguel schools involved in this study indicated that they hold summer meetings and educational workshops to address misconceptions and dispositions that undermine new teachers' effectiveness and are often resistant to change. In some cases, the summer preparation includes the reading of articles or a book to serve as a springboard for the ensuing discussions. Among the assigned readings reported by school administrators are Beverly Tatum's *Why Are All the Black Kids Sitting Together in the Cafeteria?*, Lisa Delpit's *Other People's Children,* and Ron Suskind's *A Hope in the Unseen.* Some administrators favor articles over books for reading and discussion that address specific issues that surfaced the previous academic year. Readings on White privilege, economic poverty, and the racial differences in achievement test scores were cited by several interviewees as among these topics. In many cases, consultants with experience in educating urban children and working with urban families provide workshops and ongoing discussion sessions that help beginning teachers meet the educational needs of the students. One of the school principals interviewed discussed the value that excursions into the students' neighborhoods, which include the students' elementary schools and home visits, have had for enhancing beginning teachers' understanding of the kinds of resources that children have available to them outside school.

Two of the participants in the study indicated that Ruby Payne's controversial work on urban poverty was used as a focus for teacher workshops. Using this particular work raises questions about what perspectives are being used and who is leading the conversations about race and the so-called culture of poverty that, as Gorski (2008) has pointed out, can derail the important focus on sociopolitical conditions that maintain the cycle of poverty. Well-meaning presentations meant to stimulate critical examinations and deep learning may end up further reinforcing and solidifying deficit attitudes about the children and families that the teachers are serving.

To facilitate White teachers' understanding of the issues that affect immigrant Latina/o children and families that are served in several of the NativityMiguel schools, one school hosted a full-day program led by three Latino community leaders who addressed national and local issues affecting Latina/o immigrants. Topics included struggles with the culture shock experienced and social acceptance in the United States, and immigration issues and reactions to the DREAM Act legislation (led by an immigration attorney). This *Walk in My Shoes* program, along with teachers' participation in Latino cultural events, has helped teachers structure meaningful and effective learning experiences for their students and reduce their deficit thinking.

Several schools focus significant summer workshops and discussions, as well as those held throughout the school year, on biases that the teachers bring to their work, many of which they may not be initially aware. One administrator was clear that helping young, inexperienced teachers change the way they approach the children and parents requires a great deal of ongoing reflection and conversation led by a facilitator who will challenge teachers to uncover their prejudices and misconceptions to avoid placing negative value judgments on children's behaviors. This work helps them to reframe student academic challenge or failure as something that they, the teachers, need to take responsibility for and examine how they may have contributed to that failure. One administrator indicated that the work to bring most young, inexperienced teachers to the point of being comfortable and effective urban educators can take two or more years.

At several NativityMiguel schools, beginning teachers often live together in a house located near the school (Fenzel, 2009). Together with the carefully led discussions in which they participate in their residences, the experience of living in or close to the neighborhoods in which many of their students reside helps these teachers understand the lives of their students better and even participate in the life of the community.

While in operation from 2006 to 2012, the national network of Nativity-Miguel schools offered workshops for teachers from across the country providing opportunities for teachers and administrators to engage in conversations about educating the children who attend their schools. Both authors of this chapter had the opportunity to attend many of these meetings as workshop leaders and participants. These meetings, together with our visits to and involvements with several NativityMiguel schools over the past several years, have shown us that teachers receive consistent messages that the children they are teaching are children with promise and assets rather than deficits. As the NativityMiguel Network of Schools (2009) website emphasized, the education that the students receive is reflective of the culture of the students' communities. Teachers receive consistent messages that the schools expect them to embody a perception of the students as students of promise rather than students at risk and to teach with both head and heart, which is to say with academic challenge and caring support.

William Ayers (2001) has discussed how terms such as *culturally deprived* and *at-risk* have misrepresented children of color and led teachers to hold lower expectations of their students and misrepresent their behaviors in school. NativityMiguel schools are clear in their approach to helping teachers see extraordinary potential in their students and exceptional value in their cultures. By providing ongoing professional development and regular mentoring, the school leaders also help teachers apply this understanding to the everyday educational experience that they structure for their students.

References

Allen, R., & Rossatto, C. (2009). Does critical pedagogy work with privileged students? *Teacher Education Quarterly, 36*(1), 163–180.

Ayers, W. (2001). *To teach: The journey of a teacher* (2nd ed.). New York: Teachers College Press.

Bales, B. L., & Safford, F. (2011). A new era in the preparation of teachers for urban schools: Linking multiculturalism, disciplinary-based content, and pedagogy. *Urban Education, 46,* 953–974. doi: 10.1177/0042085911400320

Conner, J. O. (2010). Learning to unlearn: How a service-learning project can help teacher candidates to reframe urban students. *Teaching and Teacher Education, 26,* 1170–1177. doi: 10.1016/j.tate.2010.02.001

Delpit, L. (1995/2006). *Other people's children: Cultural conflict in the classroom.* New York: New Press.

Delpit, L. (2006). Lessons from teachers. *Journal of Teacher Education, 57,* 220–231. doi: 10.1177/0022487105285966

Fenzel, L. M. (2009). *Improving urban middle schools: Lessons from the Nativity schools.* Albany: State University of New York Press.

Fenzel, L. M., & Flippen, G. M. (2006, April). *Student engagement and the use of volunteer teachers in alternative urban middle schools.* Paper presented at the annual meeting of the American Educational Research Association, San Francisco.

Fenzel, L. M., & Monteith, R. H. (2008). Successful alternative middle schools for urban minority children: A study of Nativity schools. *Journal of Education for Students Placed at Risk, 13*, 381–401. doi: 10.1080/10824660802427686

Gorski, P. (2008). Beyond the "culture of poverty": Resources on economic justice. *Multicultural Perspectives, 10*, 27–29. doi: 10.1080/15210960701869488

Locke, S. (2005). Institutional, social, and cultural influences on the multicultural perspectives of preservice teachers. *Multicultural Perspectives, 7*, 20–28.

McIntosh, P. (1998). *White privilege and male privilege: A personal account of coming to see correspondences through work in women's studies* (unpublished manuscript). Wellesley College, Wellesley, MA.

Mueller, J., & O'Connor, C. (2007). Telling and retelling about self and "others": How pre-service teachers (re)interpret privilege and disadvantage in one college classroom. *Teaching and Teacher Education, 23*, 840–856.

NativityMiguel Network of Schools. (2009). *Breaking the cycle of poverty through education.* Retrieved from http://www.nativitymiguelschools.org/

NativityMiguel Network of Schools. (2011, February). *Executive summary report of national data 2010.* Retrieved from http://www.nativitymiguelschools.org/

Podsiadlo, J. J., & Philliber, W. W. (2003). The Nativity Mission Center: A successful approach to the education of Latino boys. *Journal of Education for Students Placed at Risk, 8*(4), 419–428.

33

MOVING FROM THE MARGINS TO THE INTERSECTIONS

Using Race as a Lens for Conversations About Oppression and Resistance

Phyllis M. May-Machunda

S ince the mid-1990s, I frequently have taught The Dynamics of Prejudice and Oppression, an interdisciplinary general studies course, primarily for upper-class undergraduates at a predominantly white university in the upper Midwest. This course comparatively investigates racism, sexism, heterosexism, classism, and ableism as systems of oppression; identifies commonalities in the structures, dynamics, and tactics that maintain these oppressive systems; and explores effective strategies for dismantling these oppressions through processes of deep reading and discussion. The purpose of this article is to iterate lessons learned over the years of teaching this course and illuminate an approach that relies on an examination of race and racism as a foundation for revealing understandings useful in the study of other systems of oppression.

Dynamics of Prejudice and Oppression emerged out of ongoing conversations between my colleague, Suzanne Cataldi, a white feminist, who at the time was an assistant professor of Continental philosophy, and me, an African-American folklorist and an assistant professor of American Multicultural Studies. Our discussions uncovered similar desires to manage challenging classroom dynamics and student attitudes toward topics of race and gender, and to nurture critical perspectives toward these topics anchored in social justice. By comparing the resistance by students in both of our classes to exposure to issues of racism and sexism, we uncovered common themes in the experiences of targets of these oppressive systems, and in the resistive strategies of those targeted. We also embraced the need to unpack dynamics of discrimination and oppression in racism, sexism, heterosexism, classism, and ableism in ways that informed and empowered students as well as respected targeted groups. With mutual resolve, we guided students to think more critically about each of these systems of oppression, their contexts, and the ranges of constructive responses that might effectively dismantle them. We compiled interdisciplinary readings and structured the course for students to critically analyze them through writing and group dialogue. After examining definitions of prejudice, discrimination, oppression, privilege, and social identity, we reframed these concepts within frameworks of oppression, highlighting both their personal and systemic dimensions. Working collaboratively with our students, we identified and examined a spectrum of strategies that structure and perpetuate pervasive discrimination, while viewing oppression, in part, as a construction of difference in which pervasive discrimination was persistently and synergistically directed toward a group. As a result, we explored barriers to education, employment, and housing as well as vehicles for the delivery of discrimination, such as language, media imagery, violence, and legislation and judicial decisions. Students then discussed and debated current issues central to each of the systems of oppression. Through these processes, both students and instructors deepened their understandings of the dynamics, strategies, structures, and interrelationships of each form of oppression.

After team-teaching this course with me twice, Sue moved to another university and the offering of this course stalled. A couple of semesters later, I taught it once with a different assistant professor, who offered strong insights into conceptions of justice but exhibited little internalized understanding of the costs of discrimination or the power of generative dialogue to build shared understanding in the classroom.

After a few more years, I began to teach this course by myself, and biennially, I have continued to do so to the present, strengthening the course each time I offer it. In its new configuration, I have grounded the course in an understanding of systemic oppression rather than in questions of prejudice and discrimination. By placing a greater emphasis on the ways that policies, strategies, and practices link to political, social, and economic ideologies, students have been able to connect ideologies with their consequences on the lives of communities of color. This approach simultaneously lifts up the voices of students and communities of color and opens opportunities for white students to be able to move beyond feeling that they personally are blamed for their white identities, while building a foundation for all students to understand the situations and struggles of communities of color, and their stances to achieve equity and justice.

From the standpoint of systemic oppressions, I have situated the foundation of this course in perspectives of race and racism because too often the experiences of people of color have not been central to other analyses of other forms of oppression, as noted by Black feminists (Hull, Bell-Scott, & Smith, 1982; James, Foster, & Guy-Sheftall, 2009). Making the lived experiences of people of color in the complexities of their lives central to the course and ensuring that students hear the voices of those who have been targeted and traditionally voiceless are fundamental tenets of antiracism, social justice, and Black feminism, and provides a replicable strategy for the study of other systems of oppression (Adams, Bell, & Griffin, 1997; Adams, Blumenfeld, Casteneda, & Hackman, 2000; Hill Collins, 2002).

Beginning the examination of oppressions through the lenses and theories of racism and antiracism and social justice efforts and then moving into exploration of other forms of oppression provides several important tools for students' understanding of oppressive systems:

• Grounding in antiracist perspectives elucidates racial structures in ways that make it difficult for people of color to be overlooked when we expand to an examination of other oppressive systems. In this approach, students cannot assume that only people of color are raced. By exploring their own multiple social identities and locations, students begin to recognize that all people in the United States are assigned multiple identities that offer them packages of benefits or deficits that can be invoked differentially in various situations. Beginning with an exercise exploring ways all of us are socially located in the racial, gender, class, and disability structures of our society, and operate out of multiple identities in those structures, students discover that these structures and dynamics affect them personally. Students learn that building identity awareness in each area is a developmental process, and is an arena for continual growth and personal development (Hardiman & Jackson, 1992; Tatum, 2003). Students can also apply their analyses not only to their personal development but to the multicultural development of organizations and institutions in their communities and the interactions of those organizations with communities of color (Jackson & Holvino, 1988). The lessons of racial identity can shed light on and reveal questions about students' identities, roles, and relationships in other systems of oppression.

- Articulating a stance in social justice is also fundamental. Social justice is based in a belief in equity, an examination of the concepts of equality and fairness, an investigation of the ethic of caring, and an exploration of justice as both a process and a goal, culminating in a moral obligation to seek effective and appropriate solutions for dismantling oppression (Hill Collins, 2002). This stance commits to addressing injustice through transformative change.

- Through the concept of race as a social construction, students gain an understanding of the ways practices of social categorization operate. By wrestling with the idea of race as an idea marking otherness that is not based in biological attributes, students discover that the concept of race lumps together a large number of individuals who may share very few physical characteristics except arbitrary and broadly defined features. They then seek to investigate the social meanings and effects of the racial labels on those inside and outside the labeled group and, as a result, can begin to question social categories structured by other systems of oppression.

- The racial lens also highlights how marked differences operate through a hierarchical structure that rewards and accrues positive value for some, while simultaneously stigmatizing others. The racial construct in the United States provides clear examples of the bifurcated hierarchy marking people as white or nonwhite, and how, at times, that structure has flexed and morphed in order to maintain that hierarchy. Antiracism and social construction of difference theories suggest that the racial construct, like other hierarchies of oppression, is not really about perceived biological or cultural differences, such as skin color, physical features, or even minority ethnic or religious traditions. Instead, racism is the manifestation of social, economic, and political power arrangements that, through hierarchy and pervasive coverage, privilege one group over another, using physical or cultural characteristics as the marker of difference to distinguish and marginalize those who differ from the dominant group. By critiquing and reframing markings of arbitrary differences, such as those of race or gender, as structures of power, students can apply critical thinking skills to illuminate and investigate power dynamics in other systems of oppression.

- Antiracism theory suggests that the hierarchical arrangement of racial oppression generates at least three levels of power: the power that the dominant group directly or indirectly wields over the targeted group (the most commonly recognized aspect of oppressive power); race privilege, or the power that accrues benefits for the dominant group through the hierarchical arrangement; and the most potent power, the power that socializes us all into knowing the racial rules and our roles and social locations in the hierarchical arrangements (Barndt, 2007). Although the specifics differ, students rapidly begin to grasp the commonalities and unique complexities of power dynamics in other systems of oppression. The notion of privilege, so deeply explored by scholars such as McIntosh (1990), Kendall (2006), Rothenberg (2000, 2004), and Wise (2008), among others, illuminates that hierarchies of oppression are about establishing, controlling, and maintaining power and access to resources to benefit the group with the most valued characteristics. Exploration of the concept of privilege in the racial construct thus can shed light on ways dominant group privilege, as a package of unearned benefits, works and is bestowed on those who support and conform to the ideals and standards of the dominant group in other systems of oppression.

• Systemic oppression is kept in place through strategies that work similarly across systems of oppression. A few selected strategies from systemic racial oppression illustrate this point: *invisibility,* or a taking for granted of the privileges of the dominant group as well as obliviousness to circumstances and experiences of people from the targeted side of the hierarchy; *normalization,* that the racial rules and routines are unquestioningly accepted because most people assume that this is the way things are or are supposed to be; *marginalization,* or isolation of those targeted and stigmatized; and *socialization,* which makes sure that the rules of interaction for privileged and targeted groups are taught, internalized, and adhered to through the numerous societal institutions and social networks such as education, religion, government, and media, reinforcing the social order. These strategies not only illustrate the dynamics of systems and institutions in racializing society, but offer insights into other systems of oppression.

• Although exploration of race and racism in isolation allows for a focused and detailed examination of race as a social construction and is a critical first step, no racialized experience is solely about race alone, because no person has race as their singular social location. The process of moving from the margins of oppression to its intersections is a key component of this course. Intersections highlight the interdependence of various systems of oppression and allows students to realize that even within a system of oppression, not all participants have similar experiences, an idea vividly articulated in James et al. (2009). Black feminist thought advocates for examination of both the simultaneity of oppressions particularly affecting women of color and also the multiplicities of experiences within any group (Hill Collins, 2002). When we move from the margins of race alone to its intersections with gender, sexual orientation, ability, and class, we complexify racialized experiences and deepen the understanding of the dynamics of oppression across various systems.

• Finally, becoming aware of the costs of oppression calls for discovering community traditions of resistance and effective, transformative strategies for systemic change. Students need ways to direct the emotional investments from their newly acquired understandings of oppression toward positive change. Because diagnosis determines treatment, students seek to identify remedies that appropriately address the underlying structures that generate systemic racism and other oppressions. Like strategies of oppression, these strategies of resistance, dismantlement, and transformative change may have unique qualities in different systems of oppression, but they also share commonalities across those systems.

I believe these lessons have helped me reduce student resistance to thinking about oppression. In fact, many students seem to welcome the opportunity to gain skills in addressing issues of racism and oppression and acquire tools for embracing antiracism and antioppression. In addition to offering practical and critical thinking skills, I think this course develops emotional and social interactional competencies. Several students have told me that this course has been life changing for them, and I too have been enriched by the transformative journey I share with them through this course, and as a result, acknowledge that my own teaching skills and understandings have become stronger from this journey.

References

Adams, M., Bell, L. A., & Griffin, P. (Eds.). (1997). *Teaching for diversity and social justice: A sourcebook*. New York: Routledge.

Adams, M., Blumenfeld, W. J., Castaneda, C., & Hackman, H. W. (Eds.). (2000). *Readings for diversity and social justice: An anthology on racism, antisemitism, sexism, heterosexism, ableism, and classism*. New York: Routledge.

Barndt, J. R. (2007). *Understanding and dismantling racism: The twenty-first century challenge to white America*. Minneapolis, MN: Fortress Press.

Hardiman, R., & Jackson, B. W. (1992). Racial identity development: Understanding racial dynamics in college classrooms and on campus. In M. Adams (Ed.), *Promoting diversity in college classrooms: Innovative responses for the curriculum, faculty, and institutions. New directions for teaching and learning* (Vol. 52, pp. 21–37). San Francisco: Jossey Bass.

Hill Collins, P. (2002). *Black feminist thought: Knowledge, consciousness, and the politics of empowerment* (2nd ed. rev.). New York: Routledge.

Hull, G. T., Bell-Scott, P., & Smith, B. (1982). *All the women are white, all the blacks are men, but some of us are brave: Black women's studies.* Old Westbury, NY: Feminist Press.

Jackson, B., & Holvino, E. (1988). Developing multicultural organizations. *Journal of Religion and the Applied Behavioral Sciences, 9*(2), 14–19.

James, S. M., Foster, F. S., & Guy-Sheftall, B. (2009). *Still brave: The evolution of black women's studies.* New York: Feminist Press.

Kendall, F. E. (2006). *Understanding white privilege: Creating pathways to authentic relationships across race.* New York: Routledge.

McIntosh, P. (1990). Unpacking the knapsack of white privilege. *Independent School, 49*(2), 31–36.

Rothenberg, P. S. (2000). *Invisible privilege: A memoir about race, class, and gender.* Lawrence: University Press of Kansas.

Rothenberg, P. S. (2004). *White privilege: Essential readings on the other side of racism.* New York: Worth.

Tatum, B. D. (2003). *"Why are all the black kids sitting together in the cafeteria?" And other conversations about race.* New York: Basic Books.

Wise, T. J. (2008). *White like me: Reflections on race from a privileged son.* Brooklyn, NY: Soft Skull Press.

LETTERS TO OUR TEACHERS

Black and Latino Males Write About Race in the Classroom

Yolanda Sealey-Ruiz and Chance W. Lewis

Teachers, I realize that there is a pink elephant in almost every educational setting that we refuse to acknowledge . . . and that is race. That word seems to bring out virulent feelings in people.

—Gerald, twelfth grade

Any teacher who has received a personal letter from a student is familiar with the special feelings it engenders. Whether the letter's content praises us for how we've made a difference in the student's life or admonishes us for something we could have done differently in the classroom, most teachers are moved by the fact that someone who learned with us and from us takes the time to write us a letter. In an era where texting, tweeting, and posting to Facebook have become the common modes of communication, the meaning of a personal letter is not lost on teachers. No matter the weight of words or intent of the student's thoughts, the personal letter is inherently rich with meaning; it is a medium that connotes intimacy, purpose, and resolve—writing a letter to someone takes much more commitment than sending a text or making a telephone call.

As a form of communication, letter writing provides a way for the writer to put onto the page what may not be possible to verbalize to the intended in person. It should be no surprise, then, that a letter can be an effective tool for students who are marginalized in schools to have their voices heard.

The authors of this chapter are all too familiar with a segment of our school population whose voices are routinely silenced in our classrooms—Black and Latino males. Our many years of teaching in K–12 settings, and our current work in schools that serve Black and Latino boys, prompted us to create an assignment intended to help amplify the voices of some of our high school Black and Latino male students. We asked ten of them to use the pen to tell their teachers, past and present, how they feel about the ways race has positively or negatively affected their classroom learning experiences. They were asked to muse about one teacher or a collective of teachers who had taught them in high school. We instructed them to speak from the heart, and what the letters of these young men made clear was the following: (a) a desire to be respected, (b) a belief that teachers should have high expectations for them, and (c) the need to have conversations about the way race affects their lives in and out of school.

The purpose of this chapter is to share the perspectives of this group as a way to learn what troubles Black and Latino male high school students most about race in the classroom. The voices of the ten letter writers can help teachers understand why it is important to talk about the notion of race, particularly with students of color within this gender and age group. Furthermore, it can offer an instructional practice that can solicit generative conversations around race in the classroom.

Letter Writing to Communicate a Purpose

When we think of letters that changed our society, we may immediately think of Dr. Martin Luther King, Jr.'s *Letter from a Birmingham Jail.* Nearly fifty years ago, on Good Friday in 1963, Dr. King and a group of Blacks marched into downtown Birmingham to protest segregation laws and were arrested. Eight White clergymen in Birmingham wrote a letter asking the Blacks in the town to cease demonstrations. Their letter appeared in the town's main newspaper. In response, King wrote a letter from his Birmingham cell—a letter that marked a turning point in the American Civil Rights Movement. His purpose for writing his letter was clear:

> I think I should indicate why I am here in Birmingham, since you have been influenced by the view that argues against "outsiders coming in." I

have the honor of serving as president of the Southern Christian Leadership Conference, an organization operating in every southern state, with headquarters in Atlanta, Georgia. We have some eighty-five affiliated organizations across the South, and one of them is the Alabama Christian Movement for Human Rights. Frequently we share staff, educational and financial resources with our Affiliates. Several months ago the affiliate here in Birmingham asked us to be on call to engage in a nonviolent direct action program if such were deemed necessary. We readily consented, and when the hour came we lived up to our promise. So I, along with several members of my staff, am here because I was invited here. I am here because I have organizational ties here.

But more basically, I am in Birmingham because injustice is here. . . . Moreover, I am cognizant of the interrelatedness of all communities and states. I cannot sit idly by in Atlanta and not be concerned about what happens in Birmingham. Injustice anywhere is a threat to justice everywhere.

In his letter, Dr. King is speaking to a particular audience (eight White clergymen) about a specific problem (racial inequality) and calling for a clear answer (an equal society). The authenticity and directness in which his letter is written reveals a clear sense of purpose and a desire to connect with his audience around a solution to the racial divide that exists (then and now) in America. There is an urgency in Dr. King's letter, an expression that if the audience of his letter doesn't move toward creating positive changes for the Blacks oppressed under Jim Crow laws in Birmingham, there would be further protests and negative outcomes for both the writer (and who he represents) and the audience (the White clergy and White America).

We find this same sense of urgency in the letters of the ten youth who share their missives here. Like King, these young men have a clear sense of purpose and a specific call to action for their audience. The themes that were consistent in the letters included (a) teachers' low expectations, (b) feelings of both invisibility and hypervisibility, (c) disappointment with the way teachers were not living up to their teaching responsibility, and (d) feeling misunderstood. We understand that reading the findings of this study may prove to be upsetting to teachers, particularly those who work hard with all of their students, including their Black and Latino males. However, the question teachers should ask themselves as they read, no matter how difficult it is to do so, is whether they might be culpable or how they might make a difference in changing their students' realities.

Letter Writing as a Means of Validating One's Perspective

In 1963 when James Baldwin published his address, "A Talk to Teachers," in the *Saturday Review* after delivering it as a speech in New York City, America's race relations were in a fragile state. As an active member of the Civil Rights Movement, but not a teacher himself, Baldwin expressed an urgency for teachers of the Negro child to "go for broke." "A Talk to Teachers," which reads as a letter to educators, conveys a warning, as did *A Letter from Birmingham Jail,* and forebodes the consequences of continued inequality in America:

> Let's begin by saying that we are living through a very dangerous time. Everyone in this room is in one way or another aware of that. We are in a revolutionary situation, no matter how unpopular that word has become in this country. . . . To any citizen of this country who figures himself as responsible—and particularly those of you who deal with the minds and hearts of young people—must be prepared to "go for broke." Or to put it another way, you must understand that in the attempt to correct so many generations of bad faith and cruelty, when it is operating not only in the classroom but in society, you will meet the most fantastic, the most brutal, and the most determined resistance. There is no point in pretending that this won't happen. (Baldwin, 1985, p. 325)

In her article "Goin' for Broke: Reaping the Rewards of Teaching Toward Cultural and Linguistic Diversity," Haddix (2010) expounds on Baldwin's cry for teachers to "go for broke." As she reflects on her own "talk to teachers," she writes, "My task like Baldwin's is to impress upon today's audience of new and practicing teachers that there is a lot at stake. For too many education is a matter of life or death" (p. 84).

The youth* who responded to this assignment were given the directive, "What would you say if you had the opportunity to speak from your heart to your teachers about issues of race in school? Please start your letter with Dear Teacher(s):" Although this assignment was given in a class of eleventh and twelfth graders where students were accustomed to discussing controversial topics, the explicit opportunity to write a letter to a teacher about the contentious topic of race was a first for all of them. As part of their racial literacy development (Sealey-Ruiz, 2011), the students were given one class period to write a letter "from the heart"—revealing the first feelings that

---

*All student names are pseudonyms.

come to mind—to a specific teacher or a group of teachers they've had during their years in high school. This assignment was treated as a brainstorming–freewriting assignment. Students were given ten minutes to jot down words and phrases to use in their letters. Then they used the remaining class period (thirty minutes) to write their letters. The students were not given the usual opportunity to work on multiple drafts of their work; however, students are now deciding whether to continue working on their letters and "go public" by sharing them with other teachers in their school as a way to make their perspectives clear and their desires known. Writing letters can be a most effective way to share one's perspective and be explicit about what the writer expects from the reader.

This letter writing project occurred during the first week of a new school semester. It was the first assignment given to a group of young men, most of whom had taken a customized English class with the first author. The ten students who contributed letters to this project were students at an alternative high school on the East Coast. The students, all of whom self-identify as Black or Latino, are members of UMOJA, an all-male, in-school mentoring program designed to develop students' academic and social skills. Sunset Hills Academy-East (SHAE)† is one of four public schools in a consortium that serves undercredited and overaged, mostly Black and Latino students. The first author has taught the young men in this mentoring program for three years. The course, UMOJA Readers and Writers (URW), seeks to encourage and center the voices and perspectives of these students who are usually silenced in their other classes and in society at large. In this class, students were presented with a culturally responsive pedagogy meant to inspire their critique of society and their schooling experiences.

The letters are not directed solely at the teachers at SHAE. Because SHAE is a transfer school that serves older high school students, many of the students, including the young men in the URW class, have attended one or more high schools before arriving to SHAE. Some of the letters reflected learning experiences in other educational settings.

Framing the Letters Project

Examining the experiences of African-American PhD students at a predominantly White institution provided keen insight for the authors' understanding of the themes that emerged from the letters. In their article "The

---

†Pseudonym.

Experiences of African American Ph.D. Students at a Predominately White Carnegie I-Research Institution," Lewis, Ginsberg, Davies, and Smith (2004) present data from their study that illuminates the four themes present in the analysis of these letters: (a) teachers' low expectations of Black students, (b) feeling of invisibility and hypervisibility, (c) disappointment at the teachers for not fulfilling their duties, and (d) feeling misunderstood. Each theme is discussed in this chapter.

Teachers' Low Expectations of Black Students

Similar to the students in the Lewis et al. study (2004), and a common sentiment expressed by male students of color in schools, the students who wrote letters to their teachers expressed frustration about the low expectations their teachers had for them. Understanding these low expectations to be directly tied to race, the Black students shared in classroom discussions and in their letters a belief that teachers did not expect much from them because they *are Black.* The youth harbored painful feelings and wrote in their letters about negative stereotypes teachers believe about Black students not being as smart as other students. In a letter to his former teachers, Terrell admonished them for not providing challenging work to help prepare him for the rigors of upper high school: "Can we talk about the work you asked us to do? It was baby work; stuff we did in seventh and eighth grade! Don't be asking us to do no baby work!" In his letter, Terrell continued to challenge those teachers about their expectations of higher education for him and students like him: "I bet you don't even know that most of us want to go to college and have our own dreams. Do you even care? I would like to really know why y'all don't really expect nothing for us in life?" Gerald, another senior at SHAE, was more didactic in his letter to his teachers. He wrote,

> I need you to understand that you having low expectations of me would never propel me to greatness, because no one rises to low expectations. Remember feeling sorry for us, will never allow us to grow. Meet us where we are as scholars and stop stereotyping, which continues to stagnate and contaminate.

Jamal challenged his teachers for believing that Black students were not capable of facilitating their own learning. He wrote, "We are learning that you don't think we can have a discussion about our work without you and that just ain't true. I just get tired of having to fight to be seen as a good student and not a problem you have to fix." Brady, an eleventh grade student, was much more retrospective in his critique of his teachers. As a student who had always received high honors in school, he expressed disappointment and hurt and reminded his teachers, "From the time I began my educational career, I have constantly had to prove myself, . . . and at this I excelled, which was repeatedly confirmed by my teachers telling me that I was 'different'; that I wasn't like 'the others.'" A doctoral student in the Lewis et al. study (2004) expressed similar feelings about constantly needing to prove herself to her White professors. She said, "You're kind of on your guard because as a Black person I felt like I had to do extra, better than everybody else because I didn't want anybody to say—'well, she's Black and came from the ghetto'" (p. 236). The ten writers in this study had educational experiences in their various high schools, including SHAE, that gave them reason to feel disappointed in their teachers and schools. In his letter, Elvin, a twelfth grade student, wrote,

> I am writing this letter from the heart. It is something that is both hard and good to write. I've tried to forget a lot about what made me mad about school. I've tried to forget a lot about what made me feel less than the other white students in my class. And now that I look back, and just see myself sitting in the back of the room, and remembering why you never called on me. You didn't believe I had the answers. You didn't believe that a Black kid like me could know the answers about that book in English class or that math equation. You missed so much for not believing in me. I missed so much for not believing in myself.

Alfredo, a Black and Latino eleventh grader, wrote,

> There's no way you think I can do the work. And because you don't think I am capable, I really believe that you don't like me. See, the problem with you is that you have favorites, and I ain't one of them. Believe me, everytime I step inside your classroom, I feel it. I know you don't really want me there. Your Spanish class—and it's so ironic because I'm Spanish and it is a topic I really like—is one that makes me count down the days to graduation.

Kareem, an eleventh grader, wrote to his tenth grade math teacher,

> What's the best way to say it? I'll just spell it: D-I-S-A-P-P-O-I-N-T-E-D! That's how I feel. I moved with my aunt so I could supposedly go to a

"better" school. Yeah, I may have learned a little bit more in that school, but the way I was treated set me back even more, because I ended up dropping out of the school because of the way I was treated there. It wasn't even hidden that you didn't like your Black students, especially the boys. Nobody called you on the things you would say, the way you treated us just became the normal order of business.

Feelings of Invisibility and Hypervisibility

In the first line of Ralph Ellison's 1952 epic novel *Invisible Man,* the narrator bemoans his status as a Black man in America: "I am an invisible man simply because people refuse to see me." In her book *Invisibility Blues* (1990), Michele Wallace, noted artist, activist, and Black feminist called for change of the Black person's experience in America. She discussed the 1987 New York City Marathon as a case in point. That year marked the first time a Black person (a Kenyan) won the New York City Marathon, considered to be one of the most prestigious marathons in the world; if not the most prestigious, it is certainly the most well known. Wallace observed how the White male commentators of the televised event focused on the prospects of a win for the two White male runners who were far behind the Kenyan, and practically ignored his inevitable victory even when he was less than a mile away from the finish line. Just as one of the cameras was going to show the Kenyan's clear and present victory, it cut away and brought into focus the two White males. The Kenyan was never shown crossing the finish line and triumphantly breaking through the tape. Wallace noticed that even several moments after the end of the race, the victor was not shown or even discussed on this particular television broadcast. In direct rebuttal, a group of prominent New York City Black activists and academics held a special celebration for the victor a few days later in Harlem. This invisibility in the case of the Kenyan runner, Wallace argued, happens daily to Blacks in America.

The Black and Latino students in the URW class expressed anger, frustration, and confusion at the paradoxical situation of invisibility that they find themselves in: The teachers treat them differently from White students, yet refuse to acknowledge or discuss race in the classroom. Their identity is therefore ignored and they are made to feel invisible, while at the same time, they are made very aware of their difference as students of color by the ways in which their teachers treat them. Roberto, who identifies as Puerto Rican, wrote to former teachers who he felt discriminated against Black and Latino students in his classes. He wrote, "When you mention racism, it's like saying the word *bomb*. You all act like you never heard of it or it's a curse, but yet [the punishment depends] on the color of the kid's skin . . ." Gerald directly addressed being made to feel invisible by some of his teachers. Referencing Dr. Martin Luther King, Jr.'s famous quote about judging people by the content of their character and not the color of their skin, he wrote, "If we all took heed to this then many of my brothers would not be invisible. They would be regarded so that they perhaps would not have to go to extreme lengths to be noticed." Gerald asked his current teachers to "see" him and offer help when needed: "I need you to not ignore me because of my short comings that may bring a level of embarrassment to you while I am under your tutelage while in your classroom." In a lengthy two-page letter, Derrick, an eleventh grader, wrote,

> Do you even see me unless you hear me? And all you teachers wonder why we talk loud. It's our way of being seen in a place where everyone wants to ignore us until it's time to find someone to blame for something. Then it's like magic, all the black and brown boys appear. Then the school is quick to call police officers into the school. When I was kid, they used to say the police officer is your friend—really?, not in my neighborhood. And they used to say your teacher wants what's best for you—really?, not in my school. By the way, I'm going to be a journalist. I remember how you thought I used somebody else's work, and had to prove over and over that I didn't. Well, maybe you learned that some of us are smarter than you think.

In his very brief letter, which read more like a poem, Jeremiah shared, "It's like you looked right through me / seen but unseen / known yet unknown / there but invisible / Why? Why be afraid to look me in the eyez? Are you afraid you'll see your disgust for me staring back at you?" A participant in the Lewis et al. (2004) study speaks specifically to this feeling of invisibility. A PhD student reported, "There were some faculty that initially I had the impression that they didn't even see me in the hall. I felt like I was totally invisible" (p. 235). These students, just like Gerald and the other URW students, yearned for their instructors to notice them and to "validate" them. Data from the Lewis et al. (2004) study report that several students expressed feelings of isolation on campus, and these feelings were often described as being invisible (p. 234). During a class discussion, and in his letter, Terrell commented on how he felt his aspirations and those of his peers were not acknowledged by their teachers, thus rendering them invisible when it came to identifying ambitious students. He wrote,

> Do you ever think that maybe we want the same things as the white kids in school? As your own kids? We want good education. We want good jobs. We want nice families to come home to. Why can't you see that? What makes it so difficult for you to see those of us who are really working hard and trying hard to make it? When you don't see this, Miss, it's discouraging and we end up dropping out. You are our teachers, if you don't care, then why should we care? I'm gonna graduate and when I do, I ain't never coming back here. I feel sorry for the younger kids in this school cause y'all don't really expect nothing for us in life and they gonna find out like me and my friends did after all the bs you gonna put 'em through. This school is like prison, the principal be walking around with security like she need a bodyguard. Y'all all scared of us and racist—same s—t, new day! I can't wait to get out of here.

In contrast to the feelings of invisibility that Roberto and Gerald shared, some of the young men commented on feeling hypervisible (Collins, 2008) when it came to some of their teachers. Derrick asked one of his current teachers, "Why is it that when I walk in late you have to call me out and when they [White students] walk in late you don't say nothing?" And Terrell signaled a similar singling out of Black students in one of his classes at SHAE: "I noticed that it's the same group of us who get in trouble in your class. We even talk about it with each other. We be wondering like 'damn, does Mister think we a gang or something'? It's like we guilty on sight." And Jeremiah wrote in his letter poem to his former and current teachers, "Teachers may feel bad for a student / just for his skin color. Teachers look at 'minority students' differently / Why? that shouldn't be." Devon, like Terrell, wrote about feeling "seen" only when trouble broke out at his high school. In his letter he recalled an incident that made him feel like he and the other Black boys in his high school were being unfairly targeted:

> The only time in my life I ever felt sorry about being Black was when something went down at school. I remember that day when someone started a fire in the boys bathroom, the principal went around to some of the classes, mostly the special ed classes where we were and started pulling out the Black guys one by one. It was like we were on trial. On trial for a crime we didn't even commit. But it was always like that. Whenever something was stolen, or the exit alarm went off, it was a Black kid who had to do it.

Based on this theme, we see the prevailing notion from Black and Latino youth that their invisibility in the classroom is real. By *invisibility*, we simply mean that in most situations teachers do not see this group for their true academic potential. As a result, lessons are "watered down" to meet their perceived academic levels. However, the letters tell us that these males of color want more academic challenges from their teachers. Even more dismaying, the letters reveal that teachers only see this population as the population who has the greatest likelihood of "acting out" in class. In summary, Black and Latino males are invisible when it comes to academic achievement but are hypervisible when related to classroom and school management issues. Teachers will have to reverse this trend if these males of color are to be successful.

Disappointment With Teachers for Not Fulfilling Their Duties

Clem (1986) noted, "Great teachers light the candles of greatness that will cause students to dig deep to fulfill their potential. It is the duty of the teacher to find that greatness" (p. 87). Although the students express feelings of anger and disappointment with their teachers, it is important to note that they *want* to have positive academic experiences and good relationships with their teachers. Their disappointment connects to the unmet expectations of their teachers. They hold teachers accountable for failing to provide them with a rigorous and quality education in classroom environments that are conducive to learning more about themselves and the society that they must navigate as young Black and Latino men. Even a student like Terrell, who was very critical in his letter about his teachers and educational experiences, was able to describe positive classroom experiences. Terrell talked about one teacher in particular who had a positive influence on his learning. He wrote, "So far I have only had one teacher in the past four years listen to me, care about me, about us. . . . I gave her much respect because that's what she gave me. She was young and didn't have the burnout that most of y'all older teachers have in this school." Gerald implores his teachers, "I need you to show your greatness because that will give me some reason to show mine." He went further to remind his teachers of his and other Black males' precarious existence as young males of color in America: "Remember I am in a country where no one protects me because of the color of my skin. So I have always looked to you to cover me while I am on this journey."

Brady and Jamal were very critical of those teachers who did not embrace their full responsibility and maintain high expectations of them in the classroom. Brady wrote, "Considering my experiences with regard to race and racism, I would like to express my disappointment with the way that many of my peers and I were treated. And not one of you stepped up and said anything. In my mind, this made you all complicit. Complicit in the injustice perpetrated against a child." Jamal wrote, "A lot of you let me down. You had more power than I do, and were not willing to make a difference in my education." As with the PhD students, Lewis et al. (2004) reported, "Student's [sic] perceptions of faculty-student relationships were the strongest predictors of progress in doctoral programs for minority students" (p. 233). The doctoral students in the study felt they had only themselves to rely on if they were going to be academically successful; however, if they were able to receive support early on from a faculty member, not necessarily a Black professor, they were more likely to experience academic success. And even when these young writers achieved academic success, the experiences were tarnished and charged with racism. For example, Elvin, now an eleventh grade student, wrote about being selected as the salutatorian of his ninth grade class. In a letter that he described as "hard and good to write," he wrote a letter to his ninth grade Catholic junior high school teachers:

> When I stated in my graduation speech that America's worst nightmare is someone young, Black, and intelligent, you'll remember that I explained that statement by saying that was how I felt based on my years at your school. Little did I know that after accomplishing all of this, after playing by "the rules," after making it to the top of my graduating class, it would be a problem. I was supposed to be the school's first Black valedictorian, something for which my parents and I were proud. Especially because it was not an easy road. I had to work twice as hard to receive high marks, marks which seemed to be easily given to the White kids in my classes. When I got my high grades, I had to always check that they were being recorded in the grade books. All of this, and I had to endure the racist rants of certain teachers (we were called "monkeys" by one and told by another that we wouldn't amount to anything). The NAACP was even called to come out to our school! Now tell me, does this sound like an environment that was conducive to learning? In spite of this all, I made it to the top of the class. However, through some "discrepancy with the grades," I ended up *sharing* the number two spot. And not one of you stepped up and said anything. In my mind, this made you all guilty. Guilty in an injustice perpetrated against a child.

This theme reminds us of the power teachers can ultimately have on the trajectory of students' academic achievement in the K–12 setting. Too often teachers do not stand up for their males of color. For example, the teacher has the "power" to step in and prevent a disciplinary action taken by the school, or making sure a student rightfully receives an honor that he has worked hard to achieve. We see the prevailing theme throughout the letters that illustrate how disappointed these males of color were because they know teachers had the power to make a difference but did not speak up on their behalf.

Feeling Misunderstood

The lack of culturally responsive practices by their teachers left URW students feeling frustrated and irritated that their teachers did not view them in the context of their cultural backgrounds, further exacerbating feelings of invisibility. They criticized teachers for not taking the time to get to know them and understand why some students act and react as they do in certain situations. For example, Kareem spoke to the pressures that young Black and Latino males face from street culture (Lewis & Erskine, 2008), which sometimes carries over into their school lives. He told his teacher, "Well it's like that because we are from this so call[ed] hood where everyone wants to be a thug. Some kids that didn't grow up with parents, so they use that anger towards gangs, drugs, and guns." An important point to make about Kareem's comment was his mention of *some,* and not *all* Black and Latino kids. Brady continued this theme in his letter, "In addition to the pressure of achieving academic success, there was the added burden of having to represent the entire Black race in a positive light." Devon wrote, "It really did hurt to be seen as all the same, that no matter what you did that was positive, it couldn't overcome the negative labels teachers had for you. Once you were labeled, that label stuck with you all long as you were in that school."

These youth encouraged their teachers to understand that institutionalized racism complicated their daily existence. Brady felt that using classroom discussions to help deconstruct and destroy stereotypes about Black and Latino males was something that should be tackled by his teachers. He told them, "If only you noticed that I worked hard, and made working hard seem more normal than failure. But you couldn't see it because of your racist attitude against me. Everybody holds some kind of prejudice, it would have

been important to be able to talk about these kinds of things in class."
Alfredo spoke more explicitly about why Black and Latino male students
may find themselves in situations: a possible attempt to "balance out" the
inequity that comes with being a person of color in this country. He told his
teachers, "Whites are born on the middle of the ladder [and] Blacks are born
on the bottom with three missing bars ahead." Devon echoed Alfredo's observation in his letter: "Growing up in the projects I saw too much for my
age. All type of bad things. Where I'm from all the bad things was cool so I
followed." And finally, Terrell spoke clearly to his teachers about the stereotypes they held about him in particular, and other males of color in general,
which led to their stereotyping and misunderstanding of who they are and
what they manage as males of color. He wrote, "You don't know anything
about me! You judge me because of my clothes and my swag—teachers can
be haters, too." The PhD students in the Lewis et al. study (2004) also experienced feelings of being misunderstood. Lewis et al. (2004) noted, "But
more important, there was a common belief that the faculty and university
did not understand them or their needs" (p. 235). The students wished for
teachers who had a better understanding of some of the challenges students
of color face to get to college and remain successful PhD students. Instead,
they felt there was an overwhelming insensitivity to their differences and
needs as doctoral students.

Concluding Thoughts

Several key conclusions can be drawn from this research. First, there was a
powerful notion from Black and Latino males who participated in the letter
writing assignment that they were very disappointed with their teachers for
not pushing them "academically" and for viewing them as deficient in the
classroom settings. In many cases, these males of color reported that their
teachers would hold them to very low expectations and would use various
stereotypes to impede their growth. As Terrell noted, "I bet you don't even
know that most of us want to go to college and have our own dreams. Do
you even care?" This highlights that these young men wish that their teachers
would have higher expectations of them.

Second, the feelings of invisibility and hypervisibility were common
across all of the letters from the Black and Latino males in this study. This
theme made clear that Black and Latino males had to put forth extra effort—
sometimes in negative ways—just to get noticed in the classroom. These

letters highlight the notion that these students wanted to be noticed and validated in positive ways when it comes to academics. Additionally, they also desired equal treatment in the classroom when it came to management issues that arise. These students felt they were given stricter penalties when compared with their White counterparts. In many cases, these young men felt that their teachers would let White students "get away with" actions in the classroom for which they, the Black students, would have to face disciplinary action if they committed the same type of offense. Overall, Black and Latino males in this study were very disappointed with their teachers for not fulfilling their duties as it related to them having a positive educational experience. This included a common theme in the letters that teachers did not use the power they had to stand up for them in the face of injustice, even though they witnessed injustices being perpetrated against their Black and Latino male students every day within the walls of their schools. As Brady noted, "I would like to express my disappointment with the way that many of my peers and I were treated." Jamal captured the full essence of this disappointment quite succinctly in his letter when he wrote, "You let us down."

Based on the concerns reported by the Black and Latino males in this study, we hope that this chapter will serve as a wake-up call to teachers. Many teachers across the United States believe that Black and Latino males do not want to achieve in the classroom. Fortunately, this chapter weakens that sentiment a bit; it pushes for the reality that these students are very concerned about their academic futures and hope their teachers would propel them to reach their full potential.

References

Baldwin, J. (1985). A talk to teachers. In *The price of the ticket: Collected nonfiction 1948–1985* (pp. 325–332). New York: St. Martin's Press.

Clem, W. (1986). *To light a candle: The autobiography of a professional educator.* New York: Vintage.

Collins, P. H. (2008). *Black feminist thought: Knowledge, consciousness, and the power of empowerment.* London: Routledge.

Haddix, M. (2010). Goin' for broke: Reaping the rewards of teaching toward cultural and linguistic diversity. *The Language and Literacy Spectrum, 20,* 83–90.

Ellison, R. (1952). *Invisible man.* New York: Vintage.

Lewis, C., Ginsberg, R., Davies. T., & Smith, K. (2004). The experiences of African American Ph.D. students at a predominately White Carnegie I-research institution. *College Student Journal, 38,* 231–245.

Lewis, C. W., & Erskine, K. F. (2008). *The dilemmas of being an African American male in the new millennium: Solutions for life transformation.* West Conshohocken, PA: Infinity.

Sealey-Ruiz, Y. (2011). Learning to talk and write about race: Developing racial literacy in a college English classroom. *The English Quarterly. The Canadian Council of Teachers of English Language Arts, 42*(1), 24–42.

Wallace, M. (1990). *Invisibility blues: From pop to theory.* New York: Verso.

SUGGESTED READINGS

Introduction

Julie Landsman

The Shame of the Nation: The Restoration of Apartheid Schooling in America. Jonathan Kozol, 2005. New York: Broadway.

Kozol argues that school segregation is still the rule for poor minorities, and he believes a new Civil Rights Movement will be necessary to eradicate it. He builds his case with exhaustive research and heartbreaking examples of education today.

Their Eyes Were Watching God. Zora Neale Hurston, 1937. New York: Harper Perennial.

This novel, written in African-American dialect from the South and formal English, is a brilliant example of the richness of language, culture, and history. It captures a post–Civil War town totally run by Black people and follows what happens to them as these tumultuous years go by.

June Jordan's Poetry for the People: A Revolutionary Blueprint. Lauren Muller and Poetry for the People Blueprint Collective, 1995. New York: Routledge.

This is a book that helps teachers bring students' voices to the center of the class. Now more than ever we need books that recognize the brilliance of our students and the agency they must have to negotiate a difficult world. She gives a step-by-step workshop in how to set up poetry workshops and has powerful examples of students' work to illustrate her topics.

Steve Grineski

A White Teacher Talks About Race. Julie Landsman, 2009. Lanham, MD: Rowman & Littlefield Education.

The first time I read this book I was amazed and impressed with the brutally honest approach Landsman used in her writing. Whether stories about her own personal experiences or those of her students, Landsman "shook off the covers" and allowed me to see and understand these lived realities. *A White Teacher Talks About Race* is a pivotal book for my mostly white and middle- and working-class teacher education students regarding their learning about race and racism, and privilege and oppression. Their understanding of why it is so important for teachers to make classrooms relevant for all and to help students see themselves in the curriculum deepens as a result of reading this book.

Of Borders and Dreams: A Mexican-American Experience of Urban Education. **Chris Liska Carger, 1996. New York: Teachers College Press.**

This is a provocative story of Alejandro Juarez, Jr., and his family as they attempt to negotiate the Chicago public school system, as told by Alejandro Jr.'s ESL teacher, Chris Carger. Carger uses the idea of *borders* to frame the telling of this story. Two powerful borders that limit Alejandro's opportunities, access, and participation within a failing school system are racism and classism. A real strength of this book is the questions it raises regarding culturally relevant curriculum and instruction, home-school relations, and the purposes of school. These are the kinds of questions I hope teacher education students, teacher educators, and practicing teachers consider.

Lies My Teacher Told Me: Everything Your American History Textbook Got Wrong. **James W. Loewen, 1995. New York: New Press.**

Although Loewen wrote this book nearly twenty years ago, its thesis was as important then as it is now: the real story of America must be told. All teachers need to give voice and image to the voiceless and invisible by helping their students recognize how specific groups of people have been subjected to dehumanizing practices, while making sure their students learn that many individuals who have been discriminated against have stories to tell of resistance, survival, success, contribution, and triumph. Loewen's book is a great place to begin meaningful conversations about race and racism.

Robert Simmons III

The New Jim Crow: Mass Incarceration in an Age of Colorblindness. **Michelle Alexander, 2010. New York: New Press.**

Michelle Alexander challenges us to consider the complexity of race in America. Considering the prison industrial complex as an extension of the racial caste system discussed in her book, Alexander provides a great opportunity for us to unpack the complexity of race and racism—not as an individual act of bigotry but as a system of oppression and tyranny.

Twelve Angry Men. **Gregory S. Parks and Matthew W. Hughey, 2010. New York: New Press.**

What happens when twelve African-American men from different walks of life tell their stories about racism and its impact on their lives? What happens is this: the real impact that racism has on the lives of African-American men becomes apparent, and rhetoric associated with a postracial America is destroyed.

Multiplication Is for White People: Raising Expectations for Other People's Children. **Lisa Delpit, 2012. New York: New Press.**

Dr. Delpit calls us all out for failing to educate poor children of color effectively. By weaving stories and anecdotes together, *Multiplication Is for White People* is a must-read for all those looking for solutions to, but also looking to understand, the complexity of the current educational landscape.

Chapter 1: Black Silence, White Noise

Johnnetta S. C. Ricks and Imandeep Kaur Grewal

The Grapes of Wrath. **John Steinbeck, 1939.**

This novel set in the Depression of the 1930s follows the Joad family striving to find work and a home. Vivid characters and events portray this time in US history in powerful, evocative ways.

Nigger: An Autobiography. **Dick Gregory, 1964. New York: Pocket Books.**

Published in 1964, the autobiography of comedian Dick Gregory is by turns funny, poignant, and thought-provoking.

Chapter 2: Working While White

Amy Phillips and Anita Bender

Women's Lives: Multicultural Perspectives. **Gwyn Kirk and Margo Okazawa-Rey, 2009. New York: McGraw-Hill.**

This interdisciplinary, multicultural text-reader provides an introduction to women's studies by examining women's lives in a global context and across categories of race-ethnicity, class, sexuality, disability, and age.

Chapter 3: Complicating White Privilege

Paul C. Gorski

Borderlands/La Frontera: The New Mestiza. **Gloria Anzaldúa, 1987. San Francisco, CA: Aunt Lute Books.**

Anzaldua creates a mosaic of the marginal person: a person, like herself, who exists in a state of transition, of ambivalence, of conflict; someone who is infused with many cultures yet cannot claim a single one wholly for herself.

Go Tell It on the Mountain. **James Baldwin, 1953. New York: Knopf.**
The novel examines the role of the Christian Church in the lives of African Americans, both as a source of repression and moral hypocrisy and as a source of inspiration and community. It also, more subtly, examines racism in the United States.

That's What She Said: Contemporary Poetry and Fiction by Native American Women. **Rayna Green, 1984. Bloomington, Indiana University Press.**
The poems and stories Rayna Green has chosen for this collection represent some of innovative and interesting writing and yet their authors are for the most part unrecognized outside feminist and Native American circles. This book gives readers a chance to read the voices of many writers who are unheard and unknown.

Rebellion or Revolution? **Harold Cruse, 2009. Minneapolis: University of Minnesota Press. (Originally published 1968 by William Morrow and Company, Inc.)**
Rebellion or Revolution? collects reviews and essays Cruse wrote between 1950 and 1966, examining the relevance of such figures as James Baldwin, Booker T. Washington, Albert Camus, and Josephine Baker, as well as such subjects as Marxism and the African-American community, the economics of black nationalism, and the emerging Black Power movement.

Quotes from Hinmatóowyalahtq'it (also known as Chief Joseph)
These are not available in book form but are available on the Internet.

"White Privilege: Unpacking the Invisible Knapsack." Peggy McIntosh, July/August 1989. *Peace and Freedom,* **10–12.**

Chapter 7: The Color of Our Skin

Naomi Rae Taylor

"See Baby Discriminate." (September 5, 2009). *Newsweek.*
This is a thought-provoking article on how early infants learn to notice difference in races and what this implies for our future.

The House on Mango Street. **Sandra Cisneros, 1991. New York: Vintage**
   Autobiography filled with short selections that capture ways to think about our cultural heritage from our names to our food to our home language to our place in the world.

Chapter 10: Lessons Learned

Pam Booker

The Middle Passage. **Tom Feelings, 1991. New York: Dial Books.**
   Feelings's art speaks to the soul in this magnificent visual record of the Black Diaspora in the Americas. The introduction by Dr. John Henrik Clarke provides a concise narrative of the slave trade, and then readers pause at a double-spread image of a man, woman, bird, sun, and land before the pages become horrific.

Chapter 13: Letter From a High School Student #1

Eva Mitchell

aMaze, an anti-bias education program for elementary children. See: http://childrensliteraturenetwork.org/orgs/orgpages/org_a/amaze.php

Chapter 14: Middle School Lessons Lead to Deeper Insights on Race and Class

Amy Vatne Bintliff

Stolen Childhoods. **Documentary directed by Len Morris and U. Roberto Romano, 2005.**
   At a time of increasing global insecurity, *Stolen Childhoods* reveals the risks of the world community continuing to waste these children's lives. It portrays local, national, and international solutions at work to end child labor, offering a humanitarian path to a more stable world. Available from www.stolenchildhoods.org.

Invisible Children, **at invisiblechildren.com**
   A film documenting the use of child soldiers during the long periods of war in Uganda.

Ninth Ward. Jewell Parker Rhodes, 2010. New York: Little, Brown.

In the novel a young girl named Lanesha must use her intelligence, strength, and courage to keep those close to her alive during Hurricane Katrina and the flood that followed in 2005.

Chapter 15: Disrupting School

Jehanne Beaton Zirps

"Persimmons" poem from *Rose* by Li-Young Lee, 1986. Rochester, NY: BOA Editions. Available from www.poetryfoundation.org/poem/171753

"The Things They Carried" from *The Things They Carried.* Tim O'Brien, 1990. New York: Houghton Mifflin Harcourt.

"Norma" from *The House on Mango Street.* Sandra Cisneros, 1991. New York: Vintage.

"Eleven" from *Woman Hollering Creek and Other Stories.* Sandra Cisneros, 1991. New York: Vintage.

"Rayford's Song" from *Legends From Camp.* Lawson Fusao Inada, 1993. Minneapolis, MN: Coffee House Press.

"Ditched" by J. Northrup, from *Pierced by a Ray of Sun: Poems About the Times We Feel Alone.* R. Gordon, ed., 1995. New York: HarperCollins.

"Two Plus Two or Why Indians Flunk" from *Through Indian Eyes: The Native Experience in Books for Children.* Beverly Slapin and Doris Seale, Eds., 1992. Philadelphia: New Society.

"Indian Education" from *The Lone Ranger and Tonto Fistfight in Heaven.* Sherman Alexie, 1993. New York: Perennial.

Chapter 18: Combating *Huck Finn*'s Censorship

Justin Grinage

Nigger: The Strange Career of a Troublesome Word. Randall Kennedy, 2003. New York: Pantheon.

Kennedy traces the word's history in literature, song, film, politics, sports, everyday speech, and the courtroom. He also discusses its plastic, contradictory, and volatile place in contemporary American society.

Chapter 24: The Pinocchio in Black America
Ben Mchie

The Souls of Black Folk. W. E. B. Du Bois, 1903.
This classic work defines the situation of African Americans in the United States. Written in 1903, it is still relevant to our times, depicting the "double consciousness" that is part of black American life.

Chapter 25: Hip-Hop and Conversation
Jennifer Skoglund
Songs:

"Where Is the Love?" by the Black Eyed Peas. From *Elephunk*, 2003.
"One Tribe" by the Black Eyed Peas. From *The E.N.D.*, 2009.
"City High Anthem" by City High. From *City High*, 2001.
"My Story" by Sean McGee.
"It's a New Day" by will.i.am. Digital download single, 2008.
"Changes" by Common. From *Universal Mind Control*, 2008.
"We Are the World 25 for Haiti," single by Artists for Haiti, 2010.

Chapter 26: "I Know My Brother and He Is Good"
Kristien Zenkov, Marriam Ewaida, Megan R. Lynch, Athene Bell, James Harmon, and Anthony Pellegrino

Through Students' Eyes project (www.throughstudentseyes.org)
We asked over 400 Cleveland; Washington, DC; northern Virginia; and Sierra Leon–area high school and middle school students to consider these questions and answer them with photographs and text. We offer this site to students, teachers, and teacher educators worldwide who are interested in increasing student achievement in urban centers.

Chapter 28: Outside the Bubble
Rachel Rycerz

Poetry Out Loud: National Recitation Contest (www.poetryoutloud.org)
Created by the National Endowment for the Arts and the Poetry Foundation, Poetry Out Loud is administered in partnership with the State Arts

Agencies of all fifty US states, the District of Columbia, the US Virgin Islands, and Puerto Rico.

"Hope is a thing with Feathers" by Emily Dickinson
www.poemhunter.com/emily-dickinson

"Still I Rise" by Maya Angelou
www.poemhunter.com/still-i-rise

A Christmas Carol. **Charles Dickens, 1843.**
    Ebenezer Scrooge, Tiny Tim, Bob Cratchit, and the Ghosts of Christmas Past, Present, and Future are all characters many of us are familiar with. This story in its ability to ask us to look at our lives and our futures can be used to open self-analysis for students of all ages.

"The Ballad of Emmett Till" by Bob Dylan, 1962.
    This is a song by American musician Bob Dylan about the murder of Emmett Till. Till, a fourteen-year-old African American, was killed on August 28, 1955, by two white men, reportedly after flirting with a white woman. In the song's lyrics, Dylan recounts the murder and trial.

Chapter 31: Reflections on Teaching and Learning About Antiracism

Sue Peterson and Tracy Clark

Lies My Teacher Told Me: Everything Your American History Textbook Got Wrong. J. W. Loewen, 2007. New York: New Press.
    This book critically examines twelve American history textbooks and concludes that textbook authors propagate factually false, Eurocentric, and mythologized views of history.

Why Are All the Black Kids Sitting Together in the Cafeteria? B. Tatum, 1997. New York: Basic Books.
    Dr. Tatum provides us with a new way of thinking and talking about race through the lens of racial identity. She explains that all of us have a racial identity and must strive to affirm it.

Chapter 32: Preparing NativityMiguel Teachers to Work With Children of Color From High-Poverty Environments

L. Mickey Fenzel and Melodie Wyttenbach

Other People's Children. **Lisa Delpit, 1995. New York: New Press.**

In a radical analysis of contemporary classrooms, Lisa Delpit develops ideas about ways teachers can be better "cultural transmitters" in the classroom, where prejudice, stereotypes, and cultural assumptions breed ineffective education.

A Hope in the Unseen: An American Odyssey from the Inner City to the Ivy League. **Ron Suskind, 1998. New York: Broadway.**

Despite many low moments and setbacks, Cedric Jennings's story from poor schooling in Washington, DC, to Brown University is one that involves the complexity of class and race and education at all levels in the United States.

Chapter 34: Letters to Our Teachers

Yolanda Sealey-Ruiz and Chance W. Lewis

"A Talk to Teachers" by James Baldwin, 1985. From *The Price of the Ticket: Collected Nonfiction 1948–1985* (pp. 325–332) by James Baldwin.

A powerful essay of advice to teachers teaching children of all races and cultures.

A Letter From Birmingham Jail. **Martin Luther King, Jr., 1963.**

Available from www.uscrossier.org/pullias/king-jr-

A classic letter wherein King argues for nonviolence from his jail cell.

Invisibility Blues: From Pop to Theory. **Michele Wallace, 1990. New York: Verso.**

Michele Wallace poses the historical and conceptual questions that an emergent black feminist theory addresses. She begins with a consideration of the work of her mother, the artist Faith Ringgold, and moves on to recollections of her own early life in Harlem and an account of her development as a writer in the 1970s. She examines the collective legacy with which black artists—from Zora Neale Hurston and Ntozake Shange to Spike Lee and Michael Jackson—must contend in carving out a distinctive cultural practice.

ABOUT THE CONTRIBUTORS

Editors

Steven Grineski started his teaching career in 1975 as an elementary school teacher. In 1984 he joined the Minnesota State University Moorhead (MSUM) faculty and earned his doctorate from the University of North Dakota in 1989. While at MSUM Steve served as Dean of Education, Chairperson for Secondary Education and Foundations, Director of Faculty Development, and taught in several different departments and regularly in the local public schools. Currently he is Professor in the School of Teaching and Learning and teaches in the Foundations of Education program, while serving as field experience liaison between the MSUM Teacher Education and the Moorhead, Minnesota, Alternative Education programs. Steve has made over 100 presentations at state, regional, and international conferences; and published over 75 articles and 4 books in diverse areas including cooperative learning, critiquing corporate school reform, alternative education, holistic approaches to teacher education, critical perspectives about instructional technology, talking about race and racism, and the history of education. Steve and his wife Lee are parents to daughters Abby and Sara and privileged grandparents to Noah, Libby, and Caleb.

Julie Landsman taught in the Minneapolis public schools for 25 years. She has taught at Carleton College and has been an adjunct professor at Hamline University in St. Paul as well as St. Thomas and Metro State. Her books *Basic Needs: A Year With Street Kids in a City School*; *A White Teacher Talks About Race*; and, most recently, *Growing Up White: A Veteran Teacher Reflects on Racism*, are memoirs about her days in Minneapolis Public Schools. She has coedited six books on race, culture, and education. Julie has been a featured speaker on White privilege in the United States and in other countries including Thailand, Sweden, and France. She is a firm believer in stories as the key to understanding.

Robert Simmons III, a native of Detroit, is an assistant professor in the School of Education at Loyola University Maryland, the director of the Center for Innovation in Urban Education, and an associated faculty member of the African and African American Studies program. A member of the nationally recognized social justice collaborative Edchange (www.edchange.com) and a columnist for the *The Village Celebration* (www.thevillagecelebration .com), Robert is a former middle school science teacher in the Detroit Public Schools. During his teaching and administrative career in Detroit, Minnesota, and the Dominican Republic, Robert was nominated twice as the Walt Disney National Teacher of the Year and once for the Whitney and Elizabeth MacMillan Foundation Outstanding Educator Award. Robert has been a fellow with the Woodrow Wilson Fellowship Foundation and participated in the Japan Fulbright Memorial Fund. As a contributing author to both the first edition of *White Teachers/Diverse Classrooms* (Stylus Publishing) in 2006 and its second edition in 2011, much of his work explores the experiences of African American boys in public and Catholic schools, the teaching practices of African American male teachers utilizing hip-hop in classrooms, urban education, and the role of race in understanding the social context of schooling. Aside from lectures on his research and commentary on race and education, Robert is a renowned motivational speaker who openly shares his life experiences in Detroit during the height of the crack cocaine epidemic, the mental incarceration he experienced for much of his life due to the physical incarceration of his father, and the significant challenges he faced leaving his childhood home in a neighborhood where drugs and drug dealers were the norm to attend an elite Jesuit high school.

Foreword Author

William Ayers, Distinguished Professor of Education and Senior University Scholar at the University of Illinois at Chicago (retired), has written extensively about social justice; democracy and education; the cultural contexts of schooling; and teaching as an essentially intellectual, ethical, and political enterprise. His recent books include *To Teach: The Journey in Comics* and *Teaching the Taboo*.

Contributors

Fardousa Hassan Ahmed is currently a freshman in Normandale Community College's Pre-Dental and Business Programs. Fardousa was one of the first students to participate in South High's s.t.a.r.t. initiative and acted as cochair in the 2011–2012 school year.

Stacy Amaral is a 66-year-old woman who describes herself as a Jew Rican or Puerto Jew. She has worked as a teacher, school counselor, and medical and educational interpreter. Shirley and she continue their friendship and still try to find ways to keep sane while staying in the fight.

Carlo Balleria is from Minneapolis, Minnesota, and became involved in racial issues at South High School as a part of Students Together Against Racial Tensions. He is currently studying physics at the University of Puget Sound. He hopes race is not to be an issue for his kids.

Brigid Beaubien is an associate professor at Eastern Michigan University. She earned her PhD at Wayne State University and is a former Detroit Public School teacher.

Athene Bell is the district literacy specialist in Manassas City Public Schools (VA), previously taught English to adolescents in grades six through eight, and recently finished her PhD in Education at George Mason University.

Anita Bender is director of the Women's Center and the Rainbow Dragon Center at Minnesota State University Moorhead. She is program coordinator for MSUM's antiracism initiative and is adjunct instructor in the Women's & Gender Studies Program.

Amy Vatne Bintliff is a teacher and researcher who has taught language arts and reading in Minnesota and Wisconsin. She is a trained restorative justice Circle Keeper and human rights educator. She is the author of *Re-engaging Disconnected Youth: Transformative Learning Through Restorative and Social Justice Education* (Peter Lang, 2011.)

Pam Booker was a classroom teacher for twenty years, teaching kindergarten and first and second grade in a large urban school district and later in a voluntary integration collaborative. Pam currently works in a first-ring suburban school district as a supervisor in their Office of Equity and Integration.

Tracy Clark, MSW, is an assistant professor of Social Work at Minnesota State University Moorhead. She teaches, and infuses social justice and antiracism into, multiple social work practice courses. She also cotaught an antiracism course.

Marcellus Davis is the program director of Integration and Equity for Robbinsdale Area Schools in Minnesota. He has over ten years of experience working toward educational equity in both K–12 and higher education.

Marriam Ewaida is a middle school literacy coach and a former secondary English/ESOL teacher. Marriam is currently a PhD student in Literacy and Educational Leadership at George Mason University. She is committed to studying the literacy experiences of immigrant youth.

L. Mickey Fenzel is a professor in the School of Education at Loyola University Maryland. He holds a PhD in developmental psychology from Cornell and is the author of *Improving Urban Middle Schools: Lessons From the Nativity Schools.*

Jennifer Godinez is associate director of the nationally recognized policy, research, and advocacy organization, Minnesota Minority Education Partnership, Inc. (MMEP). She can be followed frequently on Twitter at @JGodi.

Cindy Gomez-Schempp is cofounder of the People's Press Project, a media justice non-profit; an editor/writer; educator; translator; and mother. Her background is in leadership on discrimination, social justice, worker rights, disability, and youth.

Paul C. Gorski is an associate professor at George Mason University where he teaches in the Social Justice concentration and minor. He provides guidance to schools all over the world on equity and diversity.

Ilsa Govan, cofounder of Cultures Connecting, LLC (www.culturesconnecting.com), has more than fifteen years' experience as a classroom teacher and social justice activist. She is also co-coordinator of WE-ACT, a group of European American educators who meet to discuss and engage in critical, cross-cultural practice.

Imandeep Kaur Grewal is currently a PhD candidate at Eastern Michigan University and is passionate about issues of gender, poverty, and children's rights—particularly right to education. She is a former teacher at the Rudolf Steiner School of Ann Arbor.

Justin Grinage is a PhD student at the University of Minnesota, studying Culture and Teaching. He also teaches English and coordinates the Advancement via Individual Determination (AVID) program at a high school in the Anoka-Hennepin school district.

James Harmon teaches English in the Euclid City School District (OH) and is cofounder of Through Students' Eyes (www.throughstudentseyes.org). He is an Apple Distinguished Educator, a Google Certified Teacher, and an educational technology instructor at Baldwin Wallace University.

Valerie Hill-Jackson is a 2012–2013 Fulbright fellow, 2001–2002 AERA/Spencer fellow, and a Geraldine R. Dodge fellow for outstanding teaching. Dr. Hill-Jackson is a social entrepreneur and international speaker.

Alexander Hines is the director of Inclusion and Diversity for Winona State University. He has experience working in higher education specializing in diversity, inclusion, students of color recruitment and retention, and Black male identity development.

Caprice D. Hollins has over fifteen years of experience working with ethnically diverse populations, providing mental health services, facilitating workshops, and teaching graduate courses. After serving in Seattle Public Schools, Dr. Hollins started Cultures Connecting, LLC (www.culturesconnecting.com).

Ok-Hee Lee is an associate professor in the School of Teaching and Learning at Minnesota State University Moorhead. Her professional interest areas include postmodernist perspectives in early childhood education, curriculum, and instruction, and teacher education.

Adam Levner is executive director and cofounder of Critical Exposure, a nonprofit that teaches youth to use the power of photography and their own voices to become effective advocates for school reform and social change.

Chance W. Lewis is the Carol Grotnes Belk Distinguished Professor and Endowed Chair of Urban Education at the University of North Carolina at Charlotte. Dr. Lewis is the executive director of the University of North Carolina at Charlotte's Urban Education Collaborative, publishing a new generation of research on improving urban schools.

Megan R. Lynch is an English as a Second Language (ESL) teacher and enrolled in the PhD in Education program at George Mason University. Her interests include at-risk youth, ESOL policy, and education leadership.

Phyllis M. May-Machunda, PhD, is a folklorist, a professor and former chair of American Multicultural Studies at Minnesota State University Moorhead, a SEED facilitator, and cofounder of a regional higher education, antiracism initiative in the Midwest.

Jennifer McCary earned a BFA in Art Education and Stone Sculpture, and an MA in College Student Personnel from Bowling Green State University. When she is not working, she is spending time with her family.

Rose McGee is a professional storyteller, poet, playwright, motivational speaker, and entrepreneur. As staff member with Minnesota Humanities Center, she trains, facilitates, and witnesses the power of story and the importance of implementing *absent narratives* into our social construct.

Ben Mchie is an educational consultant, historian, lecturer, archivist, author, and expert in multimedia. In 2000, he founded the African American Registry (www.aaregistry.org). The Registry acts out its mission in three ways: service, products, and programs.

Eva Mitchell became active with racial justice work in South High School in Minneapolis, where she cofounded a student group to build connections across racial and cultural differences. She is currently a student at St. Olaf College in Northfield, Minnesota.

Cheryl Moore-Thomas is a tenured associate professor and the associate dean of the School of Education at Loyola University Maryland. Cheryl has taught, published, and worked in the areas of multicultural counseling, identity development, and college access.

Ruth Newton is an assistant professor at Minnesota State University Moorhead. She has a master's degree in Elementary Education and a doctorate in Education with an emphasis in Teacher Education.

Anthony Pellegrino is assistant professor of history/social studies secondary education at George Mason University. His research interests include the experiences of pre-service social studies teachers and multimodal instructional strategies to enhance social studies engagement.

Sue Peterson received her BSW from Minnesota State University Moorhead and her MSW degree from the University of Minnesota. She is currently director of the Social Work Program at Minot State University in North Dakota.

Amy Phillips is an assistant professor of Social Work at the University of North Dakota. She has been involved in antiracism work for twelve years.

Johnnetta S. C. Ricks is an instructor at Eastern Michigan University (EMU) and a PhD candidate in EMU's Educational Studies program. She is a former high school mathematics teacher for Detroit Public Schools.

Rachel Rycerz taught English and reading at School of the Arts in Chicago. She currently lives in northern California, and recently created and performed the one-woman show *Ready or Not, Here Comes Mama: Lullabies and Broadway.*

Yolanda Sealey-Ruiz is an assistant professor of English Education at Teachers College, Columbia University. Her research interests include racial literacy development in urban teacher education, critical English education for Black and Latino high school males, and the educational narratives of Black female college reentry students.

Jennifer Skoglund has been teaching classroom music in Minneapolis public schools since 2000. She earned a Master of Arts in Music Education from the University of St. Thomas in St. Paul, Minnesota. Ms. Skoglund has studied hip-hop music and culture throughout her teaching career.

Naomi Rae Taylor is a lecturer in Hamline University's School of Education. She teaches graduate and undergraduate courses and supervises teacher candidates. Taylor is also an associate with the Center for Excellence in Urban Teaching. She is a former Saint Paul Public School teacher and is working on her dissertation with a focus on intercultural competency.

Kate Towle won St. Paul Foundation's 2011 Facing Race Idea Challenge. Through her initiative, Project s.t.a.r.t. Leadership (www.projectstart.wordpress.com), she is helping Minnesota school districts talk about race and engage students to close equity gaps.

Kenneth Turner is currently an assistant principal at an urban middle school. Kenneth has 20 years of educational experience in both K–12 and higher education.

Jennifer Scaturo Watkinson is an assistant professor in the school counseling program at Loyola University Maryland. A former elementary school counselor, Dr. Watkinson's research interests include school counselor leadership and culturally responsive counseling practices.

Linda Williams is an associate professor in the Department of Teacher Education at Eastern Michigan University. She earned her PhD in Curriculum, Teaching, and Educational Policy from Michigan State University, specializing in Literacy Studies.

Omah Williams is a doctoral student in the multicultural education program in the Teaching, Learning and Culture Department at Texas A&M University and graduate assistant in the Center for Math and Science Education.

Shirley Williams, MSW, LICSW, is an adjunct faculty member at Anna Maria College in Paxton, Massachusetts, where she teaches on race, culture, and issues of diversity and mental health in the Social Work Department. She has provided psychotherapy to adults and families in Worcester for over 25 years.

Melodie Wyttenbach has experience in urban education as a teacher, school principal, and program coordinator for the NativityMiguel Network of Schools. She is currently pursuing her doctorate in Educational Leadership and Policy Analysis from the University of Wisconsin–Madison.

Laura Zelle is director of Tolerance Minnesota at the Jewish Community Relations Council of Minnesota and the Dakotas (JCRC), where she has been on staff since 2005. Laura oversees the daily operations of the program.

Kristien Zenkov is associate professor of education at George Mason University. He is cofounder of Through Students' Eyes and the author of more than 90 articles, book chapters, and books on youths' perspective on school.

Jehanne Beaton Zirps has worked as a secondary social studies teacher in the Minneapolis public schools for twenty years. She is currently working on her doctorate in Social Studies Education and Teacher Education from the University of Minnesota.

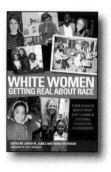

White Women Getting Real About Race
Their Stories About What They Learned Teaching in Diverse Classrooms
Edited by Judith M. James and Nancy Peterson
Foreword by Julie Landsman

For many White women teachers and teachers in training—who represent the majority of our teaching force today—the issue of race is fraught with discomfort. It may challenge assumptions, evoke a sense of guilt, or give rise to a fear of making mistakes or saying the wrong thing.

This book presents the first-person stories of White women teachers who tell us not only how they have grappled with race in diverse classrooms, but how they continue to this day to be challenged by issues of color and privilege.

In approaching chapter authors for this book, the editors asked the writers to ask themselves, "Will my well-being and sense of self be at risk if I tell this story?" Recognizing what's at stake, they wanted writers who would be real with themselves.

The women in this book hope that their stories will resonate with readers, help them feel less alone, and give them courage to begin a dialogue with colleagues, friends, staff, and administrators around race concerns.

Sty/us

22883 Quicksilver Drive
Sterling, VA 20166-2102

Subscribe to our e-mail alerts: www.Styluspub.com

Also available from Stylus

White Teachers / Diverse Classrooms
Creating Inclusive Schools, Building on Students' Diversity, and Providing True Educational Equity
Edited by Julie Landsman and Chance W. Lewis

"The second edition of *White Teachers, Diverse Classrooms* adds seven essays to 14 of the original chapters. In the first edition, the editors selected essays about pedagogical methods that might close the achievement gap between white and African American students. The new edition contains sevena rticles describing approaches for teachers working with Latino, Asian, or Native American students. Summing Up: Recommended."—*Choice*

Acclaim for the first edition:

"Black and White teachers here provide an insightful approach to inclusive and equitable teaching and illustrate its transformative power to bring about success."—*Education Digest*

"Practical advice for teachers and administrators on ways to improve the education of students of color, emphasizing that low expectations are the worst form of racism."—*Education Week*

"This is a very good book for teachers to put on their shelves; I recommend its use at the university level as a teaching tool as well."—*Multicultural Review*

Cultivating Social Justice Teachers
How Teacher Educators Have Helped Students Overcome Cognitive Bottlenecks and Learn Critical Social Justice Concepts
Edited by Paul C. Gorski, Kristien Zenkov, Nana Osei-Kofi, and Jeff Sapp
Foreword by David Stovall

"Few challenges in teacher preparation are as salient as teaching the central, troubling concepts of social justice that many profoundly resist learning. With theoretical nuance, pedagogical savvy, and highly relate-able examples and self-reflections, *Cultivating Social Justice Teachers* shows the possibilities for doing what often seems impossible. This book is one that no teacher educator—or any educator—can or should do without."
—*Kevin Kumashiro, author of* Bad Teacher!: How Blaming Teachers Distorts the Bigger Picture

"Packed with honest stories that document the missteps, mistakes, and rethinking of courses that focus on issues of social justice, *Cultivating Social Justice Teachers* offers all of us—professors, teachers, researchers, and students—strategies for teaching and learning how to face the inevitable bumps and obstacles that get in the way of full inclusion and understanding of multiple perspectives. Engaging in brave and frank discussions, the editors and authors of this text are a model of what is needed if we are to change how teachers are prepared to teach in our diverse classrooms."—*Sonia Nieto, Professor Emerita, School of Education, University of Massachusetts, Amherst*